The **Rough Guide** to

Shanghai

written and researched by

Simon Lewis

NEW YORK • LONDON • DELHI

www.roughguides.com

Contents

Shanghai's building boom colour section following p.48

China's regional cuisines colour sect following p.112

Colour maps following p.224

◄◄ Pudong skyline from the Bund ◄ Nanjing Dong Lu

Introduction to

Shanghai

In the Roaring Twenties, Shanghai was a place of opportunity, famous for its style and decadence. Now, after decades of postwar neglect, the city has shaken off its communist mothballs, and exactly the same is true today. The great metropolis is undergoing one of the fastest economic expansions that the world has ever seen. Evidence of building is everywhere: there are three thousand skyscrapers now, more than in New York, and two thousand more are on their way. Suddenly Shanghai has China's largest stock exchange and the world's first commercial Maglev (magnetic levitation) train system; soon it will boast the world's tallest building, and even its largest ferris wheel. By 2020, it is fully expected to be the richest economic region in the world.

It's not surprising then that your initial impression of the city will be of bustle and upheaval, ubiquitous construction, ferociously crowded streets, and traffic chaos. Faced with all those ads, neon signs, showcase buildings and vast shopping plazas, it's hard to imagine that you are in a communist country. Indeed, though dissent is quashed, as ever, outside the political arena anything goes these days, and consumer capitalism and instant gratification appear to be the prevailing ideologies; witness all the gleaming new restaurant and nightlife districts, the enthusiastic embrace of fashion, clubbing and fine cuisine, the gay bars and red-light zones.

Yet despite the rampant modernity, evidence of Shanghai's short and inglorious **history**, when it was carved by foreign powers into autonomous concessions, is everywhere, and parts of the city appear distinctly European. Looking like a 1920s vision of the future, prewar Art Deco buildings – relics of hated foreign imperialism, now ironically protected as city monuments – abound, standing in the shadows of brazen skyscrapers that share the same utopian aesthetic.

And Shanghai maintains its **international character**. The Shanghainese

> **Faced with all those ads, neon signs, showcase buildings and vast shopping plazas, it's hard to imagine that you are in a communist country.**

have always felt apart from the rest of the country and looked abroad for inspiration as well as business; now, you'll find more English spoken here than in any other mainland city, see foreign mannerisms such as handshaking and air-kissing, and observe the current obsession with international luxury brands. But look

Fact file

• Shanghai Municipality encompasses 6,300 square kilometres, which includes Shanghai city, eight surrounding districts and thirty islands.

• The city is **governed** by the Communist Party of China but enjoys a surprising degree of autonomy, to a degree which has begun to worry the central government in Beijing.

• The official **language** is Mandarin, but locals can also speak a dialect called Shanghainese.

• The **population** of Greater Shanghai is 21 million, which includes 4 million migrant workers.

• Shanghai is the third busiest **port** in the world, after Singapore and Hong Kong. The Shanghai region, including the adjoining provinces of Jiangsu and Zhejiang, accounts for almost a third of China's foreign **exports**, and a fifth of its **manufacturing output** is produced here. Each year, the city attracts a quarter of all China's foreign **investment**, more than any single developing country.

▲ The Maglev train

closely and you'll also find a distinctly **Chinese identity** asserting itself, whether in the renewal of interest in traditional entertainments such as opera and acrobatics or in the revival of old architectural forms brought up-to-date for the city's young elite.

Like Hong Kong, its model for economic development, Shanghai does not brim with obvious attractions. Rather, its pleasures lie in some less expected pursuits. Unlike most Chinese cities, Shanghai is actually a rewarding place to **wander** aimlessly: it's fascinating to stroll the elegant Bund, explore the pockets of colonial architecture in the former French Concession or get lost in the choking alleyways of the Old City, where traditional life continues much as it always has. The **art scene** is world class, and you can visit both flashy new art centres and ramshackle complexes of studios in abandoned factories. But perhaps the city's greatest draw is its emphasis on indulgence, and it's hard to resist its many temptations. The **restaurant** scene is superb, with every Chinese and most world cuisines represented; whether you treat yourself to the latest outrageous concoction at a celebrity restaurant or slurp noodles in a neighbourhood canteen, you may well find eating to be the highlight of your trip. There are so many great places to go for **nightlife**, from dive bars to slick clubs featuring international DJs, that some visitors rarely see daylight. And the **shopping** possibilities, at shiny malls, trendy boutiques and dusty markets, are endless; make sure you leave plenty of space in your suitcase.

> Whether you treat yourself to the latest outrageous concoction at a celebrity restaurant or slurp noodles in a neighbourhood canteen, you may well find eating to be the highlight of your trip.

▲ M on the Bund

What to see

Irst stop on every visitor's itinerary is the famous **Bund**, an impressive strip of colonial edifices lining the west bank of the Huangpu River. As well as allowing you an insight into the city's past, a wander along the riverside affords a glimpse into its future – the awesome, skyscraper-spiked skyline on the other side.

Taking a river tour from here will give you a sense of the city's scale. Heading west from the Bund down the old consumer cornucopia of **Nanjing Dong Lu** will bring you to **People's Square**, the modern heart of the city, and home to a cluster of world-class museums, all worth a few hours of your time, and the leafy and attractive Renmin Park. Continuing west onto Nanjing Xi Lu brings you to the modern commercial district of **Jing'an**, where a couple of worthwhile temples, and the fantastic Moganshan Art District, provide welcome respite from all the relentless materialism.

7

Heading south from People's Square brings you to delightful **Xintiandi**, an upscale dining district housed in renovated traditional buildings, and a good introduction to the civilized pleasures of the **former French Concession**, which stretches west of here. As well as the best (and most exclusive) shopping, hotels and dining, on these incongruously European looking streets you'll find a host of former residences of Shanghai's original movers and shakers.

But Shanghai's history was not all about the foreigners, as you'll find if you explore the **Old City**, south of the Bund, where most of the Chinese lived during the Concession era. The old alleys are being torn down at speed, but you'll still find plenty of evidence of a distinctly Chinese way of life in the elegant old Yu Gardens, the bustling shopping bazaar that's grown up around them, and a clutch of backstreet temples. By way of contrast, across the river in **Pudong** you'll see very little that's less than a decade old; come here for the views from the elegant Jinmao Tower. A clutch of sights on the city's further reaches are worthy of exploration, among them Duolun Culture Street in the far north, Century Park in the east, and Longhua Temple in the southwest.

▲ Shikumen housing near Taikang Lu, Old French Concession

After a week you might have had enough of Shanghai's hectic pace, in which case head out to the hinterland, which offers countryside, historic buildings and a chance to slow down. The tranquil Buddhist island of **Putuo Shan** and the cities of **Suzhou**, famous for gardens and silk, and **Hangzhou**, with its gorgeous lake, are well worth an overnight stop, while for a day-trip, don't miss a jaunt around one of the sleepy **canal towns**, such as Zhouzhuang or Tongli.

▲ The Bund at night

When to go

▼ Market

The best times to visit Shanghai are in **spring** and early summer (late March till the end of May) and **autumn** (mid-September till the end of October). During these times, you can expect warm temperatures, blue sky and infrequent rain.

Summer (June to mid-September) is unpleasantly hot and humid, yet you might need to carry an extra layer of clothes for when you go inside as it's common to find air-conditioning left on its fiercest setting. During the "Plum Flower Rain" season from mid-June to early July expect frequent showers, and up till September heavy storms are common – you'll certainly need an umbrella.

Winters are chilly and windy, though the temperature rarely drops below freezing and snow is uncommon. January is the coldest month.

Try to avoid visiting during the two "Golden Week" **holidays** – the first week of May and the first week of October – when pretty much the whole country is on holiday and tourist attractions become fearsomely busy. The city is lively during the run up to **Chinese New Year**, which falls between mid-January and mid-February, but travel during this time is tricky and expensive as most people are going home. New Year itself is best avoided as just about everyone stays at home with their family and most businesses are shut.

Climate

	Jan	Feb	Mar	Apr	May	Jun	Jul	Aug	Sep	Oct	Nov	Dec
Average daily temperature												
max (°C)	8	8	13	19	25	28	32	32	28	23	17	12
min (°C)	1	1	4	10	15	19	23	23	19	14	7	2
max (°F)	46	46	55	66	77	82	90	90	82	74	63	54
min (°F)	34	34	39	50	59	66	74	74	66	57	45	36
Average rainfall												
mm	48	58	84	94	94	180	147	142	130	71	51	36

17
things not to miss

It's not possible to see everything that Shanghai has to offer on a short trip – and we don't suggest you try. What follows is a selective taste of the city's highlights: fascinating museums, spectacular buildings and a few ways just to indulge yourself. They're arranged in five colour-coded categories, which you can browse through to find the very best things to see and experience. All highlights have a page reference to take you straight into the guide, where you can find out more.

01 Jinmao Tower observation deck Page **90** • The views of the city are magnificent from this lofty eyrie inside one of its most beautiful buildings.

02 Yu Garden Page **65** • This classical garden of pavilions, ponds and rockeries is a calm oasis at the heart of an olde-worlde Chinatown style shopping centre.

04 Yufo Temple Page **83** • This lively temple, wreathed in incense smoke, is home to two very holy, and very beautiful, jade Buddha statues.

03 Tailoring Page **140** • Tailored clothes to any design you can think of, all for a tiny fraction of the price you'd pay at home – Shanghai's ultimate bargain.

05 **The Bund** Page **48** • This strip of grand colonial mansions is fast becoming China's Champs-Élysees.

06 **Renmin Park** Page **61** • A bucolic beauty spot at the heart of the city, with a lovely lotus pond and bamboo groves.

07 **Moganshan Art District** Page **84** • This old factory is a hive of studios and galleries, making it the hottest spot in the city's vibrant art scene.

09 **Fake market** Page **137** • You know it's wrong but you can't resist. Stock up on name-brand knock-offs at bargain prices. A steal in more ways than one.

08 **Xintiandi** Pages **70** & **118** • Upscale dining in a beautiful rebuilt neighbourhood of traditional *shikumen* (stone-gate) houses.

10 **Taikang Lu Art Street** Pages **75** & **115** • The *Kommune* is just one of many places to pause along this charming alleyway of boutiques and little cafés that has grown out of an artists colony.

14

11 **Shanghai Museum** Page **58** • One of the best collections of paintings, jade, bronzes and other antiquities in the country, housed in one of the city's most stylish buildings.

12 **Xi Hu** Page **163** • Hangzhou's charming lake, dotted with islands, crossed by causeways, and lined with pavilions and pagodas, is one of China's most famous beauty spots.

13 **Spa treatment** Page **31** • Indulge yourself at one of Shanghai's world-class spas, such as the Banyan Tree. Because you're worth it (and it's much cheaper than at home).

14 **Xiaolongbao** See *China's regional cuisines* **colour section** • These delicious dumplings are available from both street vendors and fancy restaurants.

15 **Face Bar** Page **125** • Sip a sundowner in the company of the city's movers and shakers at this glamorous cocktail lounge.

17 **Propaganda Poster Centre** Page **78** • This evocative museum relates the bad old days of collective farms, Five-Year Plans and pigtails.

16 **Acrobatics** Page **130** • Good old-fashioned entertainment with performers in spangly costume and plenty of oohs and aahs.

Basics

Basics

Getting there

Shanghai now has direct flights from many European capitals as well as from a number of American and Australian cities. The cost of flights varies with the season, with fares at their highest between Easter and October, around Christmas and New Year, and just before the Chinese New Year (which falls between mid-January and mid-February).

You can often cut costs by going through a **specialist flight agent** – either a consolidator, who buys up blocks of tickets from the airlines and sells them at a discount, or a **discount agent**, who may also offer special student and youth fares plus travel insurance, rail passes, car rentals, tours and the like. Prices quoted below assume midweek travel – flying at weekends tends to be slightly more expensive.

Flights from the UK and Ireland

The only nonstop flights to Shanghai **from the UK** are with Virgin, British Airways and China Eastern, leaving from London Heathrow (11hr). It's not a problem to fly from other UK airports or **from the Republic of Ireland**, though you'll either have to catch a connecting flight to London or your airline's hub city.

Fares for direct flights from the UK start at around £350 in low season, rising to around £650 in high season. If you're flying from the Republic of Ireland, reckon on €950 in low season, €1400 at peak times. Indirect flights can work out cheaper; Air China and Lufthansa, both of which stop in Frankfurt, are worth considering, as is Aeroflot, which stops over in Moscow. Less fancied airlines such as Qatar Airlines offer the most competitive fares, though you may have a lengthy stopover.

Flights from the US and Canada

There's no shortage of flights to Shanghai **from the US and Canada**, with direct flights from San Francisco, Chicago, Los Angeles, New York, Vancouver, Detroit and Toronto, operated by Northwest Airlines, United Airlines, Air China and China Eastern. It takes around thirteen hours flying time to reach Shanghai from the west coast; add seven hours or more to this if you start from the east coast. In low season, expect to pay around US$850/Can$1200 from the west coast or US$1200/Can$1850 from the east, less for an indirect flight. In high season if you book your ticket early you probably won't need to pay more than US$200/Can$320 above these low-season fares.

Flights from Australia, New Zealand and South Africa

From Australia, there are direct flights to Shanghai from Sydney and Melbourne (about 11hr) with China Eastern and Qantas, but you can usually expect to pay over Aus$1000. The cheapest flights are with carriers such as Malaysia Airlines and Royal Brunei, costing around Aus$750 in low season, with a stopover in Hong Kong. Flying from Perth to Shanghai can cost as little as Aus$800 in high season.

There should soon be direct flights from Auckland to Shanghai; until then, flying **from New Zealand** will involve a stopover. Flights cost around NZ$2000 in high season.

Flying **from South Africa** also requires a change of planes. A flight from Johannesburg with a stopover in Hong Kong will cost around ZAR10,000 in high season.

Airlines, agents and operators

Online booking

Many airlines and discount travel websites allow you to book your tickets online, cutting out the costs of agents and middlemen.

Fly less – stay longer! Travel and climate change

Climate change is the single biggest issue facing our planet. It is caused by a build-up in the atmosphere of carbon dioxide and other greenhouse gases, which are emitted by many sources – including planes. Already, flights account for around 3–4 percent of human-induced global warming: that figure may sound small, but it is rising year on year and threatens to counteract the progress made by reducing greenhouse emissions in other areas.

Rough Guides regard travel, overall, as a global benefit, and feel strongly that the advantages to developing economies are important, as are the opportunities for greater contact and awareness among peoples. But we all have a responsibility to limit our personal "carbon footprint". That means giving thought to how often we fly and what we can do to redress the harm that our trips create.

Flying and climate change

Pretty much every form of motorized travel generates CO_2, but planes are particularly bad offenders, releasing large volumes of greenhouse gases at altitudes where their impact is far more harmful. Flying also allows us to travel much further than we would contemplate doing by road or rail, so the emissions attributable to each passenger are greater. For example, one person taking a return flight between Europe and California produces the equivalent impact of 2.5 tonnes of CO_2 – similar to the yearly output of the average UK car.

Less harmful planes may evolve but it will be decades before they replace the current fleet – which could be too late for avoiding climate chaos. In the meantime, there are limited options for concerned travellers: to reduce the amount we travel by air (take fewer trips, stay longer!), to avoid night flights (when plane contrails trap heat from Earth but can't reflect sunlight back to space), and to make the trips we do take "climate neutral" via a carbon offset scheme.

Carbon offset schemes

Offset schemes run by ⓦ**climatecare.org**, ⓦ**carbonneutral.com** and others allow you to "neutralize" the greenhouse gases that you are responsible for releasing. Their websites have simple calculators that let you work out the impact of any flight. Once that's done, you can pay to fund projects that will reduce future carbon emissions by an equivalent amount (such as the distribution of low-energy lightbulbs and cooking stoves in developing countries). Please take the time to visit our website and make your trip climate neutral.

ⓦ**www.roughguides.com/climatechange**

ⓦ**www.expedia.co.uk** (in UK), ⓦ**www .expedia.com** (in US), ⓦ**www.expedia.ca** (in Canada)
ⓦ**www.flychina.com** (in US)
ⓦ**www.lastminute.com** (in UK)
ⓦ**www.opodo.co.uk** (in UK)
ⓦ**www.orbitz.com** (in US)
ⓦ**www.travelocity.co.uk** (in UK), ⓦ**www .travelocity.com** (in US), ⓦ**www.travelocity.ca** (in Canada)
ⓦ**www.zuji.com.au** (in Australia), ⓦ**www.zuji .co.nz** (in New Zealand)

Airlines

Aeroflot UK ☎020/7355 2233, US ☎1-888-340-6400, Canada ☎1-416/642-1653, Australia

☎02/9262 2233; ⓦwww.aeroflot.co.uk, ⓦwww .aeroflot.com.
Air Canada UK ☎0871 220 1111, Republic of Ireland ☎01/679 3958, US and Canada ☎1-888-247-2262, Australia ☎1300 655 767, New Zealand ☎0508/747 767; ⓦwww .aircanada.com.
Air China UK ☎020/7744 0800, US ☎1-800-982-8802, Canada ☎1-416/581-8833, Australia ☎02/9232 7277; ⓦwww.airchina.com.cn.
Air France UK ☎0870 142 4343, US ☎1-800-237-2747, Canada ☎1-800 667-2747, Australia ☎1300390 190, South Africa ☎0861/340 340; ⓦwww.airfrance.com.
Air Pacific UK ☎0870 572 6827, US ☎1-800-227-4446, Australia ☎1800 230 150, New Zealand ☎0800 800 178; ⓦwww.airpacific.com.

Alitalia UK ☎0870 544 8259, Republic of Ireland ☎01/677 5171, US ☎1-800-223-5730, Canada ☎1-800-361-8336, New Zealand ☎09/308 3357, South Africa ☎011/721 4500; ⊛www.alitalia.com.

All Nippon Airways (ANA) UK ☎0870 837 8866, Republic of Ireland ☎1850 200 058, US and Canada, ☎1-800-235-9262; ⊛www.anaskyweb.com.

American Airlines UK ☎0845 7789 789, Republic of Ireland ☎01/602 0550, US and Canada ☎1-800-433-7300, Australia ☎1800 673 486, New Zealand ☎0800 445 442; ⊛www.aa.com.

Asiana Airlines UK ☎020/7514 0201, US ☎1-800-227-4262, Australia ☎02/9767 4343; ⊛www.flyasiana.com.

British Airways UK ☎0870 850 9850, Republic of Ireland ☎1890 626 747, US and Canada ☎1-800-AIRWAYS, Australia ☎1300 767 177, New Zealand ☎09/966 9777, South Africa ☎011/441 8600; ⊛www.ba.com.

Cathay Pacific UK ☎020/8834 8888, US ☎1-800-233-2742, Canada ☎1-800-268-6868, Australia ☎13 17 47, New Zealand ☎09/379 0861, South Africa ☎011/700 8900; ⊛www.cathaypacific.com.

China Airlines UK ☎020/7436 9001, US ☎1-917-368-2003, Australia ☎02/9231 5588, New Zealand ☎09/308 3364; ⊛www.china-airlines.com.

China Eastern Airlines UK ☎0870 760 6232, US ☎1-626/1583-1500, Canada ☎1-604/689-8998, Australia ☎02/9290 1148; ⊛www.flychinaeastern.com.

China Southern Airlines US ☎1-888-338-8988, Australia ☎02/9231 1988; ⊛www.cs-air.com.

Delta UK ☎0845 600 0950, Republic of Ireland ☎ 01/407 3165, US and Canada ☎1-800-221-1212, Australia ☎1300 302 849, New Zealand ☎09/977 2232; ⊛www.delta.com.

Emirates UK ☎0870 243 2222, US and Canada ☎1-800-777-3999, Australia ☎03/9940 7807, New Zealand ☎05/836 4728, South Africa ☎0861/363 728; ⊛www.emirates.com.

Iberia UK ☎0870 609 0500, Republic of Ireland ☎0818 462 000, US ☎1-800-772-4642, South Africa ☎011/884 5909; ⊛www.iberia.com.

JAL (Japan Airlines) UK ☎0845 774 7700, Republic of Ireland ☎01/408 3757, US and Canada ☎1-800-525-3663, Australia ☎02/9272 1111, New Zealand ☎09/379 9906, South Africa ☎011/214 2560; ⊛www.jal.com.

KLM (Royal Dutch Airlines) UK ☎0870 507 4074, Republic of Ireland ☎1850 747 400, Australia ☎1300 392 192, New Zealand ☎09/921 6040, South Africa ☎011/961 6727; ⊛www.klm.com.

Korean Air UK ☎0800 413 000, Republic of Ireland ☎01/799 7990, US and Canada ☎1-800-438-5000, Australia ☎02/9262 6000, New Zealand ☎09/914 2000; ⊛www.koreanair.com.

Lufthansa UK ☎0870 837 7747, Republic of Ireland ☎01/844 5544, US ☎1-800-399-5838, Canada ☎1-800-563-5954, Australia ☎1300 655 727, New Zealand ☎0800 945 220, South Africa ☎0861/842 538; ⊛www.lufthansa.com.

Malaysia Airlines UK ☎0870 607 9090, Republic of Ireland ☎01/6761 561, US ☎1-800-552-9264, Australia ☎13 26 27, New Zealand ☎0800 777 747, South Africa ☎011/8809 614; ⊛www.malaysia-airlines.com.

Northwest/KLM US ☎1-800-225-2525, ⊛www.nwa.com.

PIA (Pakistan International Airlines) UK ☎0800 587 1023, US and Canada ☎1-800-578-6786; ⊛www.piac.com.pk.

Qantas Airways UK ☎0845 774 7767, Republic of Ireland ☎01/407 3278, US and Canada ☎1-800-227-4500, Australia ☎13 13 13, New Zealand ☎0800 808 767 or 09/357 8900, South Africa ☎011/441 8550; ⊛www.qantas.com.

Qatar Airways UK ☎0870 770 4215, US ☎1-877-777-2827, Canada ☎1-888-366-5666, Australia ☎386/054 855, South Africa ☎011/523 2928; ⊛www.qatarairways.com.

Royal Brunei UK ☎020/7584 6660, Australia ☎1300 721 271, New Zealand ☎09/977 2209; ⊛www.bruneiair.com.

SAS (Scandinavian Airlines) UK ☎0870 6072 7727, Republic of Ireland ☎01/844 5440, US and Canada ☎1-800-221-2350, Australia ☎1300 727 707; ⊛www.flysas.com.

Singapore Airlines UK ☎0844 800 2380, Republic of Ireland ☎01/671 0722, US ☎1-800-742-3333, Canada ☎1-800-663-3046, Australia ☎13 10 11, New Zealand ☎0800 808 909, South Africa ☎011/880 8560; ⊛www.singaporeair.com.

Swiss UK ☎0845 601 0956, Republic of Ireland ☎1890 200 515, US ☎1-877-3797-947, Canada ☎1-877-559-7947, Australia ☎1300 724 666, New Zealand ☎09/977 2238, South Africa ☎0860 040 506; ⊛www.swiss.com.

Thai Airways UK ☎0870 606 0911, US ☎1-212/949-8424, Australia ☎1300 651 960, New Zealand ☎09/377 3886, South Africa ☎011/455 1018; ⊛www.thaiair.com.

United Airlines US ☎1-800-UNITED-1, ⊛www.united.com.

US Airways UK ☎0845 600 3300, Republic of Ireland ☎1890 925 065, US and Canada ☎1-800-428-4322; ⊛www.usairways.com.

Vietnam Airlines UK ☎0870 224 0211, US ☎1-415-677-0888, Canada ☎1-416/599-2888,

Australia ☎02/9283 9658; ⊛www
.vietnamairlines.com.
Virgin Atlantic UK ☎0870 380 2007, US
☎1-800-821-5438; Australia ☎1300 727 340,
South Africa ☎011/340 3400; ⊛www
.virgin-atlantic.com.

Agents and operators

China Highlights China ☎+86/773 2831999,
⊛www.chinahighlights.com. China-based company
that offers a set of three- and four-day tours of
Shanghai and the surrounding area.
China Odyssey China ☎+86/773 5854000,
⊛www.chinaodysseytours.com. Operates short
city tours, or longer trips that take in other
destinations in China.
North South Travel UK ☎01245/608291,
⊛www.northsouthtravel.co.uk. Friendly, competitive
travel agency, offering discounted fares worldwide.
Profits are used to support projects in the

developing world, especially the promotion of
sustainable tourism.
On the Go Tours UK ☎020/7371 1113, ⊛www
.onthegotours.com. Runs group and tailor-made tours
that include Shanghai as part of a jaunt around China.
STA Travel UK ☎0871 2300 040, US ☎1-800-
781-4040, Australia ☎134 STA, New Zealand
☎0800 474 400, South Africa ☎0861/781 781;
⊛www.statravel.com. Worldwide specialists in
independent travel; also student IDs, travel insurance,
car rental, rail passes, and more. Good discounts for
students and under-26s.
Trailfinders UK ☎0845 058 5858, Republic of
Ireland ☎01/677 7888, Australia ☎1300 780 212;
⊛www.trailfinders.com. One of the best-informed
and most efficient agents for independent travellers.
Travel China Guide US and Canada ☎1-800-
892-6988, all other countries ☎+800 6668 8666;
⊛www.travelchinaguide.com. A Chinese company
with a wide range of three- and four-day group tours
of Shanghai and around.

Arrival

Whatever your arrival point in Shanghai, you are almost guaranteed a further long
journey into the centre. Fortunately, there are good bus and metro connections to
speed you to your final destination, and very few shady cabbies, though you
should always catch a licensed cab from a taxi rank.

By air

Arriving by air from abroad, you'll touch
down at glossy, new **Pudong International
Airport** (PVG), 40km east of the city along
the mouth of the Yangzi River. There is an
ATM machine just after customs, before
baggage reclamation, and it's a good idea to
get money out here as the banks downstairs
in the arrivals hall charge a hefty ¥50
commission on currency exchanges. You'll
be pestered in the arrivals hall by charlatan
taxi drivers; ignore them and instead make
for the official **taxi** rank, on your right as you
go out, opposite exit 15. A cab into the
centre should cost around ¥140 and take
just under an hour.

The most convenient public transport into
town is the **airport bus**, which leaves from
opposite the exit gates. There are eight

routes, with departures every fifteen minutes
from 6am to 7.30pm, and a reduced service
afterwards; tickets cost around ¥20.
Remember to use the toilet in the arrivals
hall before you board as the journey into
town takes around an hour and a half. Bus
#2 is generally the most useful as it goes to
the Jing'an Temple metro stop in the city
centre. Bus #1 goes to Hongqiao Airport
(see opposite); bus #3 runs to Xujiahui; bus
#4 heads to Hongkou Stadium, in the north;
bus #5 makes for Shanghai Railway Station;
bus #6 goes to Zhongshan Park; and bus
#7 to Shanghai South Railway Station. The
only one with a drop off in Pudong is bus
#5 (at Dongfang Hospital).

If you're heading straight out of the city,
make for exit 18, opposite which **long-
distance coaches** depart hourly for Suzhou,

Shanghai transport terminals

Airports		
Pudong Airport	浦东机场	*pǔ dōng jī chǎng*
Hongqiao Airport	虹桥机场	*hóng qiáo jī chǎng*
Train stations		
Shanghai Station	上海火车站	*shānghǎi huǒchē zhàn*
Shanghai South Station	上海火车南站	*shāng hǎi huǒ chē nán zhàn*
Bus stations		
Qiujiang Lu Bus Station	虬江路汽车站	*qiú jiāng lù qì chē zhàn*
Hengfeng Lu Bus Station	恒丰路汽车站	*héng fēng lù qì chē zhàn*

Hangzhou and other destinations; tickets cost around ¥50 to each of these places.

The fastest and most romantic way to get into town is on the **Maglev** (see box below), and there are ladies in uniforms to usher you in the right direction. The Maglev is not recommended if you have heavy luggage, though, as there are escalators and corridors to deal with both at the airport and at your arrival point at Longyang metro station.

Hongqiao Airport

Most domestic flights land at the old and tatty **Hongqiao Airport** (SHA), 20km from the Bund. From here, a taxi to Nanjing Xi Lu costs about ¥45, taking about 45 minutes, and to the Bund about ¥60. At busy times such as Friday night, you could wait more than an hour for a cab at the rank, so walk to departures and pick up one that's just dropped someone off. Buses leave from the car park: bus #1 goes to Pudong Airport; the airport shuttle goes to Jing'an Temple subway stop in the city centre; bus #925 makes for People's Square; and the #941 heads to the main train station.

By train and bus

The main train station – **Shanghai Railway Station**, and often called the "new station" – is in the north of the city. Its vast concrete forecourt is always a mass of encamped migrants, and it's not a particularly safe place to hang around at night. The best way to get out of the station area is by metro (lines #1, #3 and #4 run through it) or taxi, the latter not likely to cost more than ¥15–20 into the city. There's an official rank outside the station. If you've come from Hangzhou you'll arrive at **Shanghai South Station**, which is on metro lines #1 and #3.

Hardly any tourists arrive in Shanghai by bus; if you do you'll be dropped in the remote outskirts of the city. Some services use the bus station on **Qiujiang Lu**, next to the Baoshan Lu metro station; a few private buses terminate at the main train station itself; or you may arrive at nearby **Hengfeng Lu Station** over the road from the Hanzhong Lu metro station. Generally speaking, though, it's potluck where you end up.

The Maglev

The most glamorous way to get into town from Pudong is on the world's only commercial **Maglev train** (daily 7am–9pm; every 20min), suspended above the track and propelled by the forces of magnetism. It whizzes from Pudong International Airport to Longyang Lu metro station, in eight minutes, accelerating to 430km per hour in the first four minutes, then immediately starting to decelerate. As there's no friction, the ride is smooth, and as you near top speed – there's a digital speedometer in each cabin – the view from the windows becomes an impressionistic blur. Tickets cost ¥50 one way, and ¥40 if you show a plane ticket. Never mind that the Maglev terminal is three minutes' walk from the airport, and that Longyang Lu is still a long way from the centre of town – you may never get another chance to go this fast on land.

Leaving Shanghai by plane

International and domestic **plane tickets** can be bought from any hotel or travel agent for a small commission, or online at ⓦwww.elong.net; the ticket will be delivered without extra charge a few hours after you book it and you pay the delivery boy. You'll need to provide a phone number to confirm the booking. **Departure tax** is included in the ticket price.

To get to **Hongqiao Airport** (Ⓣ62688899), which handles most domestic flights, take a cab (¥60 or so from the centre; 45min), bus #941 from Shanghai train station (just over 1hr) or the airport shuttle bus (which will take rather less) from the terminal at 1600 Nanjing Xi Lu, opposite Jing'an (every 30min; daily 6am–7.30pm; ¥20).

The fastest way to get to **Pudong International Airport** (Ⓣ68341000) is to take the metro to Longyang Lu on line #1 and then get the Maglev (see p.23). Otherwise, take an airport bus (details as for Hongqiao Airport). A taxi will cost around ¥140.

The following **airlines** have offices in Shanghai. For websites, see pp.20–22.

Aeroflot Donghu Hotel, Donghu Lu Ⓣ64158158.

Air China 24H Room 101B, Changfeng Centre, 1088 Yan'an Xi Lu (near Fanyu Lu) Ⓣ52397227.

Air France Room 3901, Ciro's Plaza, 388 Nanjing Xi Lu Ⓣ400 8808808.

All Nippon Airways (ANA) Shanghai Centre, 1376 Nanjing Xi Lu Ⓣ62797000.

Asiana Airlines 2000 Yan'an Xi Lu Ⓣ62709900.

Cathay Pacific Room 2104, 138 Shanghai Plaza, Huaihai Zhong Lu Ⓣ63756000.

China Eastern Airlines 200 Yan'an Xi Lu Ⓣ62472255.

China Southern Airlines 227 Jiangsu Lu Ⓣ62262299.

JAL (Japan Airlines) 7th Floor, Huaihai International Plaza, 1045 Huaihai Zhong Lu Ⓣ62883000.

KLM/Northwest Airlines Room 207, Shanghai Centre, 1376 Nanjing Xi Lu Ⓣ68846884.

Korean Air 2099 Yan'an Lu Ⓣ62758649.

Lufthansa 3rd Floor, 1 Building, Corporate Avenue, 222 Hubin Lu Ⓣ53524999.

Malaysia Airlines Suite 560, Shanghai Centre, 1376 Nanjing Xi Lu Ⓣ62798607.

Qantas Airways 32nd Floor, K. Wah Centre, 1010 Huaihai Zhong Lu, near Xiangyang Nan Lu Ⓣ800 8190089.

Singapore Airlines Plaza 66, Tower 1, 1266 Nanjing Xi Lu Ⓣ62887999.

Thai Airways Unit 105, Kerry Centre, 1515 Nanjing Xi Lu Ⓣ52985555.

United Airlines Room 3301, Central Plaza, 381 Huaihai Zhong Lu Ⓣ33114567.

Virgin Atlantic Suite 221, 2nd Floor, 12 The Bund Ⓣ53534600.

Getting around

Shanghai's infrastructure groans under tremendous demands, but is holding up, for the moment. The subway is fast, air-conditioned and easy to navigate. Taxis are cheap and plentiful and drivers are honest, which means that it's easy to avoid the overcrowded bus system.

Cycling is a good way to get around, though bikes are banned on most of the major roads in the daytime. **Walking** is more rewarding than in most Chinese cities – there are few of the tedious boulevards that tend to characterize Chinese city centres – but the sheer density of the crowds can be intimidating. Crossing the road is more stressful than it should be as traffic is allowed to turn right even when the green man is flashing – you really have to stay on your toes. It is impossible to hire a car without a Chinese driving licence – and anyway you'd have to be nuts to voluntarily drive these streets. But if you're short on time, there are plenty of **tours** of Shanghai on offer, and this can be a great way to see the sights. Finally, for details of **boat** travel within Shanghai, see p.54 and p.86, and for information on travelling around Shanghai's hinterland by train see box, p.149.

By metro

The clean, modern **metro** operates from 5.30am to 11pm, and includes both underground and light rail lines. The system is easy to find your way around: station entrances are marked by a red "M" logo, all stations and trains are well signed in English and stops are announced in both English and Chinese over an intercom when the train pulls in.

There are four **lines** at present, with nine more to open in the next decade, but only two are particularly useful for tourists. Line #1 runs north–south, with useful stops at the railway station, People's Square, Changshu Lu (for the Old French Concession), Xujiahui and Shanghai Stadium. Line #2 runs east–west with stops at Jing'an Temple, Henan Lu and, in Pudong, Lujiazui and the Science and Technology Museum. The lines intersect at the enormous People's Square station

(take careful note of the wall maps here for which exit to use). Lines #3 and #4 are much less used by visitors, and mainly serve commuters. They intersect with line #1 at Shanghai Stadium and at the railway station – but if you want to change be prepared for a lot of walking.

Tickets cost from ¥3 to ¥7, according to the distance travelled. They can be bought either from touch-screen machines (there's an option for English) or from vendors. Alternately, you can purchase a ¥70 stored-value card for ¥100 (you get ¥30 back when you return it) at stations and convenience stores, but you'd need to be in the city for at least a couple of weeks to make it worthwhile.

By bus

Shanghai has more than a thousand **bus** lines and buses run frequently, every few minutes. Still, they are often overcrowded, and you should be careful of pickpockets. Buses operate from 5am to 11pm, after which time night buses take over. **Fares** are ¥1 on old buses, ¥2 on the new, air-conditioned buses; you pay on board. There are onboard announcements in English, but be careful not to miss your stop as the next one will likely not be for another kilometre.

Services with numbers in the 300s are night buses; those in the 400s cross the Huangpu; and anything over 800 is air-conditioned. Most large fold-out city maps show bus routes, usually as a red or blue line with a dot Indicating a stop. **Sightseeing buses** for tourist sights in the outskirts leave from the Shanghai Stadium (see p.27).

By taxi

Taxis are ubiquitous (until you need one when it's raining) and very cheap – the rate is ¥2 per km, a little more after 10pm, with a

Useful Shanghai bus routes

North–south

#18 (trolleybus) From Lu Xun Park, across Suzhou Creek and along Xizang Lu.

#41 Passes Tianmu Xi Lu, in front of the main train station and goes down through the Old French Concession to Longhua Park.

#64 From the main train station, along Beijing Lu, then close to the Shiliupu wharf to the south of the Bund.

#65 From the top to the bottom of Zhongshan Lu (the Bund), terminating in the south at the Nanpu Bridge.

East–west

#3 From the Shanghai Museum across the Huangpu River to the Jinmao Tower.

#19 (trolleybus) From near Gongping Lu wharf in the east, passing near the *Pujiang Hotel* and roughly following the course of the Suzhou Creek to the Jade Buddha Temple (Yufo Si).

#20 From Jiujiang Lu (just off the Bund) along Nanjing Lu, past Jing'an Temple, then on to Zhongshan Park subway stop in the west of the city.

#42 From Guangxi Lu, near People's Square then along Huaihai Lu in the Old French Concession.

#135 From Yangpu Bridge in the east of the city to the eastern end of Huaihai Lu, via the Bund.

#911 From the Yu Garden to Huaihai Lu.

---

minimum charge of ¥11, or ¥14 at night. Drivers rarely speak English so you'll need your destination written down in Chinese characters. Otherwise, if you're heading anywhere near an intersection, just say the name of the two roads.

The driver should flip the meter down as he accelerates away – if he doesn't, say *dabiao*. Having a map open on your lap deters unnecessary detours but you shouldn't be paranoid as Shanghai cabbies are a decent bunch on the whole. If you get into a dispute with one, take his number, written on the sign on the dashboard – just the action of writing it down can produce a remarkable change of behaviour.

The best **taxi company** is Dazhong (☏63185666) – look at the characters on the cab roofs. Their well-trained drivers wear uniforms and white gloves and drive newish Santanas. Dazhong will also hire out cabbies at a day rate (around ¥600).

By bicycle

Cycling is a great way to get around the city but cyclists need to be wary as traffic is not well disciplined. Pedestrians provide the biggest hazard, though, with a tendency to step right out in front of you. Ringing your bell will elicit no response, so you need to yell – shouting in English gets a better response than trying to do it in Chinese (perhaps it sounds more alarming). Note that major thoroughfares are closed to cyclists between 7.30am and 5pm.

The only place to **rent a bike** is the *Captain Hostel* (see p.104) and they'll only rent to guests. You can buy cheap city bikes at Carrefour (see p.136), however, starting from about ¥200. Their fold-ups (¥360 or so) are perfectly adequate for city riding and you can chuck it in the boot of a taxi at the end of the day. Good-quality bikes are available from Bohdi Bikes (Suite 2308, Building 2, 2918 Zhongshan Bei Lu ☏32260000, ☒www .bohdi.com.cn; Caoyang Lu metro).

Tours

The government-run tourist office, CITS (see p.42), runs a wide range of tours and trips, as well as tickets for onward travel, but rather better value is the private company **Jinjiang Tours** (161 Changle Lu, by the *Jinjiang Hotel*; ☏64151188). Their convenient day-long coach tour of Shanghai whizzes round all the staples –

Street names

All Shanghai's east–west streets are named after Chinese cities; north–south roads are named after provinces. The name is usually followed by a direction – **bei** (north), **nan** (south), **xi** (west), **dong** (east) and **zhong** (middle) – then the word for street, usually **lu** but occasionally **jie**; so Maoming Bei Lu (Maoming North Street), as it heads south, turns into Maoming Nan Lu (Maoming South Street).

Old French Concession, People's Square, Jade Buddha Temple, Yu Garden, the Bund and Pudong – for a reasonable ¥250 (including lunch but excluding entrance fees). Their English-speaking staff will also arrange tours to other sights in the city centre or further afield. **The Sightseeing Bus Centre** next to the Shanghai Stadium (by entrance 5), in the far south of the city, is the place to head for tours of the outlying areas, such as to the local canal towns (see p.151). Tickets can be bought up to a week in advance. See also Agents and operators on p.22.

The media

Sadly, China's opening up has not resulted in any softening of the Communist Party's authoritarian instincts, and all media is heavily censored. Journalists and even bloggers who fail to toe the party line are slung in jail, often on a charge of "revealing state secrets". Change might come from an unexpected source: now that Shanghai has one of the world's largest stock exchanges, accurate financial reporting has become vital. The loudest calls for press freedom are coming from the dry-as-dust financial papers, and those who rely on them, who are marshalling the only argument that might have any weight with the government – that they're threatening economic development.

Newspapers and magazines

Xinhua, the Chinese news agency, is a mouthpiece for the state, whose propaganda you can read in the English-language **newspapers**, *China Daily* and *Shanghai Star*, available from most newsagents, including the ones on subway platforms. Both have a handy section listing mainstream cultural events.

Imported publications (sometimes censored) such as *Time*, *Newsweek*, the *Far Eastern Economic Review* and Hong Kong's *South China Morning Post* can be bought at the bookshops of four- and five-star hotels and are sometimes available at the Charterhouse bookstore (see p.146). If you are moving or doing business here, you'll find

plenty of books offering help and advice at the Foreign Language Bookstore (see p.146). Gourmands will also find in-depth dining guides.

You can pick up glossy free **leaflets**, containing basic tourist information at the upmarket hotels and at the airport. Much more useful, though, are the free **magazines** aimed at the expat community, such as *City Weekend* (Ⓦwww.cityweekend.com.cn/shanghai), *Hint* (Ⓦwww.hintmagazinesh.com), *Time Out Shanghai* and the once great but now rather pedestrian *That's Shanghai* (Ⓦwww.thatssh.com). All have listings sections including restaurants, club nights and art happenings, with addresses written in *pinyin* and Chinese, but no maps. The magazines are free, and you can pick them up at most expat hangouts such as the Old French Concession, Xintiandi or *Barbarossa* in Renmin Park. For a list of online resources, with comprehensive listings and maps, see p.43.

Radio

On the **radio** you're likely to hear the latest ballads by pop-robots from the Hong Kong and Taiwan idol factories, or versions of Western pop songs sung in Chinese. The BBC World Service can be picked up at 12010, 15278, 17760 and 21660kHz. VoA can be tuned into on 5880, 6125, 9760, 15250, 15425, 17820 and 21840kHz.

Television

There is the occasional item of interest on Chinese **television**, though you'd have to be very bored to resort to it for entertainment. Domestic travel and wildlife programmes are frequently shown, as are song-and-dance extravaganzas, the most

entertaining of which feature dancers in weird fetishistic costumes. Gung-ho Chinese war films, in which the Japanese are shown getting mightily beaten, at least have the advantage that you don't need to speak the language to understand what's going on. The present rage is for *Pop Idol*-type shows where the audience chooses the winner by phone-in – the only time that Chinese citizens get to vote. These shows are fiercely popular with teenage girls, who form clans based around their favourite. The winner tends to be a feisty and androgynous-looking girl.

CCTV9 is an English-language channel, with a news programme at 10pm nightly. The local broadcaster SBN has a news update at 10pm daily, in English. CCTV5 is a sports channel and often shows European football games. Satellite TV in English is available in the more expensive hotels. Most mid- and top-range hotels will have ESPN, BBC and CNN.

Festivals and public holidays

The rhythm of festivals and religious observances that used to mark the Chinese calendar was interrupted by the Cultural Revolution, and only now, nearly forty years on, are old traditions beginning to re-emerge. The majority of festivals celebrate the turning of the seasons or propitious dates, such as the ninth day of the ninth lunar month, and are times for gift-giving, family reunions and feasting.

Traditional **festivals** take place according to dates in the Chinese lunar calendar, in which the month starts when the moon is a new crescent, and the middle of the month is marked by the full moon; by the Gregorian calendar, these festivals fall on a different date every year.

Public holidays have little effect on business, with only government departments and certain banks closing. However, on New Year's Day, during the first three days of the Chinese New Year, and on National Day, most businesses, shops and sights will be shut, though some restaurants stay open.

January/February

New Year's Day (Jan 1).
Spring Festival (Starts between late Jan and mid-Feb) Chinese New Year celebrations extend over the first two weeks of the new lunar year (see box opposite).

March

Guanyin's Birthday Guanyin, the goddess of mercy and probably China's most popular Buddhist deity, is celebrated on the nineteenth day of the second lunar month; festivities are held at the Yufo and Baiyunguan temples.

Spring Festival

The **Spring Festival**, usually falling in late January or the first half of February, is marked by two weeks of festivities celebrating the beginning of a new year in the lunar calendar (and is thus also called Chinese New Year). In Chinese astrology, each year is associated with a particular animal from a cycle of twelve – 2008 is the Year of the Rat, for example – and the passing into a new astrological phase is a momentous occasion. There's a tangible sense of excitement in the run-up to the festival, when Shanghai is perhaps at its most colourful, with shops and houses decorated with good-luck messages and stalls and shops selling paper money, drums and costumes. However, it's not an ideal time to travel – everything shuts down, and most of the population is on the move, making travel impossible or extremely uncomfortable.

The first day of the festival is marked by a family feast at which *jiaozi* (dumplings) are eaten, sometimes with coins hidden inside. To bring luck, people dress in red clothes (red being regarded as a lucky colour) – a particularly important custom if the animal of their birth year is coming round again – and each family tries to eat a whole fish, since the word for fish is a homonymn for surplus. Firecrackers are let off to scare ghosts away and again on the fifth day, to honour Cai Shen, god of wealth. Another ghost-scaring tradition you'll notice is the pasting up of images of door gods at the threshold.

The most public expression of the festivities – a must for visitors – is at the **Longhua Temple** (see p.98), held on the first few days of the festival. There are food and craft stalls and plenty of folk entertainments such as stilt walkers and jugglers. The highlight is on the evening of the first day, when the Longhua bell is struck.

April

Qingming Festival (April 4 & 5). "Tomb Sweeping Day" is the time to visit the graves of ancestors, leave offerings of food, and burn ghost money – fake paper currency – in honour of the departed.

May

Labour Day (May 1). Labour Day marks the start of a week-long national holiday, during which all tourist sights are extremely busy.

Youth Day (May 4). Commemorating the student demonstration in Tian'anmen Square in 1919, which gave rise to the nationalist, anti-Imperialist May Fourth Movement. Go to the First National Congress of the CCP and you'll see hordes of youths being indoctrinated.

June

Children's Day (June 1). Most school pupils are taken on excursions at this time, so if you're visiting a popular tourist site, be prepared for mobs of kids in yellow baseball caps.

September/October

Moon Festival Marked on the fifteenth day of the eighth lunar month, this is also known as the Mid-Autumn Festival. It's a time of family reunion, celebrated with fireworks and lanterns; in Shanghai there is an evening parade along Huaihai Lu. Moon cakes, containing a rich filling of sweet paste, are eaten: all the fancier restaurants will have them on the menu.

Double Ninth Festival Nine is a number associated with yang, or male energy, and on the ninth day of the ninth lunar month qualities such as assertiveness and strength are celebrated. It's believed to be a good time for the distillation (and consumption) of spirits.

National Day (Oct 1). On which everyone has a week off to celebrate the founding of the People's Republic, and state TV is even more dire than usual, packed with programmes celebrating the achievements of the Communist Party. During the "golden week" expect massive crowds everywhere – it's not a convenient time to travel.

November

The Shanghai International Arts Fair sees a month of cultural programming at the city's arts venues, but it's at its best when the Art Biennale is in town (2008 and 2010; see p.129 and Ⓦ www .artsbird.com).

Sport and activities

2008 is of course China's Olympic year, and a passion for athletics has become almost a patriotic duty. But the most visible forms of exercise are fairly timeless; head to any public space in the morning and you'll see citizens going through all sorts of martial arts routines, playing ping pong and street badminton, even ballroom dancing. Sadly though, facilities for organized sport are fairly limited.

Spectator sports

The Chinese say they're good at "small" ballgames, such as squash, badminton and of course table tennis, at which they are world champions, but admit room for improvement in the "big" ballgames, such as **football**. Nevertheless, Chinese men follow foreign soccer avidly, particularly foreign teams with Chinese players, such as (at the time of writing) Manchester City. English, Spanish and German league games are shown on CCTV5 and BTV. The standard of the domestic football league is improving, and decent wages have attracted a fair few foreign players and coaches. In season (mid-March to November) Shenhua, Shanghai's best team, play every other Sunday at the Hongkou Stadium in the north of the city (see p.96). Tickets cost ¥15 and can be bought on the day, either from the kiosk or from a tout.

In the southwest of the city, Shanghai Stadium is one of China's largest, and is mostly used for pop concerts, though it will host some of the football games in the 2008 summer **Olympics**; check the official website (ⓦen.beijing2008.cn) for tickets and dates.

Shanghai has an impressive new **Formula One** track at Jiading, west of the city (ⓦwww.icsh.sh.cn). Races are held there every September; tickets start at ¥30.

Activities

Golf

There are plenty of courses outside the city; the most prestigious is the Shanghai West Golf Club (☎0512/57203888, ⓦwww .shanghaiwest.com). The Lujiazui Golf Club in Pudong (☎68871200, ⓦwww.lujiazui-golf .com) has a driving range and organizes competitions at city courses.

Gyms and yoga

Most large hotels have **gyms**, with facilities at the *Westin* and *Pudong Shangri-La* being particularly impressive. Good private gyms include Megafit in the basement of the Hong Kong Plaza at 300 Huaihai Zhong Lu and Total Fitness on the 5th floor at 819 Nanjing Xi Lu, near Taixing Lu (☎62553535).

Yoga has taken off in a big way with the smart set (though they wouldn't be seen dead practising the similar homegrown tradition of *tai ji*). The most fashionable yoga studio is Yplus at 299 Fuxing Xi Lu, near Huashan Lu (☎63406161, ⓦwww.yplus.cn).

Swimming

Try the Olympic-size pool in the International Gymnastic Centre at 777 Wuyi Lu (Mon–Fri 3.30–9.30pm, Sat & Sun 8.30am–9.30pm; ☎51083583) or the smaller Pudong Pool at 3669 Pudong Nan Lu (Mon–Fri 3.30–9pm, Sat & Sun 9am–9pm; ☎58890101). For fun, you can't beat the water park Dino Beach (June–Sept; ¥150), with its slides and wave machines, at 78 Xinzhen Lu, near Gudai Lu, Qibao town (☎64783333); take bus #763 from Xinzhuang subway stop, at the end of line #1. Rather incongruously, there are sometimes indie music gigs and rave parties here (entrance fee is halved after 6pm).

Massage and spas

Shanghai has superb massage and spa facilities, with something for all budgets. They are the perfect places to go to unwind from the stresses of a noisy, overcrowded city, for a post-work gossip or even to cap a night out on the town. They are generally open from 10am till midnight, but many open later.

Every neighbourhood has a **foot masseur** – you can spot one by the poster of big feet in the window. For around ¥25 you'll get your toes and legs bathed, then thoroughly rubbed and pummelled for around forty minutes. For a little extra they'll paint your nails or squeeze your blackheads. Above this, there are plenty of mid-range places, which offer a reasonably priced service in a fairly clinical environment. At the upper end of the scale, the city has some fantastic **spas**, where attention has been lavished on decor and ambience and well-trained staff speak English. Look out for discounts and special offers advertised in the expat magazines.

Massage

Dragonfly 206 Xinle Lu ☏54055351; 20 Donghu Lu ☏54050008. This popular chain offers aroma oil massage (¥200 for 1hr) to relieve muscular aches and restore energy, as well as shiatsu and Chinese massages. There's even a hangover relief massage (Y240 for 2hr). Open till 2am.

Green Massage 58 Taicang Lu, near Jinan Lu ☏53860222. Offers shiatsu and cupping among a wide range of inexpensive treatment massages, which start at around ¥80. Handily located just around the corner from Xintiandi.

Huimou Massage No.1, Lane 117, Ruijin Er Lu ☏64664857. Foot massage ¥60, body massage ¥80, and an aroma oil massage is ¥178. They can also arrange house calls, for which the same rates apply plus the cost of return taxi fare.

Sunshine 161 Changle Lu, near Ruijin Yi Lu ☏64158222. Foot massage chain – they start at ¥40. Open till 2am.

Yiheyuan Massage 656 Jianguo Xi Lu ☏54651265. Inexpensive foot, body, aroma oil and traditional Chinese massages.

Spas

Banyan Tree Spa 3rd Floor, The Westin Shanghai, 88 Henan Zhong Lu ☏63351888, Ⓦwww.banyantreespa.com. Choose from a á la carte menu of oil massages: Balinese, Swedish, "Island Dew", sports and Hawaiian Lomi Lomi. Prices start at ¥780 for 1hr.

Evian Spa 2nd Floor, Three on the Bund, 3 Zhongshan Dong Yi Lu ☏63216622. Try the Lomi Lomi massage (¥980 for 1hr 30min), Indian head massage (¥600 for 1hr) or even the colour hydrotherapy underwater massage (¥320 for 30min). Also offer facials, manicures and pedicures.

Hilton Spa Hilton Hotel, 250 Huashan Lu ☏62480000. Reasonably priced, no-nonsense and a bit more clinical than the other top-end places, this place is popular with men. Chinese and Swedish massage and facials, from ¥400.

Mandara Spa JW Marriott Hotel, 6th Floor, Tomorrow Square ☏67986799, Ⓦwww.mandaraspa.com. Specialities include a hot stone massage (¥880 for 2hr) and something called a coffee energizer (¥420 for 1hr), which involves being scrubbed with freshly ground coffee beans. The Yin & Yang (¥780/1hr 30min) is a foot massage combined with a facial.

Culture and etiquette

Shanghai is cosmopolitan and sophisticated, and its inhabitants on the whole well mannered – there's certainly much less spitting and queue jumping than elsewhere in China. But because the streets are so crowded there is a widespread public brusqueness that can take some getting used to. Pushy vendors will shout at you, jump in front of you or even tug your arm, and it takes a while to train yourself to simply ignore them, as the locals do.

As for personal appearance, skimpy **clothing** is fine (indeed fashionable), but looking scruffy will only induce disrespect. All foreigners are – correctly – assumed to be comparatively rich, so why they would want to dress like peasants is quite beyond the Chinese.

Shaking hands is not a Chinese tradition, though it is now fairly common between men. Businessmen meeting for the first time exchange business cards, with the offered card held in two hands as a gesture of respect – you'll see polite shop assistants doing the same with your change.

If you visit a Chinese house, you'll be expected to present your hosts with a **gift**, which won't be opened in front of you – that would be impolite. Imported whisky and ornamental trinkets are suitable as presents, though avoid giving anything too practical as it might be construed as charity.

For **restaurant** etiquette, see p.112. **Smoking** is widespread, and though pricier restaurants have no smoking sections, cafés and bars don't. **Public toilets** are of the squat variety, and on the whole sanitary. But if you blanch at going local, visit any decent hotel – there are always Western-style toilets in the lobby. The characters you will need to learn are:

toilet	厕所	cèsuǒ
man	男	nàn
woman	女	nǚ

Sex and gender issues

Women travellers in Shanghai usually find the incidence of sexual harassment much less of a problem than in other Asian countries. Chinese men are, on the whole, deferential and respectful. Being ignored is a more likely complaint, as the Chinese will generally assume that any man accompanying a woman will be doing all the talking.

In terms of sexual mores pretty much anything goes in Shanghai these days, though public displays of homosexual behaviour will raise an eyebrow (see Gay and lesbian Shanghai, p.127, for more). **Prostitution**, though illegal, has made a big comeback – witness all the new "hairdressers", saunas and massage parlours, every one a brothel. Single foreign men are likely to be approached inside hotels; it's common practice for prostitutes to phone around hotel rooms at all hours of the night, so disconnect the phone. Bear in mind that China is hardly Thailand – consequences may be unpleasant if you are caught with a prostitute – that AIDS is common and the public largely ignorant of sexual health issues. Condoms are widely available, however.

Travelling with children

Children in China are, on the whole, indulged and pampered, and thanks to the one child policy, each "little emperor" is accompanied by six doting adults – his or her parents, plus two sets of grandparents. It's common to see little brats doing whatever the hell they like, but they have a lot less fun when they're old enough to be thrown into China's education sweatshop, where it's also made clear to them that when they grow up they're expected to look after those six adults in their dotage.

Foreigners with kids can expect to receive lots of attention from curious locals – and the occasional admonition that the little one should be wrapped up warmer. Local kids don't use **nappies**, just pants with a slit at the back, and when baby wants to go, mummy points him at the gutter. Nappies are available from modern supermarkets such as Carrefour (see p.136), though there are few public changing facilities. High-end hotels have baby-minding services for around ¥150 an hour.

Sights that children would enjoy include the Ocean Aquarium, Wild Insect Kingdom and Century Park in Pudong (see p.89), the zoo (see p.100), acrobat shows (see p.130), Dino Beach (see p.30) and the Shanghai and Science and Technology museums (see p.91). If you're tired of worrying about your kids in the traffic, try taking them to pedestrianized Xintiandi, the malls, Taikang Lu or Moganshan Art District.

Travel essentials

Costs

Though there's a minority in Shanghai who throw their money around – and plenty of places to spend it – it's quite possible to live cheaply, with most locals surviving on salaries of around ¥3000 a month.

Generally, your biggest expense will be accommodation. Food and transport, on the other hand, are cheap. The minimum **daily budget** you can comfortably maintain is around US$20/£10/¥150 a day, if you stay in a dormitory, get around by bus, and eat in local restaurants. On a budget of US$50/£25/¥400 a day, you'll likely have a better time, staying in a modest hotel, taking taxis, and eating in good restaurants. To stay

in an upmarket hotel and eat in the trendiest places you'll need a budget of around US$150/£75/¥1200 a day.

It used to be government policy to **surcharge foreigners** on public transport fares and admission tickets for sights. This is no longer the case but the practice lives on, and you might find price discrimination being exercised by unscrupulous shopkeepers. **Discounts** on some admission prices are available to students in China on production

> **Tipping** is never expected, and though you might sometimes feel it's warranted, resist the temptation – you'll set an unwelcome precedent.

of the red Chinese student identity card or ISIC card. An international youth hostel card gets a small discount at hostels.

High-end restaurants and hotels add a ten or fifteen percent **service charge** (annoyingly though, it rarely goes to the staff).

Crime and personal safety

The main problem likely to affect tourists visiting Shanghai is **getting scammed** (see box below). In terms of personal safety, Shanghai is safer than most Western cities but you do need to take care as tourists are an obvious target for petty **theft**. Passports and money should be kept in a concealed money belt, and it's a good idea to keep around US$200 separately from the rest of your cash, together with your traveller's cheque receipts, insurance policy details, and photocopies of your passport and visa. Be wary on buses, the favoured haunt of pickpockets.

Warning: scam artists

Getting scammed is the biggest threat to foreign visitors, and there are so many professional con artists targeting tourists that you can expect to be approached many times a day at places such as **Yuyuan Bazaar**, around **People's Square** and on **Nanjing Dong Lu**.

Commonly, a sweet-looking young couple, a pair of girls, or perhaps a kindly old man, will ask to practise their English or offer to show you round. After befriending you – which may take hours – they will suggest some refreshment, and lead you to a teahouse. Following a traditional-looking **tea ceremony** you will be presented with a bill for thousands of yuan, your new "friends" will disappear or pretend to be shocked, and some large gentlemen will appear. In another variation, you will be coaxed into buying a painting (really a print) for a ridiculous sum. So remember: never drink with a stranger if you haven't seen a price list.

Hotel rooms are on the whole secure, dormitories less so – in the latter case it's often fellow travellers who are the problem. Most hotels should have a safe, but it's not unusual for things to go missing from these.

On the street, flashy jewellery and watches will attract the wrong kind of attention, and try to be discreet when taking out your cash. Not looking obviously wealthy also helps if you want to avoid being ripped off by street traders and taxi drivers, as does telling them you are a student – the Chinese have a great respect for education, and much more sympathy for foreign students than for tourists.

The police

The police, or **PSB** (Public Security Bureau) are recognizable by their dark blue uniforms and caps, though there are a lot more around than you might at first think, as plenty are undercover. They have wider powers than Western police forces, including establishing the guilt of criminals – trials are often used only for deciding the sentence of the accused, though China is beginning to have the makings of an independent judiciary. Laws are harsh, with execution – a bullet in the back of the head – the penalty for a wide range of serious crimes, from corruption to rape, though if the culprit is deemed to show proper remorse, the result can be a more lenient sentence.

The police also have the job of looking after foreigners, and you'll most likely have to seek them out for visa extensions (see p.36), to get a loss report, or complain when you've been scammed in a teahouse. They can be surprisingly helpful, but are often officious. A convenient police station is at 499 Nanjing Xi Lu, beside the Chengdu Bei Lu overpass.

Emergency numbers

Police ☎110
Fire ☎119
Ambulance ☎120
Note though that in an emergency you are generally better off **taking a taxi** (see p.37) to the nearest hospital than calling for an ambulance.

Customs allowances

You're allowed to **import** into China up to 400 cigarettes, two litres of alcohol, twenty fluid ounces (59ml) of perfume and up to 50g of gold or silver. You can't take in more than ¥6000, and foreign currency in excess of US$5000 or the equivalent must be declared. It's illegal to import printed or filmed matter critical of the country, but don't worry too much about this, as confiscation is rare in practice.

Note that **export restrictions** apply on any items over 100 years old that you might buy in China – though as you'd be hard pressed to buy anything that old in Shanghai, you needn't be unduly concerned about the process – the "antiques" you commonly see for sale are all fakes.

Electricity

The electricity supply runs on 220 volts, with the most common type of plug dual flat prong. Adaptors are widely available from neighbourhood hardware stores, or any of the tech malls (see p.144).

Entry requirements

Visa applications

To enter China, all foreign nationals require a visa, available worldwide from Chinese embassies and consulates and through specialist tour operators and visa agents, and online.

Single-entry tourist visas (L) must be used within three months of issue, and cost US$30–50 or the local equivalent. The standard L visa is valid for a month, but the authorities will usually grant a request for a two- or three-month visa if asked (which costs the same), though they might refuse at times of heavy tourist traffic. To apply for an L visa you have to submit an application form, either one or two passport-size photographs, your passport (which must be valid for at least another six months from your planned date of entry into China, and have at least one blank page for visas) and the fee. If you apply in person, processing should take between three and five working days. Postal applications are not accepted. You'll be asked your occupation – it's not wise to

admit to being a journalist or writer as you might be called in for an interview. At times of political sensitivity you may be asked for a copy of any air tickets and hotel bookings in your name.

A **business visa** (F) is valid for six months and can be for either multiple or single entry; you'll need an official invitation from a government-recognized Chinese organization to apply for one (except in Hong Kong, where you can simply buy one). **Twelve-month work visas** (Z) again require an invitation, plus a health certificate from your doctor.

Students can get an F visa if they have an invitation or letter of acceptance from a college in Shanghai, though this is only valid for six months. If you're intending to study for longer than six months, you need to fill out an additional form, available from Chinese embassies and online, and will also need a health certificate; then you'll be issued with an X visa which allows you to stay and study for up to a year.

Chinese embassies and consulates

Australia 15 Coronation Drive, Yarralumla, Canberra, ACT 2600 ☏ 02/6273 4780, ☒ au.china -embassy.org. Also consulates at 77 Irving Rd, Toorak, Victoria (visa & passport enquiries ☏ 03/9804 3683), 539 Elizabeth St, Surry Hills (☏ 02/9698 7929), 39 Dunblane St, Camperdown, New South Wales (☏ 02/8595 8000) and 45 Brown St, East Perth (☏ 02/9222 0321).
Canada 515 St Patrick St, Ottawa, Ontario K1N 5 ☏ 1-613/234 2682, ☒ www.chinaembassy canada.org. Visas can also be obtained from the consulates in Calgary, Toronto and Vancouver.
New Zealand 2–6 Glenmore St, Wellington ☏ 04/474 9631, plus a consulate in Auckland ☏ 09/525 1589; ☒ www.chinaconsulate.org.nz.
Republic of Ireland 40 Ailesbury Rd, Dublin 4 ☏ 01/269 1707.
South Africa 220 Hill St, Arcadia, Pretoria ☏ 027/1234 24194, ☒ www.chinese-embassy .org.za.
UK 31 Portland Place, London W1B 1QD ☏ 020/7631 1430; consulate at Denison House, Denison Rd, Victoria Park, Manchester M14 5RX ☏ 0161/224 7480; ☒ www.chinese-embassy.org.uk.
USA 2300 Connecticut Ave NW, Washington DC 20008 ☏ 1-202-328-2517, ☒ www.china-embassy .org. Also consulates in Chicago, Houston, Los Angeles, New York and San Francisco.

Getting visas in Hong Kong

In Hong Kong, it's easier to obtain Chinese visas that are valid for longer than the usual thirty-day period. For a sixty- or ninety-day multiple-entry visa, issued in two days, visit the China Travel Service (CTS) at 78–83 Connaught Rd or 27–33 Nathan Rd. Note that these visas are valid from the date of issue, not the date of entry. You can get a six-month multiple-entry business visa at Shoestring Travel, in the same building as CTS at 27–33 Nathan Rd, for HK$600/US$80. No invitation letter is required, just a business card. For a next-day, no-questions-asked, one-year business visa (HK$1300/US$160), visit Forever Bright Trading Ltd, 707 New Mandarin Plaza, Tower B, 14 Science Museum Rd.

Nationals of most countries can stay in Hong Kong without a visa for up to three months.

Visa extensions

Once in China, a **first extension** to a tourist visa, valid for a month, is easy to obtain; most Europeans pay ¥160 for this, Americans a little less. To apply for an extension, go to the gleaming "Aliens Entry Exit Department" of the PSB (Public Security Bureau) at 1500 Minsheng Lu, in Pudong, near Yinchun Lu (Science and Technology Museum subway stop; Mon–Fri 9–11.30am and 1.30–4.30pm). The visa office is on the third floor. You'll need a passport photo (a shop offers a photo service on the ground floor), proof of your address in Shanghai – so take some hotel receipts – and proof that you have plans to leave the country, so show a plane ticket if you have one. The officious staff will keep your passport for five working days – note that you can't change money, or even book into a new hotel, while they've got it. **Subsequent applications** for extensions will be refused unless you have a good reason to stay such as illness or travel delay. They'll reluctantly give you a couple of extra days if you have a flight out of the country booked.

Don't overstay your visa even for a few hours – the fine is ¥500 per day, and if you're caught at the airport with an out-of-date visa the hassle that will follow may mean you miss your flight.

Health

The most common health hazard in Shanghai is the **cold and flu infections** that strike down a large proportion of the population in the winter months, but **diarrhoea** can also be a problem. It usually strikes in a mild form while your stomach gets used to unfamiliar food, but can also be a sudden onset accompanied by stomach cramps and vomiting, which indicates food poisoning. In both instances, get plenty of rest, drink lots of water, and in serious cases replace lost salts with oral rehydration solution (ORS); this is especially important with young

Foreign consulates in Shanghai

Your consulate can help if you have lost your passport, need some local reading material or are moving here and need some advice.

Australia 22nd floor, 1168 Nanjing Xi Lu ☎52925500, ⓦwww.shanghai.china.embassy.gov.au.

Canada Room 604, West Tower, Shanghai Centre, 1376 Nanjing Xi Lu ☎62798400, ⓦgeo.international.gc.ca/asia/china.

New Zealand 15th floor, Qihua Building, 1375 Huaihai Zhong Lu ☎64711127, ⓦwww.nzembassy.com/home.cfm?c=19.

Republic of Ireland 700A Shanghai Centre, 1376 Nanjing Xi Lu ☎62798729, ⓦwww.embassyofireland.cn/ireland/consulate.htm.

South Africa Room 2706, 220 Yanan Zhong Lu ☎53594977.

United Kingdom Room 301, West Tower, Shanghai Centre, 1376 Nanjing Xi Lu ☎62797650, ⓦwww.uk.cn/bj/index.asp?city=4.

USA 1469 Huaihai Zhong Lu ☎64336880, ⓦshanghai.usconsulate.gov.

children. Take a few sachets with you, or make your own by adding half a teaspoon of salt and three of sugar to a litre of cool, previously boiled water. While down with diarrhoea, avoid milk, greasy or spicy foods, coffee and most fruit, in favour of bland foodstuffs such as rice, plain noodles and soup. If symptoms persist, or if you notice blood or mucus in your stools, consult a doctor.

To avoid stomach complaints, eat at places that look busy and clean and stick to fresh, thoroughly cooked food. Beware of food that has been pre-cooked and kept warm for several hours. Shellfish is a potential hepatitis A risk, and best avoided. Fresh fruit you've peeled yourself is safe; other uncooked foods may have been washed in unclean water. Shanghai's **tap water** can be a little suspect, so try to avoid drinking it. Boiled or bottled water is widely available.

Finally, note that though Shanghai is a pretty permissive place, there is widespread ignorance of sexual health issues. Always practise safe sex.

Hospitals, clinics and pharmacies

Medical facilities in Shanghai are pretty good: there are some high-standard international clinics, big hotels have a resident doctor, and for minor complaints, there are plenty of pharmacies that can suggest remedies. Most doctors will treat you with Western techniques first, but will also know a little Traditional Chinese Medicine (TCM).

Chinese **hospitals** sometimes charge high prices for simple drugs and procedures that aren't necessary – they'll put you on a drip just to administer antibiotics – so be wary of price gouging. In an emergency you're better off taking a cab than waiting for an ambulance – it's quicker and will work out much cheaper. Some English is spoken at the Ruijin Hospital (197 Ruijin Er Lu; ☎64664483) and the Huashan Hospital (12 Wulumuqi Zhong Lu; ☎62489999) has a specialist foreigners' clinic on the eighth floor. The United Family Hospital on 1139 Xianxia Lu (☎51331900, ⓦwww .unitedfamilyhospitals.com) is a complete hospital staffed by doctors trained in the West. Expect to pay around ¥500 as a consultation fee at each of the above.

Expats with medical insurance tend to use **private clinics** such as World Link (Suite 203 Shanghai Centre; ☎62797688, ⓦwww .worldlink-shanghai.com) and the International Medical Centre (551 Pudong Nan Lu, by Pudong Dadao; ☎58799999); both the above also provide dental treatment.

Pharmacies are marked by a green cross. Be wary of backstreet pharmacies as counterfeit drugs are common (check for spelling mistakes in the packaging or instructions). There is a 24-hour pharmacy at 201 Lianhua Lu, Changning (☎62941403), and another outside the Huashan Hospital (see above). Watson's (daily 9am–9pm) is a good brand to head for over-the-counter medicines. There are large branches at 787 Huaihai Zhong Lu and 616 Nanjing Dong Lu, in the basements of the Times Square Mall on Huaihai Lu, Raffles Mall on Fuzhou Lu and Westgate Mall on Nanjing Xi Lu.

Medical resources for travellers

In the UK and Ireland

MASTA (Medical Advisory Service for Travellers Abroad) UK ☎0870 606 2782, ⓦwww .masta-travel-health.com. Forty clinics across the UK. **Tropical Medical Bureau** Republic of Ireland ☎1850 487674, ⓦwww.tmb.ie.

In the US and Canada

Canadian Society for International Health ⓦwww.csih.org. Extensive list of travel health centres in Canada.
CDC ☎1-877-394-8747, ⓦwww.cdc.gov. Official US government travel health site.
International Society for Travel Medicine ⓦwww.istm.org. A full list of clinics worldwide specializing in travel health.

In Australia, New Zealand and South Africa

Netcare Travel Clinics ⓦwww.travelclinic.co.za. Travel clinics in South Africa.
Travellers' Medical & Vaccination Centre ⓦwww.tmvc.com.au. Website lists travellers' medical and vaccination centres throughout Australia and New Zealand.

Insurance

With medical cover expensive you'd be wise to have **travel insurance**. There's little opportunity for dangerous sports in Shanghai (unless crossing the road counts) so a standard policy should be sufficient.

Rough Guides has teamed up with Columbus Direct to offer you travel insurance that can be tailored to suit your needs. Products include a low-cost backpacker option for long stays; a short break option for city getaways; a typical holiday package option; and others. There are also annual multi-trip policies for those who travel regularly. Different sports and activities (trekking, skiing, etc) can usually be covered if required.

See our website (🖰www.roughguides.com /website/shop) for eligibility and purchasing options. Alternatively, UK residents should call ☎08700 339988; Australians should call ☎1300 669 999 and New Zealanders should call ☎0800 559911. All other nationalities should call ☎+44 8708 902843.

Internet

Shanghai has plenty of **Internet cafés**, usually full of kids playing Counterstrike. They're generally located in backstreets, not on the ground floor, and never signposted in English – look for the net character, two crosses inside an "n" (see p.194). Prices are cheap (at around ¥3 an hour), and they are open 24 hrs, but are also heavily regulated – you are required to show your passport before being allowed near a computer. There are a couple on Nanyang Lu, behind the Shanghai Centre, and another on Yunnan Nan Lu, just south of the intersection with Huaihai Zhong Lu. Shanghai Library at 1555 Huaihai Zhong Lu (Hengshan Lu metro; 7am–2am) has a ground-floor room full of computers at ¥4/hr.

All large **hotels** have business centres where you can get online, but this is expensive, especially in the classier places (around ¥30/hr). Better value are the **backpacker hostels** (see p.104 for details), where getting online costs around ¥5/hr or is free. But the best deal is to tote a **laptop** – just about every café has free WiFi, as does *McDonalds*.

Laundry

All hotels provide a laundry service for around ¥50–100, depending on how classy the hotel is. Hostels have a self-service laundry. There are very few public launderettes.

Living and working in Shanghai

If you want to stay on in Shanghai, first you'll need a **residence permit**, which your employer will help you sort out. You have to show your passport and Z (working) visa, health certificate, employment certificate, work permit and your employer's business licence at the main PSB (see p.34). The issued green card is then valid for a year.

Foreigners are now allowed to reside anywhere in the city, though most live in housing targeted at them. Rent in these districts is expensive, usually at least US$2000 a month, which gets you a tolerable imitation of a Western apartment. Living in ordinary neighbourhoods is much cheaper: a central, furnished two-bedroom apartment can cost around US$500 a month. The easiest way to find an apartment is through a real-estate agent, who will usually take a month's rent as a fee. There

---

The new Great Wall of China

If the Chinese regime was discomfited by news faxes sent from abroad during the Tian'anmen massacre in 1989, imagine the headache the Internet is giving them. Tireless as ever in controlling what its citizens know, the government has built a sophisticated **firewall** – nicknamed the new Great Wall of China – that blocks access to undesirable websites. The way this is administered shifts regularly according to the mood of the powers that be. In general, you can be pretty sure you won't be able to access the BBC, CNN, the White House, or anything about Tibetan freedom or democracy, though newspaper websites tend to be left unhindered. You can get around the great firewall by using a proxy server, though it will make loading times slow. Try installing tor (🖰tor.eff.org) into your browser (it works well with Firefox), or simply go through the proxy 🖰www .anonymouse.org.

are plenty of agents, and many advertise in the expat magazines. When you move in you must register with the local PSB office.

Teaching and other work opportunities

Various schemes are run to place foreign teachers in Chinese educational institutions – contact your nearest Chinese embassy (see p.35 for addresses) for details, or the organizations given below. Some employers ask for a TEFL (Teaching English as a Foreign Language) qualification, though a degree, or simply the ability to speak the language as a native, is usually enough. You can also study for your TEFL in Shanghai (details at ⓦ www .windsorschools.co.uk/tefl-shanghai.html).

Teaching at a **university**, you'll earn about ¥2500 a month, more than your Chinese counterparts do, though your workload of around twenty hours a week is correspondingly heavier. The pay isn't enough to allow you to put much aside, but is bolstered by on-campus accommodation. Contracts are generally for one year. Most teachers find their students keen, hardworking, curious and obedient. However, avoid talking about religion or politics in the classroom, as this could get you into trouble.

You'll earn more – up to ¥150 per hour – in a **private school**, though be aware of the risk of being ripped off (you might be given more classes to teach than you've signed up for, for example). Check out the institution thoroughly before committing yourself.

There are plenty of jobs available for foreigners in Shanghai, with a whole section of expat society surviving as actors, cocktail barmen, "Chinglish" correctors, models, freelance writers and so on – the bottom section. To really make any money here, you

need to either be employed by a foreign company or start your own business.

Studying

Private schools aimed at teaching business people how to get by in **Chinese** include the Panda School (☎62376298, ⓦ www .pandachinesetraining.com) and Mandarin House (☎62882308, ⓦ www.mandarinhouse .cn). Both offer a wide range of courses and private tuition. Enjoy Mandarin (☎52300060, ⓦ www.enjoymandarin.com) has a course in Chinese culture – chess, calligraphy and so on – as well as language.

Useful resources

Chinatefl ⓦ www.chinatefl.com. Gives a good overview of English teaching opportunities in the Chinese public sector.
Council on International Educational Exchange ⓦ www.ciee.org. Exchange programmes for US students of Mandarin or Chinese studies, with placements in Shanghai.
Teach Abroad ⓦ www.teachabroad.com. Website on which you can post your CV.
Zhaopin ⓦ www.zhaopin.com. Huge jobs site, in Chinese and English.

Mail

Main **post offices** are open seven days a week between 9am and 7pm; smaller offices may close for lunch or at weekends. The International Post Office is at 276 Suzhou Bei Lu (7am–10pm daily). This is where poste restante letters end up (have letters addressed to you c/o Poste Restante, GPO, Shanghai). There are other convenient post offices inside the Shanghai Centre on Nanjing Xi Lu and on Huangpi Bei Lu at the intersection with Jiangyin Lu.

The Chinese **postal service** is on the whole fairly reliable, with letters and parcels taking a couple of weeks to reach Europe or the US. Overseas postage rates are becoming expensive; a postcard costs ¥4.2, while a standard letter is ¥6. As well as at post offices, you can post letters in green **postboxes**, or at tourist hotels, which usually have a postbox at the front desk. Envelopes can be frustratingly scarce; try the stationery sections of department stores. Stamps can be bought at post offices.

An Express Mail Service (**EMS**) operates to most countries and to most destinations within China and is available from all post offices. Besides cutting delivery times, the service ensures the letter or parcel is sent by registered delivery – though note that the courier service of DHL (38 Huaxiang Lu, ☎52277770) is rather faster, and costs about the same.

To send **parcels**, turn up at any post office with the goods you want to send and the staff will sell you a box to pack them in for ¥15 or so. Once packed, but before the parcel is sealed, it must be checked at the customs window in the post office. A 1kg parcel should cost upwards of ¥70 to send surface mail, or ¥120 by airmail to Europe. If you are sending valuable goods bought in China, put the receipt or a photocopy of it in with the parcel, as it may be opened for customs inspection farther down the line.

Maps

A large foldout **map** of the city can be handy. In general, the free tourist maps – available in large hotels and printed inside tourist magazines – don't show enough detail. A wide variety of city maps are available at all transport hubs and from street vendors, hotels and bookshops, with the best selection available from the Foreign Language Bookstore on Fuzhou Lu (see p.146). With the city changing so fast, it's important to check that your map is up to date.

Money

Chinese **currency** is formally called the **yuan** (¥), more colloquially known as renminbi (RMB) or kuai; a yuan breaks down into units of ten jiao. Paper money was invented in China and is still the main form of exchange, available in ¥100, ¥50, ¥20, ¥10, ¥5 and ¥1 notes. Unlike in the rest of China, you'll receive a lot of ¥1 coins in Shanghai – this is because China's mint is here. The yuan is kept pegged to the dollar at just over ¥8 to $1, which works out at ¥15 to £1, ¥10 to €1; it's an artificially low rate designed to keep Chinese exports competitive and is good news for visitors as it means everything's cheap.

China is suffering from a rash of **counterfeiting**. Check your change carefully, as the locals do – hold ¥50 and ¥100 notes up to the light and rub them; fakes have no watermarks and the paper feels different.

Banks and ATMs

Banks are usually open seven days a week (9am–noon & 2–5pm), though foreign exchange (there's generally a particular counter for this, marked in English) is sometimes only available Monday to Friday. All banks are closed on New Year's Day, National Day, and for the first three days of the Chinese New Year, with reduced hours for the following eleven days.

Cirrus, Visa and Plus cards can be used to make cash withdrawals from **ATMs** operated by the Bank of China, the Industrial and Commercial Bank of China, China Construction Bank and Agricultural Bank of China. Note that most ATMs are located inside banks or shopping centres, so close when they do; there are 24-hour ATMs in the Hong Kong Plaza on Huaihai Zhong Lu and next to Citibank on the Bund. Your bank back home will in all likelihood charge a fee on each withdrawal, with a minimum of around US$3, so it's best to get large amounts out; the maximum for each withdrawal is ¥2500. Keep your exchange receipts and when you leave you can change your renminbi into dollars or sterling at any branch of the Bank of China.

Traveller's cheques and foreign currency

Traveller's cheques are a convenient way to carry your funds around, as they can be replaced if lost or stolen – for which contingency it's worth keeping a list of the serial numbers separate from the cheques. They also attract a slightly better rate of exchange than cash. Available through banks and travel agents, they can be cashed only at branches of the Bank of China and at tourist hotels.

It's still worth taking along a small quantity of **foreign currency** – such as US, Canadian or Australian dollars, or British pounds or euros – as cash is more widely exchangeable than traveller's cheques. Don't try to change money on the **black market** as you'll almost certainly get ripped off.

Credit cards and wiring money

China is basically a cash economy, and **credit cards**, such as Visa, American Express and MasterCard, are only accepted at big tourist hotels and the fanciest restaurants, and by some tourist-oriented shops; there is usually a four percent handling charge. It's straightforward to obtain cash advances on a Visa card at many Chinese banks (though the commission is a steep three percent). Visa cardholders can also get cash advances using ATM machines bearing the "Plus" logo. For **lost or stolen cards**, call ☏62798082 (Amex), ☏10 800 110 7309 (Mastercard) or ☏63236656 (Visa).

It's possible to **wire money** to Shanghai through Western Union (ⓦwww.western union.com); funds can be collected from one of their agents in the city, in post offices and the Agricultural Bank of China.

Opening hours

Offices and **government agencies** are open Monday to Friday, usually from 8am to noon, then from 1 to 5pm; some open on Saturday and Sunday mornings too. **Museums** are either open all week or are shut on one day, usually Monday. The best time to sightsee is during the week, as all attractions are swamped with local tourists at weekends.

For post office hours, see p.39; for banking hours, see opposite; and for restaurant, bar and shop opening hours, see the Eating (p.111), Drinking and nightlife (p.123) and Shopping (p.135) sections.

For dates of public holidays, see p.28.

Phones

Local calls are free from landlines, and long-distance **China-wide calls** are fairly cheap. Note that everywhere in China has an area code which must be used when phoning from outside that locality. The area code for Shanghai (**021**) has been excluded from listings in this book but must be added if you're dialling from outside the city.

A cheap way to make **international calls** is with **IC card phones**, which you'll find in every hotel lobby, and in booths on the street. IC cards (*I-C kǎ* in Mandarin) are sold at every little store and in hotels, in units of ¥20, ¥50 and ¥100, and can also be used for long-distance calls (¥0.2 for 3min). There's a fifty percent discount when used after 6pm and at weekends. You will be cut off when the credit left on the card drops below the amount needed for the next minute.

An even cheaper option is the **IP (Internet Phone) card**, which can be used from any phone, and comes in ¥50 and ¥100 denominations (though the card is always discounted). You dial the number on the card, then instructions in Chinese then English ask you to dial a PIN printed beneath a silver strip on the card, which activates the account; finally you call the number you want. Rates can be as low as ¥2.4 per minute to the USA and Canada, ¥3.2 to Europe. The cards are widely available, but some are China-only, so ask for a *guoji* card if you want to make international calls.

Note that calling from **tourist hotels**, whether from your room or from their business centres, will attract a surcharge and may well be extortionate.

Calling mainland China from abroad

To **call mainland China from abroad**, dial your international access code, then 86 (China's country code), then the area code, minus the initial zero of the regional code (so for Shanghai call 21, not 021), then the rest of the number.

Calling home from Shanghai

To **call abroad from Shanghai** and
the rest of mainland China dial ⊕00,
then the country code (see below),
then the area code, omitting the initial
zero (if any), then the number.
UK ⊕44
Ireland ⊕353
US & Canada ⊕1
Australia ⊕61
New Zealand ⊕64
South Africa ⊕27

Mobile phones

Your home **cellular phone** may already be
compatible with the Chinese network (visitors
from North America should ensure their
phones are GSM/Triband), though note that
you will pay a premium to use it abroad, and
that callers within China have to make an
international call to reach you. Alternatively,
once in Shanghai you can buy a GSM SIM
card from any China Mobile shop or street
kiosk, which – as long your phone is
unlocked – allows you to use your phone as
though it's a local mobile (you will have a
new number). The SIM card costs around
¥100, with some variation in price according
to how lucky the digits are – favoured sixes
and eights bump up the cost, unlucky fours
make it cheaper. You'll also need to buy

Guanxi

Guanxi is a **mobile city guide**,
accessible via phone text (SMS)
messaging, that's particularly useful
when (as often happens) you're
finding it hard to communicate with a
cabbie. From your mobile, text "sh"
and a space (for Shanghai), then the
name of the place you want to go to,
to ⊕95882929, and you'll be
instantly texted back the venue
address in English. Reply to that with
a "C", and the address will be texted
to you in Chinese. Text "sh huaihai lu
thai restaurants" and you'll get a list
of all the Thai restaurants on Huaihai
Lu. Each text costs around ¥1.

prepaid cards to pay for the calls. Making
and receiving domestic calls this way costs
¥0.6 per minute; an international call will cost
around ¥8 a minute.

You can also **rent mobile phones** – look
for the ads in expat magazines or ask at your
hotel. The cheapest phones **to buy** will cost
around ¥400; make sure the staff change
the operating language into English for you.

Photography

The Chinese are pretty relaxed about having
their picture taken, and the staff at museums
and attractions surprisingly accommodating.
For places to buy photographic equipment,
see p.144. Colour film and processing is
widely available, though not particularly
cheap; it costs about ¥1 a print.

Time

Shanghai, like the rest of China, is eight
hours ahead of GMT, thirteen hours ahead of
US Eastern Standard Time, sixteen hours
ahead of US Pacific Time and two hours
behind Australian Eastern Standard Time. It
does not have daylight saving time.

Tourist information

The official China Tourist Service, **CITS**, at
1227 Beijing Xi Lu (Mon–Fri 9am–6pm;
⊕62898899, Ⓦwww.cits.net), is pretty
useless at supplying information, being
geared mainly towards getting you to buy
one of its tours; otherwise, you'll just be
handed a few leaflets. They can also,
however, sell tickets for onward travel. There
are small CITS offices that can sell tickets
and book you on CITS tours at 1699 Nanjing
Xi Lu (⊕62483259) and 149 Jiujiaochang
Lu (⊕63555032), on the west side of the
Yuyuan Bazaar.

There's plenty of **online information** about
China in general and Shanghai specifically,
though as a general rule, avoid websites run
by official agencies such as CITS as they're
dry as dust.

Travel advice

Australian Department of Foreign Affairs
Ⓦ www.dfat.gov.au, Ⓦ www.smartraveller.gov.au.
British Foreign & Commonwealth Office
Ⓦ www.fco.gov.uk.

Canadian Department of Foreign Affairs ⓦwww.dfait-maeci.gc.ca.
Irish Department of Foreign Affairs ⓦwww .foreignaffairs.gov.ie.
New Zealand Ministry of Foreign Affairs ⓦwww.mft.govt.nz.
South African Department of Foreign Affairs ⓦwww.dfa.gov.za.
US State Department ⓦwww.travel.state.gov.

Other useful websites

Shanghai Guide ⓦwww.shanghaiguide.com. Not really a guide, but a mishmash of reviews and observations with the occasional gem, and a lively forum.

Shanghaiist ⓦwww.shanghaiist.com. A scatty forum with lots of quirky local gossip; entertaining and informative.

Sinomania ⓦwww.sinomania.com. A California-based site with links to current Chinese news stories and a good popular music section, with MP3s available.

Smartshanghai ⓦwww.smartshanghai.com. The definitive nightlife site, with plenty of restaurant reviews too; up to date, with events listings, bitchy user reviews, maps to show where venues are (a rare plus) and a personals section.

Yesasia ⓦwww.yesasia.com. Online shopping for Chinese movies, CDs, books, collectables and so on.

Zhongwen.com ⓦwww.zhongwen.com. A dictionary site useful for students of Chinese and anyone struggling to communicate in Chinese.

Travellers with disabilities

In China the disabled are generally hidden away, so attitudes are not very sympathetic and little special provision is made. As it undergoes an economic boom, Shanghai resembles a building site, with uneven, obstacle-strewn paving, intense crowds and vehicle traffic, and few access ramps. Commendably, a huge effort has been made to make pavements and subway stations friendly to **the blind**.

Wheelchair users will generally find public transport inaccessible, though a few of the upmarket hotels have experience in assisting disabled visitors; in particular, Shanghai's several Holiday Inns (☎63538008) and Hiltons (☎62480000) have rooms designed for wheelchair users.

Given the situation, it may be worth considering an **organized tour**. Make sure you take spares of any specialist clothing or equipment, extra supplies of drugs (carried with you if you fly), and a prescription including the generic name – in English and Chinese characters – in case of emergency. If there's an association representing people with your disability, contact them early on in the planning process. The official representative of the disabled in Shanghai is the Disabled Person's Federation at 189 Longyang Lu (☎58733212, ⓦwww .shdisabled.gov.cn).

The City

The City

1

The Bund and Nanjing Dong Lu

Shanghai's signature skyline, and the first stop for any visitor, is **the Bund**, a strip of grand colonial edifices on the west bank of the Huangpu River, facing the flashy skyscrapers of Pudong on the opposite shore. The product of the city's commercial frenzy at the beginning of the twentieth century, this was where the great trading houses and banks built their headquarters, each trying to outdo the last in the pomp of their edifices. Today it's the most exclusive chunk of real estate in China, with pretensions to becoming the nation's Champs-Elysées; the world's most luxurious brands have recently set up shop, and there are a clutch of celebrity restaurants and some rather good hotels.

Having strolled the length of the Bund and soaked up some history, visitors can get a first taste of the frantic pace of Shanghai's modern consumerism on the roads that lead from it back towards People's Square – **Nanjing Dong Lu** and **Fuzhou Lu**.

The Bund	外滩	*wài tān*
Broadway Mansions	上海大厦	*shàng hǎi dà shà*
Russian Consulate	俄罗斯领事馆	*é luó sī lǐng shì guǎn*
Pujiang Hotel	浦江饭店	*pǔ jiāng fàn diàn*
Main Post Office	国际邮局	*guó jì yóu jú*
Waibaidu Bridge	外白渡桥	*wài bái dù qiáo*
Huangpu Park	黄浦公园	*huáng pǔ gōng yuán*
Bund Tourist Tunnel	外滩观光隧道	*wài tān guān guāng suì dào*
Peace Hotel	和平饭店	*hé píng fàn diàn*
18 The Bund	外滩18号	*wài tān shí bā hào*
Customs House	上海海关	*shàng hǎi hǎi guān*
Five on the Bund	外滩5号	*wài tān wǔ hào*
Three on the Bund	外滩3号	*wài tān sān hào*
Huangpu Cruise Dock	黄浦江游览船	*huáng pǔ jiāng yóu lǎn chuán*
Nanjing Dong Lu	南京东路	*náng jīng dōng lù*
Fuzhou Lu	福州路	*fú zhōu lù*
Raffles Mall	莱福士广场	*lái fú shì guǎng chǎng*

The Bund

Though the row of European buildings along the Huangpu River has since 1949 been known officially as Zhongshan Lu, and locals know it better as Wai Tan (literally "outside beach"), it will always be **the Bund** to foreigners. The northern end starts from the confluence of the Huangpu and the Suzhou Creek, by **Waibaidu Bridge**, and runs south for 1500m to Jinling Dong Lu, formerly Rue du Consulat. You can get here by taking metro line #2 to Nanjing Dong Lu subway station and walking east along Nanjing Dong Lu itself, which will bring you to the **Peace Hotel**, around a third or the way down the strip.

Named after the Anglo-Indian term for the embankment of a muddy foreshore, the Bund was old Shanghai's commercial heart, with the river quays on one side, the offices of the leading **banks** and **trading houses** on the other. These sturdy marble-and-granite structures, built in a mongrel mix of Anglo-Oriental styles ranging from Italian Renaissance and neo-Grecian to Moorish, were both a celebration of Western commercial enterprise and a declaration of dominance. During Shanghai's riotous heyday this was also a hectic working **harbour**, where vessels from tiny sailing junks to ocean-going freighters unloaded under the watch of British (and later American and Japanese)

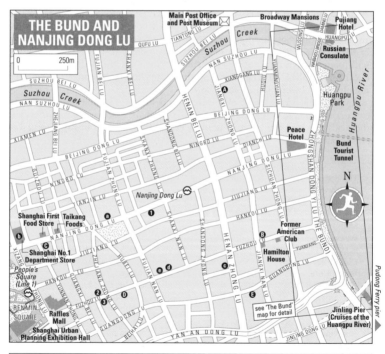

ACCOMMODATION		EATING AND DRINKING		SHOPS AND MARKETS	
24K Hotel	D	Ajisen	1 Wang Baohe **3**	Design Bookshop **e**	Shanghai No. 1
Le Royal Méridian	C	Lao Zhenxing	2 Westin Bakery **E**	Foreign Language	Department Store **b**
Metropole	B	The Stage,		Bookstore **d**	Silk King **a**
Mingtown Hikers Hostel	A	Westin	**E**	Nantai Costume	
Westin	E			Company **c**	

High hopes:
Shanghai's building boom

Since the early 1990s Shanghai has been growing faster than anywhere else in the world, ever – at one point, a quarter of the world's cranes were in use here. In the rush to globalize, the city has become something of a construction free-for-all, a playground for some of the most celebrated names in architecture. The result has been some of the world's most ambitious building projects – from spectacular high-rises to brand-new futuristic cities.

A global city

▲ The Bank of China building

The first phase of Shanghai's reconstruction began in the 1980s, when China first started opening up. Prevailing talk was of creating "capitalism with Chinese characteristics", and accordingly scores of international-style concrete-and-glass high-rises were built and given a Chinese twist, such as a pagoda-shaped "hat" atop the tower. The template was the **Bank of China** (see p.51) on the Bund, built in 1934, though in truth the original is more successful than any of its imitators.

In the 1990s, with Shanghai attempting to become a global city, thirty percent of new projects were awarded to foreign architects. They usually attempted at least a nod towards Chinese culture; one recurring theme has been use of squares atop circles, as a reference to the Chinese idea that the earth is square, heaven round – this is notable in French architect Jean-Marie Charpentier's **Shanghai Grand Theatre** (see p.60). The most effectively Sinicized building has to be the **Jinmao Tower**, whose proportions are built around the number eight – associated with prosperity in Chinese culture – and whose tiered form constantly references pagoda design. Other experiments have been unsuccessful, however – the "moon gate" (a traditional element in Chinese gardens) originally designed to form the apex of the **World Financial Centre**, for example, was taken for a Japanese flag, and had to be redesigned.

Furthermore, Shanghai's architectural revolution has not been without its critics. In China's Wild West business environment, planning decisions are made in minutes and zoning laws are light. Inconveniently located residents are brushed aside with minimal compensation as their homes are bulldozed. The architects themselves complain that their projects are bedevilled by cost-cutting and copying. And to cap it all, the city is becoming a victim of its own success: the heavy new build area around Lujiazui is currently sinking at a rate of 1.5cm a year.

Still, construction continues at a frantic pace. Exciting new developments to look out for include the revamp of the southern stretch of the Huangpu river in time for the 2010 **World Expo** and a reconstructed **north Bund zone**, with a giant ferris wheel at the centre. To get a taste of what these new areas will look like, head to the Shanghai Urban Planning Exhibition Hall (see p.60).

◀ Shanghai Grand Theatre

Architectural Wonders of Shanghai

Jinmao Tower (1998; right) This beautiful tapering tower uses the formal language of Chinese pagodas to make a powerful statement; the enormous barrel-vaulted atrium, lined with staircases arrayed in a spiral, is the city's most spectacular interior (see p.90).

Jiushi Corporation Headquarters (2000) The glass facade of Norman Foster's forty-storey tower, in the South Bund area, curves elegantly to make the most of fantastic views across the Huangpu. It is also one of the most eco-friendly buildings in Shanghai.

Tomorrow Square (2002; below) One of the city's characteristic landmarks, thanks to the pincers on the roof. The building is shaped like two squares on top of each other, with the upper one rotated at 45 degrees (see p.62).

Three on the Bund (2004) The interior of this stolid Neoclassical Bund building

has been deftly modernized for its conversion into an upmarket complex, with a magnificent atrium that extends from the third floor to the roof (see p.54).

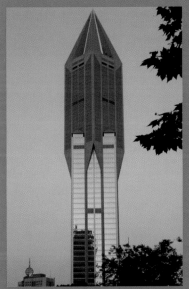

Xintiandi (1998) Restoring this run-down area of traditional shikumen houses was a daring move when every other developer was busy demolishing them. Human in scale, it's become a model for urban development that is sympathetic to local conditions (see pp.70–74).

Oriental Arts Centre (2004) French architect Paul Andreu designed this building to look like a butterfly orchid, with the petals being the exhibition halls. To strengthen the effect of something delicate and unearthly, lights on the roof change colour with the cadences of the music being played inside (see p.92).

World Financial Centre (2007) This 492-metre-high tower was once intended to be the world's tallest building. It's still a striking structure, a broad-shouldered wedge with very clean lines and a hole in the top – like God's own tent peg (see p.90).

Shanghai's satellites

Developments within the city are certainly eye-catching, but the most ambitious projects are happening outside the city centre. With its population set to double over the next twenty years, and a population density four times greater than that of New York, Shanghai cannot simply built upwards – it needs to spread outwards too. Accordingly, nine new **satellite cities** are being built from scratch, each to accommodate half a million souls. Bizarrely, many of them – designed to appeal to the affluent and increasingly Westernized Chinese middle class – are direct pastiches of European cities and towns. Pujiang will have an Italian flavour; Fencheng focuses on an adaptation of Barcelona's Ramblas; Anting is a German-themed town designed by Albert Speer, the son of Hitler's favourite architect. And Thames Town, the faux-English centre to Song Jiang new town, features half-timbered Tudor-style houses,

▲ Jiushi Corporation Headquarters building

Georgian terraces and Victorian warehouses; there are even statues of Winston Churchill and Harry Potter.

Shanghai's attitude to the environment tends towards the ambivalent, but one notable exception is under construction on nearby Chongming Island. Designed by British engineering company Arup, Dongtan is set to become the world's first self-sustaining, carbon neutral **eco-city**. Buildings will be powered by solar energy, wind turbines and recycled organic material, while grass will be grown on rooftops to provide natural insulation. The city should be self-sufficient in water too, with purified rainwater the primary source.

It looks like Shanghai's cranes won't be idle for some time yet.

▼ Oriental Arts Centre

warships. Everything arrived here, from silk and tea to heavy industrial machinery. So too did wealthy foreigners, ready to pick their way to one of the grand hotels through crowds of beggars, hawkers, black marketeers, shoeshine boys and overladen coolies.

When the Communists took over in 1949 the buildings were mothballed, and though nothing was done to preserve these symbols of foreign imperialism, surprisingly little was destroyed. Now, as Shanghai rises, the street is once again a hub of commerce, though of the decidedly upmarket kind. As well as the ritziest shops, such as an Armani showcase, the buildings house Shanghai's fanciest restaurants (see p.116), though if you just want to eat, rather than have a life- (and wallet) transforming culinary experience, choice is much more limited.

Along Suzhou Creek

Before heading south for the Bund proper, it's worth taking a quick peek around the colonial edifices just north of the Waibaidu Bridge. You can't miss the hulking **Broadway Mansions**, though you may wish you could – it's a classic example of the po-faced stolidity of the Chicago School and would make a good Orwellian Ministry of Truth. When it was built in 1933, it was the highest building in Asia. During World War II it was taken over by the Japanese; it is now a dull hotel (see p.106). Its most illustrious resident was Jiang Qing (wife of Mao Zedong), who issued a decree during the Cultural Revolution banning barges and sampans from travelling up the Huangpu or Suzhou while she was asleep. If you're not staying here, you can appreciate the views by taking the lift to the eighteenth floor.

Just east, over the road, the **Russian Consulate** is one of the few Bund buildings that is used for its original purpose. The iron grilles over the windows came in useful on those occasions in the 1920s when this bastion of "Red" Soviet Russia was attacked by White Russians. In 1960, during one of the frostier periods of Sino–Soviet relations, it suffered the indignity of being turned into a bar for seamen; it returned to being a consulate in 1987.

Opposite, the rather grander **Pujiang Hotel** (formerly known as the *Astor*) was built in 1846 and enlarged in 1910, and was the city's glitziest venue until the *Peace Hotel* was built. It was also one of the few places where polite foreign and Chinese society mingled, when "tea dances" were held – with rather more whisky than tea serving as social lubricant. The original manager, a retired seaman, had the corridors painted with portholes and the rooms decorated like cabins. Today, though, with its endless wooden corridors and genteel shabbiness, the hotel has something of a Victorian public school about it. It remains worth a snoop for its grand lobby, renovated ballroom and a few relics of its past glories on display (see also p.107).

The zone north of here, known as **north Bund**, is due to be revamped as a showpiece waterfront development, complete with a ferris wheel that will be (of course) bigger than London's, with a two-hundred-metre diameter. For now, it's a bit scruffy, so instead walk a few hundred metres west along Suzhou Bei Lu to the Main Post Office, built in 1931 and easily recognizable by its clock tower. It's the only Bund building that has never been used for anything but its original function. It houses the **Shanghai Post Museum** (Wed, Thurs, Sat & Sun 9am–4pm; ¥10) on the third floor, which is more interesting than it sounds. The collection of letters and stamps is only mildly diverting, but the new atrium is very impressive, and the view of the Bund from the grassed-over roof is superb.

The riverside promenade

Creaky **Waibadu Bridge**, built by the British in 1907, is the obvious place to start an exploration of the Bund. At the outbreak of the Sino–Japanese War in 1937 it represented the frontier between the Japanese-occupied areas north of Suzhou Creek and the **International Settlement** to the south – itself a no-man's-land, it was guarded at each end by Japanese and British sentries.

The first building south of the bridge was one of the cornerstones of British interests in old Shanghai, the **former British Consulate**, once ostentatiously guarded by magnificently dressed Sikh soldiers. Right on the corner of the two waterways, on the east side of the road, **Huangpu Park** was another British creation, then the British Public Gardens, established in 1886 on a patch of land formed when mud and silt gathered around a wrecked ship. Here, too, there were Sikh troops, ready to enforce the rules which forbade Chinese from entering unless they were servants accompanying their employer. After protests the regulations were relaxed in 1928 to admit "well-dressed" Chinese, who had to apply for a special entry permit. Though it's firmly established in the Chinese popular imagination as a symbol of Western racism, there's no evidence that there ever was a sign here reading "No dogs or Chinese allowed". These days the park contains a rather unattractive stone obelisk commemorating the "**Heroes of the People**", and is also a popular spot for citizens practising *tai ji* early in the morning. Underneath the monument lurks a small **historical museum** (daily 9am–4pm; free), with a display of photographs of Shanghai past that is worth a few minutes of your time.

In contrast to the pretensions of the buildings over the road, the riverside **promenade** remains stoutly proletarian, full of out-of-towners taking the obligatory Shanghai shot of the Oriental Pearl Tower (see p.89) – and there are plenty of vendors who will take the picture for you, or sell you a plastic

▲ Tai ji in Huangpu Park

copy of it (or a yapping mechanical dog). One reason for this disparity is the almost complete disconnect between the two sides of the road; take note that the only place to cross over nearby is the underpass roughly opposite Beijing Dong Lu. This will take you past the entrance to the **Bund Tourist Tunnel**, the psychedelic gateway to Pudong.

Back on the west side of the street and walking south down the Bund, you'll pass a succession of grandiose Neoclassical edifices, once built to house the great foreign enterprises. Jardine Matheson, founded by William Jardine – the man who did more than any other individual to precipitate the Opium Wars and open Shanghai up to foreign trade (see p.176) – was the first foreign concern to buy land in Shanghai. Their former base (they lost all of their holdings in China after 1949), just north of the *Peace Hotel* at no. 27, is now occupied by the **China Textiles Export Corporation**. It's seen a lot of different nationalities come and go: in 1941 the British Embassy occupied the top floor (facing the German Embassy, just across the road), shortly after which it was requisitioned by the Japanese navy, before doing service as the American consulate.

One of the Bund's more modern structures is the **Bank of China** at no. 23, built in 1937 in the Chicago style with a Chinese hat as concession to local sensibilities. Next door, the **Agricultural Bank of China**, originally the Yokohama Bank, is rather more successful in its blend of eastern and neo-Grecian styles. Unfortunately (but hardly surprisingly) only a couple of the Japanese martial sculptures that once ornamented the facade have survived; look above the first-floor windows.

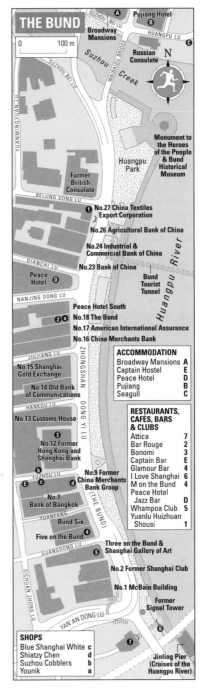

The Peace Hotel to Hankou Lu

Straddling the eastern end of Nanjing Dong Lu is one of the most famous hotels in China, the **Peace Hotel**, formerly the *Cathay Hotel*. The hotel's main building (on the north side of Nanjing Dong Lu) is a relic of another great trading house, **Sassoon's**, and was originally known as Sassoon House. Like Jardine's, the Sassoon business empire was built on opium trading, but by the early years of the last century the family fortune had mostly been sunk into Shanghai real estate, including the *Cathay* (see box below). Nicknamed "The Claridges of the Far East" it was *the* place to be seen in prewar Shanghai: Douglas Fairbanks and Charlie Chaplin were among its celebrity guests and Noel Coward is supposed to have written *Private Lives* here while laid up with flu. It boasted innovations such as telephones in the rooms before any European hotels, and had such luxuries as a private plumbing system fed by a spring on the outskirts of town, marble baths with silver taps and vitreous china lavatories imported from Britain. The *Peace* today is well worth a visit for the bar, with its legendary jazz band (see p.125), and for a walk around the lobby and upper floors to take in the splendid Art Deco elegance. There's a good view of the Bund from the balcony of the seventh-floor bar – staff will tolerate curious visitors popping in for a quick look.

The smaller wing on the south side of Nanjing Dong Lu was originally the *Palace Hotel*, built around 1906; its first floor now holds the Western-style *Peace Café*.

Victor Sassoon

"There is only one race finer than the Jews, and that's the Derby."

More than anyone, it was **Victor Sassoon** (1881–1961), infamous tycoon and *bon vivant*, who shaped Shanghai's prewar character. The Sassoons were Sephardic Jews from Iraq, whose family fortune was built by trading in India. Victor, one of the fourth generation (which included the writer Siegfried Sassoon) astonished the family by moving the company assets out of India and into China – largely, it is said, to dodge the British taxman. "Sir Victor" as he liked to be known, began pouring millions of dollars into Shanghai in the 1920s, virtually single-handedly setting off a high-rise real estate boom that was to last almost a decade. His Art Deco constructions include what have become many of the city's most distinctive landmarks, among them: Hamilton House and the *Metropole Hotel* (see p.107), facing each other at the intersection of Fuzhou Lu and Jiangxi Lu; the Cathay Theatre on Huaihai Zhong Lu (see p.75); the *Orient Hotel* on Xizang Zhong Lu near People's Square; the Embarkment Building on Suzhou Bei Lu; Cathay Mansions (now the *Jinjiang Hotel*; see p.75); and the enduring landmark of the Bund, the *Cathay Hotel* (now the *Peace Hotel*; see above).

At the *Cathay*, Victor lived in a penthouse with a 360-degree view over the city, and indulged his tastes for the finest of everything – including women. His suite had two bathtubs because, he said, he liked to share his bed but never his bath. As described by Stella Dong in *Shanghai, the Rise and Fall of a Decadent City*, his **parties** sound dazzling. At his shipwreck party, guests came dressed as if they were abandoning ship; the prize for best costume was awarded to a couple who were naked except for a shower curtain. At his circus parties, guests would come as clowns or acrobats while he, of course, played ringmaster, in top hat and tails and wielding a riding crop. Victor's world came crashing down with the Japanese invasion, though he was able to spirit most of his fortune away to the Bahamas, where he died in 1961.

Number 18 The Bund was originally the Chartered Bank of India and Australia, but today is home to the city's ritziest shops, given gravitas by the building's Italian marble columns. If you want to spot Chinese celebrities (assuming you can recognize them), this is the place to be seen. As well as top-end retail outlets such as Younik (see p.140) and Cartier, the building houses an arts space and two ventures run by the Michelin-starred Pourcell brothers – the overhyped *Sens & Bund* restaurant and swanky *Bar Rouge* (see p.124) above, which has a fantastic roof terrace with views of Pudong.

At no. 17, **American International Assurance** has returned to re-occupy the building it left in 1949. Back then it shared its tenancy with "the old lady of the Bund" – the English-language *North China Daily News*, whose motto is engraved over the ground-floor windows – "Journalism, Art, Science, Literature, Commerce, Truth, Printing". The Communists banned it from printing news in 1949, so the very last issue was given over to articles on the philosopher Lao Tzu and Hittite hieroglyphics.

The Customs House and HSBC Building

Continuing south down the Bund past neo-Grecian, Italian Renaissance and Art Deco edifices brings you to the magnificent **Customs House** at no. 13. The Chinese customs service was administered by foreigners as it was discovered that this way much less money disappeared through graft. The service was headed by an Irishman, Robert Hart, who at one point was forwarding to Beijing a third of the Qing government's revenue. The clock tower was modelled on Big Ben in London, and after its completion in 1927, local legend had it that the chimes, which struck every fifteen minutes, confused the God of Fire: believing the chimes were a fire bell, the god decided Shanghai was suffering from too many conflagrations, and decided not to send any more. During the Cultural Revolution loudspeakers in the clock tower played *The East is Red* at six o'clock every morning and evening. The original clockwork was restored in time for a visit by Queen Elizabeth II in 1986. You can step into the downstairs lobby for a peek at some faded mosaics of maritime motifs on the ceiling.

Right next to the Customs House, and also with an easily recognizable domed roofline, the former headquarters of the **Hong Kong and Shanghai Bank**, built in 1921, has one of the most imposing of the Bund facades. It's now owned by the Pudong Development Bank, who allow visitors to poke around the entrance hall. Today, HSBC is one of Britain's biggest banks, though few of its customers can be aware of its original purpose – to finance trade between Europe and China. Each wall of the marble octagonal entrance originally boasted a mural depicting the bank's eight primary locations (Bangkok, Calcutta, Hong Kong, London, New York, Paris, Shanghai and Tokyo), and the eight words of its motto: "Within the four seas all men are brothers". The four huge marble columns in the banking hall are among the largest pieces of solid marble in the world. In the far left corner was a separate bank for Chinese customers, who entered using the entrance on Fuzhou Lu – the massive door, inscribed with the initials HSBC, still stands. The Chinese character *fu* (prosperity) can be seen on the walls and in the trim, and Chinese-style abstract designs decorate the cornices and ceilings.

It's considered lucky to rub the noses or paws of the bronze lions that stand guard outside the Corinthian columns of the entranceway. These are replacements for the two originals, which were removed by the Japanese; one stands today in the historical museum (see p.89). They were officially named

"Prudence" and "Security" but nicknamed "Stephen" and "Stitt", after the bank's general managers. One lion looks belligerent, the other smiles inscrutably. There are similar pairs outside the HSBC headquarters in Hong Kong and London. Locals used to joke that the lions roared when a virgin passed – so their incessant silence said something about the relaxed morals of the Shanghainese.

The small door north of the main entrance will get you to the second floor *Bonomi* café (see p.114), a good place for a break.

South of Fuzhou Lu

Cross Fuzhou Lu, pass a couple more banking headquarters that aren't open to the public, and you'll come to some very posh addresses. Most of no. 5 (officially **Five on the Bund**) is home to the Huaxia Bank but on Guangdong Lu you'll find the entrance to the building's upscale restaurant, *M of the Bund* (see p.116). Opened in 1999, it kicked off the zone's present revival. A little further down, **Three on the Bund** is perhaps the most successful and certainly most luxurious of the new developments. There's the Shanghai Gallery of Art (see p.134), an Armani flagship store, Evian Spa (see p.31) and three swish restaurants, including *Whampoa Club* (see p.117).

Number 2 is presently unoccupied, which is a shame as it has some of the Bund's most colourful history. It was once that bastion of white male

Huangpu River tours

Even in this age of freeway projects and a sophisticated metro system, the Huangpu is still a vital resource for Shanghai – one-third of all China's trade passes through here. The river is also the city's chief source of drinking water – though, thick and brown, it contains large quantities of untreated waste, including sewage and high levels of mercury and phenol. At least it no longer serves as a burial ground – until the 1930s those too poor to pay for the burial of relatives would launch the bodies into the river in boxes decked in paper flowers.

A highlight of a visit to Shanghai, and an easy way to view the edifices of the Bund, is to take one of the **Huangpu River tours**. There are several different companies, but they all offer similar services, with boats leaving throughout the day from a wharf at the south end of the Bund, opposite Jinling Dong Lu. Tickets are available from booths at the wharf itself (daily 8am–4.30pm). One of the better boats – it's new and it doesn't have fake dragon's claws – is run by the *Captain Hostel* and leaves from jetty no. 191, at the southern end.

The hour-long round trip to the Yangpu Bridge, 15km downstream, costs around ¥45, a little more in the classier seats; a less frequent service (also lasting 1hr) heads to Pudong's Gaoqiao Bridge, but the classic cruise here is the sixty-kilometre, three-hour journey to the mouth of the **Yangzi River** and back. There are departures daily at 9am and 2pm, and tickets cost between ¥90 and ¥120, with the higher prices offering armchairs, a higher deck, tea and snacks. On this cruise, you're introduced to the vast amount of shipping that uses the port, with all the paraphernalia of the shipping industry on view, from sampans and rusty old Panama-registered freighters to sparkling Chinese navy vessels. You'll also get an idea of the colossal level of construction that is taking place on the eastern shore, before reaching the mouth of the Yangzi itself, where the wind kicks in and you'll feel like you're almost in open sea. There are also two-hour-long **night cruises**, with boats departing at 7pm and 8.30pm (¥78; ¥150 with buffet dinner). Pudong at night is lit up like a games arcade, and the new construction carries on under arc lights, so this tour is much more colourful than you might imagine. Note that tours do not run in foggy or windy weather; for current information, call ☏63744461. It is also possible to take boats tours from Pearl Dock in Pudong (see p.89).

chauvinism, the *Shanghai Club*. The club's showpiece, the 33-metre mahogany *Long Bar*, was where the wealthiest of the city's merchants and their European guests congregated for cocktail hour, with the highest-status taipans sitting closest to the window. The last building on the block, at the corner of Yan'an Dong Lu, is the **McBain Building**, also known as the Asiatic Petroleum Building. It was constructed in 1916, and features the now familiar motifs of Greek columns, Baroque pillars and a Romanesque archway.

Just across the road – finally it's possible to cross again – is a rather quaint **former signal tower**. It was closed for renovation at the time of writing, but when it reopens may show a collection of old photos (though there are rumours it will be yet another pricey restaurant). From here, it's a short walk to the boat dock for a river tour (see opposite). If you want to go west back into town, it's best to avoid dull Yan'an Dong Lu and backtrack north to Fuzhou Lu (see p.56).

The Bund to People's Square

Two kilometres west of the Bund lies another hotspot for tourists, People's Square (Renmin Guangchang). Connecting them is the consumer cornucopia of pedestrianized **Nanjing Dong Lu**, with its two major parallel arteries, dull Yan'an Lu and quirky **Fuzhou Lu**. In the days of the foreign concessions, expatriates described Nanjing Lu as a cross between New York's Broadway and London's Oxford Street. But it was also at this time that Nanjing Dong Lu and Fuzhou Lu were lined with teahouses that functioned as the city's most exclusive brothels, whose courtesans were expected, among their other duties, to be able to perform classical plays and scenes from operas, and host banquets. In a juxtaposition symbolic of prewar Shanghai's extremes, strings of the lowest form of brothel, nicknamed *dingpeng* ("nail sheds" because the sex, at less than one yuan, was "as quick as driving nails"), lay just two blocks north of Nanjing Dong Lu, along Suzhou Creek. The street was dubbed "Blood Alley" for the nightly fights between sailors on leave who congregated here.

Nanjing Dong Lu

On its eastern stretch, **Nanjing Dong Lu**'s garish neon lights and window displays are iconic; come here in the evening (before things start closing up at 9pm) to appreciate the lightshow in its full tacky splendour. If you don't want to explore by foot, a daft little electric train tootles up and down (¥2). The shopping is not what it once was, with the emphasis now firmly on cheap rather than chic, but the authorities, aware of this, intend to boot out the locals and get some international brands in.

Scammers on Nanjing Dong Lu

Take note that foreign faces on Nanjing Lu will be incessantly approached by pesky pimps, street vendors and "art students", but the most common scam is for a young guy or girl to befriend you, perhaps asking to practise their English. They'll suggest you go to a bar for a coffee or a beer, which, when the bill comes, will cost hundreds of yuan. On a single stroll up the street, this will be tried a dozen times. There are plenty of places in Shanghai where strangers are genuine, but this is not one of them. For more on this, see p.34.

Number 635 was once the glorious **Wing On** emporium, and diagonally opposite was the **Sincere**. These were not just stores: inside there were restaurants, rooftop gardens, cabarets and even hotels. Off the circular overhead walkway at the junction between Nanjing and Xizang Zhong Lu is the grandest of the district's department stores, the venerable **Shanghai No. 1 Department Store**; it's still a place of pilgrimage for out-of-towners, but is nothing like as spectacular as it was.

If you're looking for cheap clothes, you'll be spoilt for choice, but for something distinctly Chinese you'll have to look a bit harder. Your best bet for curiosities is to head to the **Shanghai First Food Store**, at no. 720. The Chinese often buy food as a souvenir, and this busy store sells all kinds of locally made gift-wrapped sweets, cakes and preserves, as well as tea and tasty pastries. Nearby **Taikang Foods** at no. 768 is another example, with a dried meat section at the back selling rather macabre flattened pig heads.

Fuzhou Lu

Heading west from the Bund along **Fuzhou Lu**, you'll first come to the nautically themed *Captain Hostel*, where taking the creaky lift to the sixth-floor bar will reward you with excellent views of Pudong (see p.124). Continue west until you reach Jiangxi Lu, and you'll see Shanghai at its most gloomily Gothamesque, thanks to twin Art Deco edifices, the **Metropole Hotel** (see p.107) and **Hamilton House**, once an apartment complex, on the south corner; both were built by British architects Palmer and Turner. In the building at the northwest corner lodged the Shanghai Municipal Council, the governing body of the International Settlement.

Fifty metres further west, the court building at no. 209 used to be the **American Club**. Georgian-style, with marble columns, it was built in 1924 with bricks shipped in from the States. After you cross Henan Zhong Lu you enter a brighter commercial area, with a medley of small stores selling art supplies, stationery, trophies, medical equipment and books, including the Foreign Language Bookstore at no. 390 (see p.146). Finally, at the end of the road, **Raffles Mall** is one of Shanghai's best (and busiest), with a juice bar and plenty of cheap, clean eateries in the basement, and a good mix of clothes stores above.

2

People's Square

I ts perimeters defined by the city's main arteries, Xizang, Nanjing and Yan'an roads, **People's Square** (Renmin Guangchang) is the modern heart of Shanghai. Like Tian'anmen Square in Beijing, it functions both as a transport hub and as home to the grand temples of culture, history and government. But in contrast to the dour totalitarianism of its Beijing counterpart, People's Square possesses a much more human feel. Instead of a concrete plain lined with po-faced edifices, Shanghai's urban centre comprises a rather haphazardly arranged park and a plaza dotted with a hotchpotch of modernist and colonial buildings (with, of course, a huge shopping mall underneath). There's an impressive clutch of sights, all within walking distance of each other. The pot-shaped **Shanghai Museum** is world class, and one of the city's highlights, while the nearby **Urban Planning Exhibition Hall** looks to the future both in its design and its contents. Just north of here, the stolid **Shanghai Art Museum** and charming little **Museum of Contemporary Art** are two of the best places in the city to view modern art. Add to that the unexpectedly peaceful **Renmin Park**, and you have one of Shanghai's most rewarding destinations. There's always one part being ripped up and improved, and some residents are snooty about the place, dismissing it as too new, flashy or proletarian; ignore them. Few places in China have such a concentration of great sights, and you'll need a full day to do them justice.

As People's Square is at the interchange of subway lines #1 and #2, the easiest way to get here is on the metro. A dozen exits cover a vast area, so work out which exit you want from the wall maps in the station, then navigate your way through the shopping mall – the low numbers bring you out in the southeast

People's Square	人民广场	*rén mín guǎng chǎng*
Renmin Dadao	人民大道	*rén mín dà dào*
Shanghai Museum	上海博物馆	*shàng hǎi bó wù guǎn*
Urban Planning Exhibition Hall	城市规划展示馆	*chéng shì guī huà zhǎn shì guǎn*
Shanghai Grand Theatre	上海大剧院	*shàng hǎi dà jù yuàn*
Shanghai Art Museum	上海美术馆	*shàng hǎi měi shù guǎn*
Renmin Park	人民公园	*rén mín gōng yuán*
Museum of Contemporary Art	上海当代艺术馆	*shàng hǎi dāng dài yì shù guǎn*
Tomorrow Square	明天广场	*míng tiān guǎng chǎng*
Jiangyin Lu	江阴路	*jiāng yīn lù*

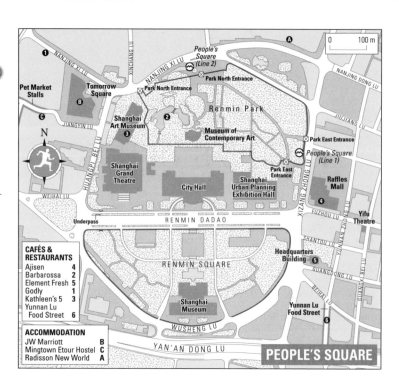

corner of the square near the museum, the high ones in the northwest near the park. There aren't many places to eat so if you're here for the day, you'll have to plan where you're having lunch (see p.113 & p.117).

The Shanghai Museum

People's Square metro station can get fearsomely busy but fortunately as you head west onto Renmin Dadao the crowds thin out dramatically. On the south side of this giant boulevard, Renmin Square is a pleasant plaza with a fountain where you might catch a few skateboarders, and tourists feeding the pigeons. At the back stands the unmistakeable showpiece **Shanghai Museum** (daily 9am–5pm; ¥20, students ¥5; audio-guide ¥40, with ¥400 deposit).

The building's form is based on a *ding*, an ancient Chinese pot, and its layout, like many Chinese buildings, is inspired by traditional cosmogony, with a square base to represent earth and a rounded roof to represent heaven. Inside, there are eleven galleries, with well-displayed pieces and plenty of explanation in English. You'll need several hours for a comprehensive tour, though some galleries can be safely skipped; the best stuff, on the whole, is on the ground and top floors. Informative leaflets are available at an information desk on the ground floor.

The ground floor

One of the museum's major highlights is its ground-floor gallery of **bronzes**, most of which are more than two thousand years old yet appear strikingly modern in their simple lines and bold imagery. The cooking vessels, containers and weapons on display were used for ritual rather than everyday purposes, and are beautifully made. Many are covered with intricate geometrical designs that reference animal shapes, while others reveal startlingly naturalistic touches – check out the cowrie container from the western Han dynasty, with handles shaped like stalking tigers and lid surmounted by eight bronze yaks. There's also a charming wine urn with a dragon spout and another shaped like an ox. A display near the entrance shows how these were made, using an early form of the "lost wax" method – the original is made in wax, then covered in plaster, after which the wax is heated and poured away to create a mould.

A crowd-pleasing pottery dog guards the entrance to the **sculpture** gallery next door. Most of the exhibits are religious figures – boggle-eyed temple guardians, serene Buddhas and the like. Look out for the row of huge, fearsome Tang dynasty heads and the figurines of dancers in flowing robes, which resemble Brancusi sculptures in their simplicity.

The first and second floors

The Tang dynasty steals the show once again in the **ceramics** gallery, which takes over the first floor. The spiky, multicoloured tomb guardians, in the shape of imaginary beasties, make the delicate glazed pots look reserved in comparison. The English text reminds you that the delicate art of porcelain was invented in China; some fine examples from the Song and Ming dynasties are on display.

On the second floor, skip the calligraphy and carved seals unless you have a special interest and check out the **painting** gallery instead. The winning dynasty here has to be the Ming, as the amazingly naturalistic images of animals from this time are much easier to respond to than the interminable idealized landscapes. Look out in particular for Bian Wenzhi's lively images of birds.

The top floor

The top floor contains the most colourful gallery, dedicated to the many **Chinese minority peoples**. To anyone who thinks of China as a monoculture, this striking assembly of the weird and wonderful will come as a shock. One wall is lined with spooky lacquered masks from Tibet and Guizhou (in southwest China), while nearby are colourfully decorated boats from the Taiwanese minority, the Gaoshan. The silver ceremonial headdresses of southwest China's Miao people are breathtaking for their intricacy, if rather impractical to wear; elsewhere, elaborate abstract designs turn the Dai lacquered tableware into art. In the section on traditional costumes, look out for the fish-skin suit made by the Hezhen people of Dongbei, in the far north. The text might insist on the "Chineseness" of all this but it's quite clear from their artefacts that these civilizations at the furthest edges of the Chinese Empire, many of them animist in their beliefs, are culturally very distant from the Han mainstream, and those from southwest China have more in common with their Thai or Laotian co-religionists.

The Ming and Qing dynasty **furniture** next door is more interesting than it sounds. The Ming pieces are balanced and gracious while those from the Qing, as illustrated in the diorama of a study room, swarm with intricate detail; they may look a little old-fashioned compared to, say, the bronzes downstairs, but there is a similar aesthetic on display – everyday objects raised to high art.

Along Renmin Dadao

Head from the museum to the north side of **Renmin Dadao**, and you are faced with some fine modern buildings, all worthy of exploration.

Shanghai Urban Planning Exhibition Hall and Shanghai Grand Theatre

It's surely revealing that one of Shanghai's grandest museums is dedicated not to the past but the future: the **Shanghai Urban Planning Exhibition Hall** (daily 9am–5pm; ¥40) is interesting for its insight into the grand ambitions and the vision of the city planners, though if you're not keen on slick propaganda presentations it can be safely skipped. Most worthy of note is the tennis court-sized model on the second floor, showing what the city will (if all goes to plan) look like in 2020. No room in this brave new world for shabby little alleyways: it's a parade ground of skyscrapers and apartment blocks in which, according to this model, the whole of the Old City (see p.63) is doomed. Look out for the giant ferris wheel on the north Bund. Other as yet unbuilt structures are shown in transparent plastic. In a video room next door you can get taken on a virtual helicopter trip around this plan, which is liable to make you giddy. Back on the first floor, there's a collection of old photographs of Shanghai from colonial times – most interesting if you've already grown somewhat familiar with the new look of these streets. Avoid the tacky "olde-worlde" cafés in the basement.

Continue west, past the frumpy City Hall, and you come to the impressive **Shanghai Grand Theatre**, distinguished by its convex roof and transparent walls and pillars – a different take on the same cosmological principles that influenced the Shanghai Museum's designers. Created by the architects responsible for the Bastille Opera House in Paris, it has ambitions of being a truly world-class theatre (see p.130). If you're just passing, there's a café on site and a good shop sells reasonably priced DVDs and CDs (see p.146).

The Shanghai racecourse

The area of People's Square was originally the site of the Shanghai racecourse, built by the British in 1862. The races became so popular among the foreign population that most businesses closed for the ten-day periods of the twice-yearly meets. They soon caught on with the Chinese too, so that by the 1920s the Shanghai Race Club was the third wealthiest foreign corporation in China. When not used for racing the course was the venue for polo and cricket matches. During World War II it served as a holding camp for prisoners and as a temporary mortuary; afterwards most of it was levelled, and while the north part was landscaped to create Renmin Park, the rest was paved to form a dusty concrete parade ground for political rallies. The former paved area has now been turned over to green grass, bamboo groves and fountains, while the bomb shelters beneath have become shopping malls. Only the racecourse's clubhouse survives, as the venue for the Shanghai Art Museum.

▲ Shanghai Art Museum

Shanghai Art Museum

Past the Grand Theatre, turning right along Huangpi Bei Lu will bring you ultimately to the **Shanghai Art Museum** (daily except Mon 9am–5pm, no entry after 4pm; ¥20; ⓦ www.cnarts.net/shanghaiart), whose distinctive clock tower was once nicknamed "Little Ben". You can see hints of its former function as the racecourse clubhouse in the equestrian detailing on the balustrades (see box opposite). It's very popular to get yourself photographed among the witty bronzes to the right of the entrance; portraits of migrant workers by Liang Shuo, they were put up for the 2000 Biennale and proved so popular that they became a permanent fixture. On the east side of the building a huge bracket, or *dougong*, of the kind usually seen on temples clings to the facade, a remnant from the 2006 Biennale.

Inside, the museum has no permanent exhibition, but its shows of contemporary art are always worth a wander round. It's a must during the Biennale every other autumn (see p.133), when it's full of work by the hottest international artists and you'll have to queue to get in. The third-floor café is okay but you'd be better off heading up to *Kathleen's 5* restaurant (see p.117) on the top floor for afternoon tea and fantastic views over the square.

Renmin Park

Just east of the Art Museum is the north gate to lovely **Renmin Park** (open 24hr; free). It's surprisingly quiet, with rocky paths winding between shady groves and alongside ponds – the only sign that you are in the heart of a modern city is the skyscrapers looming above the treetops. In the morning, the park is host to *tai ji* practitioners and joggers and old folk arrive to camp out all day playing cards.

Bearing left brings you to a small square. On weekends, this is the venue for an extraordinary **marriage market**. Hundreds of middle-aged parents mill round with printouts displaying the statistics of their children – height, education, salary – and arrange dates. Interestingly, few display photos – these people know what attributes they want for their little darling's partner, and looks are not top of the list.

Head through bamboo groves to the lotus pond and a quintessential Shanghai **view** will open out in front of you. It's a shocking architectural mash-up: from left to right, elegant modernism (MoCA; see below), then Arabian fantasy (the *Barbarossa* café; see p.113), followed by the colonial edifice that is now the Art Museum, and looming over that the corporate brutalism of Tomorrow Square (see below).

Crossing the zigzag bridge, a minute's walk to the south of *Barbarossa* brings you to the attractive, glass-walled **Museum of Contemporary Art** (MoCA; 10am–6pm; ¥20, students free; Ⓦwww.mocashanghai.org). This privately funded museum has no permanent collection but its shows are always interesting and imaginatively curated, and its three storeys make an excellent exhibition space. There's a lot of video and installation art, with a roughly equal balance between Chinese and foreign artists, and the museum holds regular talks and tours; check the website for details.

Tomorrow Square and around

Come out of the north entrance of Renmin Park, turn left and cross back over Huangpi Bei Lu and that scary, claw-roofed monolith towering over you, with a striking resemblance to Saruman's castle out of the *Lord of the Rings* films, is **Tomorrow Square**. The top floors house the *JW Marriott* hotel; head to the lobby on the 38th floor for great views over People's Square – you can see how much prettier it would be without City Hall in the middle. If you want to linger here you'll have to buy a drink (the cheapest cocktails are around ¥50).

Just behind the castle, and in stark contrast to its corporate slickness, is an area of ramshackle low rise, **Jiangyin Lu**. Heading west along here for a hundred metres or so, past the *Mingtown Hostel* (see p.105), brings you to a little **pet market**, where you can buy a cricket in a bamboo cage for ¥5 or a snake for a little more. Pot-bellied pigs are all the rage at the moment. You're not far now from the fake market (see p.138) and the food street, Wujiang Lu (see p.82).

The Old City and around

The **Old City** is that strange oval on the map, circumscribed by two roads, Renmin Lu and Zhonghua Lu, which follow the old path of the city walls. This district never formed part of the International Settlement and was known by the foreigners who lived in Shanghai, rather patronizingly, as the **Chinese City**. Based on the original walled city of Shanghai, which dated back to the eleventh century, the area was reserved in the nineteenth and early twentieth centuries as a ghetto for vast numbers of Chinese who lived in conditions of appalling squalor, while the foreigners carved out their living space around them. It's an area of about four square kilometres, and at its northern edge is not half a kilometre from the Bund – though a great distance in spirit. In modern times it has been slashed down the middle by the main north–south artery, Henan Nan Lu. The easiest approach from Nanjing Dong Lu is to walk due south along Henan Lu or Sichuan Zhong Lu.

Although tree-lined ring roads replaced the original walls and moats as early as 1912, and sanitation has obviously improved vastly since, to cross the boundaries into the Old City is still to enter a different world. The twisting alleyways are a haven of free enterprise, bursting with makeshift markets selling fish, vegetables, cheap trinkets, clothing and food. Ironically, for a tourist entering the area, the feeling is like entering a Chinatown in a Western city. It probably won't stay that way for long though; as prime real estate, the area is squarely in the sights of developers and city planners and many of the lanes have already been demolished.

The Old City	老城	*lǎo chéng*
Huaihai Dong Lu	淮海东路	*huái hǎi dōng lù*
Henan Nan Lu	河南南路	*hé nán nán lù*
Yuyuan Bazaar	豫园商城	*yù yuán shāng chéng*
Yu Gardens	豫园	*yù yuán*
Huxin Ting Teahouse	湖心亭茶馆	*hú xīn tíng chá guǎn*
Chenxiangge Nunnery	沉香阁	*chén xiāng gé*
Dajing Lu	大镜路	*dà jìng lù*
Dajing Pavilion	大镜阁	*dà jìng gé*
Baiyunguan Temple	白云观	*bái yún guān*
Confucius Temple	文庙	*wén miào*

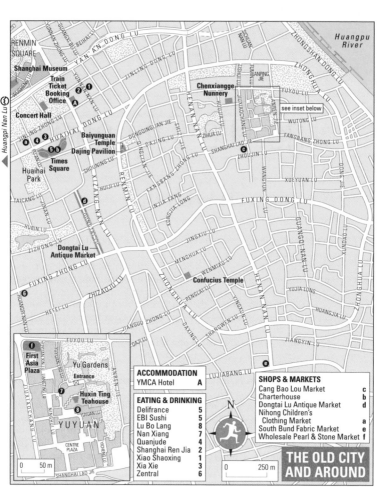

ACCOMMODATION
YMCA Hotel   **A**

EATING & DRINKING
Delifrance	5
EBI Sushi	5
Lu Bo Lang	8
Nan Xiang	7
Quanjude	4
Shanghai Ren Jia	2
Xiao Shaoxing	1
Xia Xie	3
Zentral	6

N

SHOPS & MARKETS
Cang Bao Lou Market	c
Charterhouse	b
Dongtai Lu Antique Market	d
Nihong Children's Clothing Market	a
South Bund Fabric Market	e
Wholesale Pearl & Stone Market	f

0   250 m

THE OLD CITY AND AROUND

Visitor activity centres on the tourist **Yuyuan Bazaar** and the attached **Yu Gardens**, but there are also a few charming **temples** sunk into the **alleyways**. Heading west, you abruptly re-enter the modern city when you hit **Huaihai Dong Lu**. Not far from here you'll find the shabby but intriguing Dongtai Lu Antique Market (see p.139), worth a mooch even if you're not into buying, and from here you can walk to swanky Huaihai Lu, Xintiandi and Taikang Lu Art Street, all covered in the next chapter.

Yuyuan Bazaar and Yu Gardens

The Yu Gardens lie at the centre of a touristy **bazaar** of narrow lanes lined with souvenir shops, all new but built in a style of architectural chinoiserie. Some might complain that it looks like Disneyland but Chinese tourists love it, and it gets fearsomely busy. If you need to get some souvenir **shopping** done in a hurry, this is the place to come, though watch out for tea scam artists (see p.34). You'll have to bargain hard, except at the large jewellery shops, where gold and platinum pieces are sold by weight, and the price per gram – significantly lower than in the West – is marked on the wall. Wooden signs point to the more famous shops (see p.139).

A classical Chinese garden featuring pools, walkways, bridges and rockeries, the **Yu Gardens** (Yu Yuan or Jade Garden; daily 8.30am–5.30pm; ¥40) were created in the sixteenth century by a high-ranking official in the imperial court in honour of his father. Despite fluctuating fortunes, the gardens have surprisingly survived the passage of the centuries. They were spared from their greatest crisis – the Cultural Revolution – apparently because the anti-imperialist "Little Sword Society" had used them as their headquarters in 1853 during the Taiping Uprising (see p.177). The Yu Gardens are less impressive than the gardens of nearby Suzhou (see p.153), but given that they predate the relics of the International Settlement by some three centuries, the Shanghainese are understandably proud of them. During the lantern festival on the fifteenth day of the traditional New Year, the gardens are brightened up by thousands of lanterns and an even larger number of spectators.

Garden connoisseurs will appreciate the whitewashed walls topped by undulating dragons made of tiles, the lotus ponds full of koi and the paths winding round hillocks. The first building you come to is the **Cuixiu Hall** (Hall of Gathering Grace), built as a venue for the appreciation of an impressive twelve-metre-high **rockery**; Chinese gardens are meant to be landscapes in miniature, so the rockery is something of a mini-Himalaya. The **Yuhua Tang** (Hall of Jade Magnificence) behind it has some lovely wooden screens on the doors and inside is full of Ming dynasty rosewood furniture. The huge, craggy, indented rock in front of the hall was intended for the Summer Palace in Beijing, but the boat carrying it sank in the Huangpu, so it was recovered and installed here. Chinese guides demonstrate that a coin dropped in the hole at the top can emerge from several different exits – according, so they say, to your astrological sign. The southeast section of the gardens is a self-contained **miniature garden** within a garden and tends to be rather less busy, so it's a good place to head for a sit down.

After visiting the gardens, check out the delightful **Huxin Ting** (Heart of Lake Pavilion; 8am–9pm), a two-storey teahouse on an island at the centre of an ornamental lake, reached by a zigzagging bridge. The Queen of England and Bill Clinton, among other illustrious guests, have dropped in for tea. These days it's a bit pricey at ¥50 for a cup of tea (albeit limitless), but you're welcome to poke about. Vendors on the bridge sell fish food for ¥2 so you can feed the carp.

The alleyways

A short walk west from the Yu Gardens, the **Chenxiangge Nunnery** (daily 8am–4pm; ¥10) is one of the more active of Shanghai's temples. This tranquil complex is enlivened by the presence of a few dozen resident nuns, who gather twice daily to pray and chant in the Daxiongbao Hall, under the gaze of the Sakyamuni Buddha. His gilded statue is flanked by images of 384 disciples, all supposedly the work of a single recent, still living, craftsman. As in all Chinese nunneries, the gardens are extremely well tended.

If you head west out of the bazaar (past all the construction work) you will soon find yourself in some gritty **alleyways** – the real old town, if you like. It's being torn down at a fearsome rate, but hopefully there will still be a few streets left by the time you read this. Crossing Henan Nan Lu brings you to the most interestingly ramshackle street, **Dajing Lu**, where you'll likely come across ducks being killed and plucked, laundry and cured meat hung up on the same lines, and plenty of hole-in-the-wall restaurants with their fare – crabs, toads, shrimps and the like – crawling around plastic tubs outside. Look behind you for a great Shanghai snapshot, the Jinmao Tower rising over the shabby street like a mirage – very *Blade Runner*.

▲ Confucius statue

At the end of the street is the pretty and newly renovated Taoist **Baiyunguan Temple** (daily 9am–5pm; ¥5). Worshippers light incense and burn "silver ingots" made of paper in the central courtyard – some burn paper cars and houses too. Taoist priests wander around in yellow robes with their long hair tied in a bun, well aware of those tourists who lurk hoping to snap that killer photo – monk on a mobile. In the main hall there's a huge effigy of the Jade Emperor looking judgmental. Taoism is the most esoteric of China's three big religions, and there are some weird figures of Taoist Immortals on display at the side of the hall – look for the fellow with arms coming out of his eyes.

Just next door, the **Dajing Pavilion** is a new structure built over the last surviving slice of a Ming dynasty wall. Brick markings on the wall bear the names of the two Emperors, Tongzhi and Xianfeng, who commissioned it as protection against Japanese pirates. The pavilion today contains a rather threadbare exhibition on the history of the Old City.

Confucius Temple

Sunk deep into the southwestern corner of the Old City on Wenmiao Lu is the **Confucius Temple** (daily 9am–5pm; ¥10). Confucius was a philosopher who, around 500BC, lectured on ethics and statecraft, emphasizing the importance of study and obedience. He was deified after his death and his theories provided the ideological underpinnings to the feudal Chinese state. Though Confucianism is no longer an active religion, its ideological influence on Chinese culture is obvious in the general Chinese respect for education and patriarchal authority.

Like most such temples across China, the Confucius Temple has become a park and museum. Shanghai has had a temple dedicated to Confucius since the Yuan dynasty but most of the present buildings date back to 1855, when the Small Swords Society (see p.177) made the temple a base. The only original Yuan building left is the elegant three-storey **Kuixing Pavilion**, near the entrance, which is dedicated to the god of artistic and intellectual endeavour. An appealing atmosphere of scholarly introspection infuses the complex – students wishing for good exam results tie red ribbons to the branches of the pine trees, and there's a **statue** of Confucius himself looking professorial (though it's not the recently approved "official" likeness).

In the **study hall** is an exhibition of teapots, more interesting than it sounds as some display a great deal of effort and ingenuity. One, appropriately for the venue, is in the shape of a scholar, with the spout being his book, while another is nearly a metre high – it must have been hell to pour.

The temple is never busy except on Sundays, when there is a secondhand book fair in the main courtyard. Outside, vendors sell kitschy plastic and street food.

The Old French Concession

Shanghai might be changing furiously but one thing always stays the same: the **Old French Concession** is its most charming area. More than anywhere else in the city it has retained its historic feel; when people call Shanghai the Paris of the East, this is the area they're thinking of.

The Old French Concession is predominantly low rise, thanks to a colonial ruling that no building be more than one and a half times taller than the road is wide, and lined with glorious old mansions – many of which have become restaurants, boutiques, embassies and galleries. Certain French characteristics linger here, in the local chic and in a taste for bread and sweet cakes, and in the many old plane trees providing shade. The district invites leisurely strolling, with a little shopping, people watching, a good meal and lots of coffee the order of the day.

Less crowded than Nanjing Dong Lu but more upmarket, **Huaihai Zhong Lu** is the main street running through the heart of the area. The most interesting streets are the quieter ones leading off it. To the south you'll find the **Xintiandi** development, a zone of rebuilt traditional houses (*shikumen*), housing that even critics of its yuppie ambience admit has great architectural charm, and further south, the quaint **Taikang Lu**; both are well worth exploring. Heading west from here, there are plenty of **former residences** and boutiques to poke around in the area of **Ruijin Er Lu**, **Maoming Nan Lu** and **Fenyang Lu**. As the street heads towards **Hengshan Lu**, embassies, bars and restaurants start to predominate.

A great way to explore is by **bike** (for rental places, see p.26), though note that bikes are not allowed on Huaihai Lu. Otherwise, take the metro to Huangpi Nan Lu, Shaanxi Nan Lu or Changshu Lu and walk.

Some history

Established in the mid-nineteenth century, the former French Concession lay to the south and west of the International Settlement, abutting the Chinese City (see p.63). Despite its name, it was never particularly French: before 1949, in fact, it was a shabby district mainly inhabited by Chinese and White Russians – what is now Huaihai Lu was then Avenue Joffre, after the French general, but it was nicknamed "Little Moscow". Other Westerners looked down on the White Russians as they were obliged to take jobs that, it was felt, should have been left to the Chinese (see box, p.76).

The Old French Concession	法租界	*fǎ zū jiè*
Huangpi Nan Lu	黄陂南路	*huáng pí nán lù*
Huaihai Zhong Lu	淮海中路	*huái hǎi zhōng lù*
Xintiandi	新天地	*xīn tiān dì*
Shikumen Open House Museum	石库门民居陈列馆	*shí kù mén mín jū chén liè guǎn*
First National Congress of the Chinese Communist Party	中国一大会址纪念馆	*zhōng guó yī dà huì zhǐ jì niàn guǎn*
Fuxing Park	复兴公园	*fù xīng gōng yuán*
Former Residence of Sun Yatsen	孙中山故居	*sūn zhōng shān gù jū*
Zhou Enlai's Former Residence	周恩来故居	*Zhōu ēn lái gù jū*
Taikang Lu Art Street	泰康路田子坊	*tài kāng lù tián zi fǎng*
Ruijin Er Lu	瑞金二路	*ruì jīn èr lù*
Ruijin Hotel	瑞金宾馆	*ruì jīn bīn guǎn*
Maoming Nan Lu	茂名南路	*mào míng nán lù*
Cathay Theatre	国泰电影院	*guó tài diàn yǐng yuàn*
Okura Garden Hotel	上海花园饭店	*shàng hǎi huā yuán fàn diàn*
Jinjiang Hotel	锦江之星	*jǐn jiāng zhī xīng*
Lyceum Theatre	兰心大戏院	*lán xīn dà xì yuàn*
Shaanxi Nan Lu	陕西南路	*shǎn xī nán lù*
Hengshan Moller Villa	衡山马勒墅饭店	*héng shān mǎ lè shù fàn diàn*
Julu Lu	巨鹿路	*jù lù lù*
Xiangyang Park	襄阳公园	*xiāng yáng gōng yuán*
Fenyang Lu	汾阳路	*fēn yáng lù*
Arts and Crafts Museum	手工艺博物馆	*shǒu gōng yì bó wù guǎn*
Taiyuan Villa	太原别墅	*tài yuán bié shù*
Changshu Lu	常熟路	*cháng shú lù*
Art Scene China	艺术景画廊	*yì shù jīng huà láng*
The Propaganda Poster Centre	宣传画黏画艺术中心	*xuān chuán huà nián huà yì shù zhōng xīn*
Hengshan Lu	衡山路	*héng shān lù*
Song Qingling's Former Residence	宋庆龄故居	*sòng qìng líng gù jū*

It's hard to imagine it now, but the French Concession was notorious for being low rent, for its lawlessness and for the ease with which police and French officials could be bribed – in contrast to the well-governed areas dominated by the British. This made it ideal territory for gangsters, including the king of all Shanghai mobsters, Du Yuesheng, the right-hand man of Huang Jinrong (see p.179). For similar reasons, political activists also operated in this sector – the first meeting of the Chinese Communist Party took place here in 1921, and both Zhou Enlai and Sun Yatsen, the first provisional President of the Republic of China after the overthrow of the Qing dynasty, lived here. The preserved former homes of these two in particular (see p.74) are worth visiting simply because, better than anywhere else in modern Shanghai, they give a sense of how the Westerners, and the Westernized, used to live.

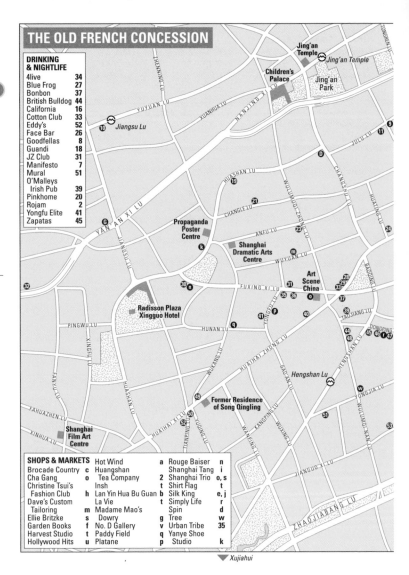

THE OLD FRENCH CONCESSION

Xintiandi

Although it might seem like an obvious idea, the **Xintiandi** development, which comprises two blocks of renovated and rebuilt *shikumen* converted into a genteel open-air mall, was the first of its kind in China. It has met with such success that now town planners all over the country are studying its winning formula. Detractors may call it a working-class neighbourhood reimagined as a yuppie playground,

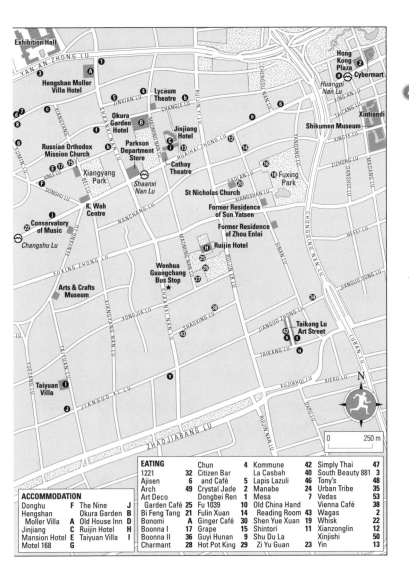

THE OLD FRENCH CONCESSION | Xintiandi

ACCOMMODATION		
Donghu	F	The Nine	J
Hengshan		Okura Garden	B
Moller Villa	A	Old House Inn	D
Jinjiang	C	Ruijin Hotel	H
Mansion Hotel	E	Taiyuan Villa	I
Motel 168	G		

EATING							
1221	32	Chun	4	Kommune	42	Simply Thai	47
Ajisen	6	Citizen Bar		La Casbah	40	South Beauty 881	3
Arch	49	and Café	5	Lapis Lazuli	46	Tony's	48
Art Deco		Crystal Jade	2	Manabe	24	Urban Tribe	35
Garden Café	25	Dongbei Ren	1	Mesa	7	Vedas	53
Bi Feng Tang	21	Fu 1039	10	Old China Hand		Vienna Café	38
Bonomi	A	Fulin Xuan	14	Reading Room	43	Wagas	2
Boonna I	17	Ginger Café	30	Shen Yue Xuan	19	Whisk	22
Boonna II	36	Grape	15	Shintori	11	Xianzonglin	12
Charmant	28	Guyi Hunan	9	Shu Du La		Xinjishi	50
		Hot Pot King	29	Zi Yu Guan	23	Yin	13

but architecturally the area is a triumph – its stone buildings have retained their charm without being chintzy and the attention to detail is fantastic. Paved and pedestrianized, with *longtang* opening out onto a central plaza, Xintiandi is a great place to wind down or linger over a coffee, with upscale restaurants and shops and plenty of outside seating for people watching. Access is subtly but strictly controlled, with security guards keeping the riffraff out, so there aren't even any art students to hassle you. The easiest way to get here is to take the metro to Huangpi Nan Lu and walk south for five minutes.

Heading into the **North Block**, you'll first have to pass the city's most popular *Starbucks*. The branch of the popular Shanghai Tang on the left is lovely, with a great tiled floor, but the prices are mind-boggling; for similar stuff at more reasonable prices visit imitators such as nearby Shanghai Trio (see p.140), or you'll find crude knock offs at the fake market (see p.138). It's also worth having a jaunt down the narrow lane on the east side; that impressive mansion is 1 Xintiandi, where its Hong Kong owners hang out and count their money. At the southern edge of the north block are two sights worth having a nose around: the **Shikumen Open House Museum** and the **First National Congress**.

After this, Xintiandi's **South Block** is rather anticlimactic, with a modern glass mall at the end rather spoiling the olde-worlde effect. Inside it, as well

▲ The Shikumen Open House Museum

as the UME International Cineplex (see p.133) and a host of luxury brands, you'll find Xintiandi's best restaurant, *Crystal Jade* (see p.118).

Shikumen Open House Museum

The **Shikumen Open House Museum** (daily 10am–10pm; ¥20), at the bottom end of the north block, does an excellent job of evoking early twentieth-century Chinese gentility. This reconstruction of a typical *shikumen* is filled with everyday objects – typewriters, toys, a four-poster bed and the like, so it doesn't look as bare as the "Former Residences" elsewhere in the city. A top-floor display details how Xintiandi came about, admitting that most of it was built from scratch. A quote on the wall is perhaps more revealing than was intended: "Foreigners find it Chinese and Chinese find it foreign."

The First National Congress of the Chinese Communist Party

On the east side of the complex, at the junction of Xingye Lu and Huangpi Nan Lu, you'll find, rather incongruously, one of the shrines of Maoist China, the **First National Congress of the Chinese Communist Party** (daily 9am–

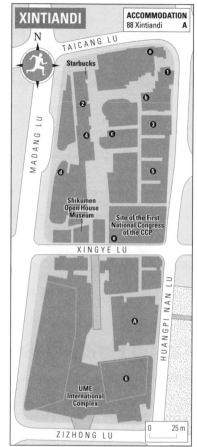

EATING & DRINKING		SHOPS & MARKETS	
Crystal Jade	6	Annabel Lee	b
KABB	2	Shanghai Tang	c
Paulaner Bräuhaus	4	Shanghai Trio	a
T8	5	Simply Life	d
Xinjishi	1	Yaoyang Teahouse	e
Ye Shanghai	3		

5pm, last admission 4pm; ¥3). The official story of this house is that on July 23, 1921, thirteen representatives of the communist cells which had developed all over China, including its most famous junior participant **Mao Zedong**, met here to discuss the formation of a national party. The meeting was discovered by a French police agent (it was illegal to hold political meetings in the French Concession), and on July 30 the delegates fled north to nearby Zhejiang province, where they resumed their talks in a boat on Nan Hu. Quite how much of this really happened is unclear, but it seems probable that there were in fact more delegates than the record remembers – the missing names would have been expunged according to subsequent political circumstances. There's a little **exhibition hall** downstairs, where relics from the period such as maps,

Shikumen

The **shikumen**, or stone-gated house, was developed in the late nineteenth century as an adaption of Western-style terrace housing to Chinese conditions. By the 1930s, such houses were ubiquitous across Shanghai, and housed eighty percent of the population. Crammed together in south-facing rows, with a narrow alley or *longtang* in between, they were all built to a similar design, with a stone gate at the front leading into a small walled yard. Some were very salubrious, others little more than slum dwellings. Those aimed at the middle classes had five rooms upstairs, five down. The least desirable room was the north-facing *tingzijian*, at the bend in the staircase; these were generally let to poor lodgers such as students and writers. Many classics of Chinese literature were composed in these pokey spaces.

As the city's population mushroomed in the twentieth century, *shikumen* were partitioned into four or five houses. In the rush to develop, most *shikumen* neighbourhoods have been demolished; those that remain are cramped and badly maintained, with archaic plumbing. Xintiandi is the single example of stylish renovation, though perhaps pastiche would be a more accurate word, as there's not much left in the area of the original houses. The *longtangs* at Taikang Lu (see opposite) and Duolun Lu (see p.94) have, however, been well preserved.

money and a British policeman's uniform and truncheon, are more interesting than the comically outdated propaganda rants. The last room has a waxwork diorama of Mao and his fellow delegates.

Fuxing Park and the Former Residences

Fuxing Park is a pleasant venue for a stroll. Locals play mahjong or perform *tai ji* under the shade of tall, fragrant plane trees and the gaze of busts of Marx and Engels. The complex at the northwestern exit is popular club *California* so at night the fountain here sees its share of frolicking.

Just outside the western exit stands the **Former Residence of Sun Yatsen**, the first president of the Chinese Republic, and his wife, Song Qing Ling (daily 9am–4.30pm; ¥8). The dry exhibition of the man's books and artefacts is nothing special, but just as an example of an elegantly furnished period house it is worth a wander round. Just north of here on Gaolan Lu, the Russian Orthodox **St Nicholas Church**, built in 1933, was turned into a factory by the Communists, then became a fancy nightclub until the Russians complained. No doubt it will be reinvented again soon, but at present it's closed.

Head south down Sinan Lu and you enter a smart neighbourhood of old houses. Five minutes' walk brings you to one you can get into, **Zhou Enlai's Former Residence**, at no. 73 (daily 9am–4pm; ¥2). Zhou was Mao's right-hand man, but – rather less harsh, and not so barmy – he has always been looked on with rather more affection than the Chairman. When he lived here he was head of the Shanghai Communist Party, and as such was kept under surveillance from a secret outpost over the road. There's not, in truth, a great deal to see, beyond a lot of hard beds on a nice wooden floor. The house has a terrace at the back with rattan chairs and polished wooden floors, and its garden, with hedges and ivy-covered walls, could easily be a part of 1930s suburban London.

Taikang Lu Art Sheet

Continuing further south along Sinan Lu from the Former Residences, the area begins to feel earthier. Head right to the end of the road and a right turn onto Taikang Lu will bring you to what no inner Shanghai working-class district can these days be without – an artsy quarter. Its entrance marked by an arch, **Taikang Lu Art Street** is an unassuming alleyway stretching north off Taikang Lu, It winds all the way to Jianguo Zhong Lu but forget trying to find it from there – the entrance is hidden.

The *shikumen* houses and 1950s factories along this narrow *longtang* have been turned into boutiques, cafés and galleries. It's quainter and artsier than Xintiandi with a little more charm. There are still plenty of local families around, who continue, boutiques or no boutiques, to hang their woolly underwear out to dry, and old folk shuffle around in their pyjamas. The art on sale tends towards the commercial, "something for the guestroom" variety, and some stores are cutesy, but others contain quirky items you won't find elsewhere; on the whole, this is the place to come for accessories such as handmade jewellery, belts, shoes and scarves, and for unique one-off pieces rather than name-brand designer labels (see Shopping, p.142).

Ruijin Er Lu and Maoming Nan Lu

Heading west, the south section of **Ruijin Er Lu** is busy and cramped but there's a wonderful escape in the form of the stately **Ruijin Hotel**, just south of Fuxing Zhong Lu. This Tudor-style country manor was home in the early twentieth century to the Morris family, owners of the *North China Daily News*; Mr Morris raised greyhounds for the Shanghai Race Club and the former Canidrome dog track across the street. The house, having miraculously escaped severe damage during the Cultural Revolution because certain high-ranking officials used it as their private residence, has now been turned into a pleasant inn (see p.109). Even if you're not a guest, you're free to walk around the spacious, quiet grounds, where it's hard to believe you're in the middle of one of the world's most hectic cities. Check out the sumptuous *Face Bar* (see p.125) and the *Art Deco Garden Café* (see p.114).

For a complete change of tone, you can exit the guesthouse onto the south end of **Maoming Nan Lu**, a raucous bar strip, though it's pretty tame during the day. Point yourself north and the street grows more salubrious with every step, until by the time you cross Fuxing Zhong Lu it's positively la-di-da, with plenty of boutiques to poke around. Keep going over Huaihai Zhong Lu and past the old **Cathay Theatre**, now a cinema (see p.133), and you'll come to one of the city's most discreetly prestigious districts.

The two plush hotels, the **Okura Garden** (see p.109) and the **Jinjiang** (see p.108), are both worth a visit for glimpses of past luxuries. The *Okura*, originally the French Club, or Cercle Sportif Français, was taken over by the Americans during World War II and converted by the egalitarian Communists into the People's Cultural Palace. Anyone can wander round the lovely gardens and go in to look at the sumptuous ceiling design of stained glass in the ballroom.

The *Jinjiang* compound opposite includes the former **Grosvenor Residence** complex, the most fashionable and pricey address in pre–World War II Shanghai.

White Russians

After the Bolsheviks took power in 1917, loyalists of the czar, known as **White Russians** to distinguish themselves from the Red Communists, first fought, then, when defeated, fled into exile. Many came to Shanghai. As stateless peoples without extra-territorial protection they were subject to Chinese laws, and suffered harsh Chinese punishments. Some had brought their family jewels and heirlooms, but most arrived with little.

The girls, ex-ballerinas and opera singers among them, could at least rely on their feminine charms; many became **"taxi girls"**, dancing for a small gratuity at night-clubs, or the mistresses of established Westerners – the divorce rates shot up as a result, particularly among the British. Other girls (as many as one in four, according to a League of Nations report), drifted into prostitution.

The lives of the men were even more precarious. Destitution forced many to earn their living in ways no other foreigner would consider, as rickshaw pullers or beggars. Ex-soldiers found work as bodyguards for Chinese gangsters. This was all terribly embarrassing to other foreigners, as it punctured a carefully constructed facade of superiority, and a scheme was mooted to have them all packed off to Australia, though it came to naught.

But the influence of the Russians was by no means all negative; as well as a certain élan, they brought a wealth of skills. Cultivated sophisticates became teachers, exposing the children of boorish merchants to cultured pastimes such as fencing and horse riding, and it was Russian musicians, ballerinas, and singers who more than anyone created the city's unique cultural scene.

The hotel has recently been modernized, but the VIP Club still retains much of its 1920s architecture and *Great Gatsby* ambience. Non-guests might be able to sneak a peek by taking the lift to the top floor of the old wing of the *Jinjiang*, where the club is located, although gaining entrance to one of the twenty astonishingly beautiful refurbished Art Deco VIP mansion rooms on the floors directly below (a snip at US$800 per night) might prove slightly more difficult. Never mind: visit the excellent and much more affordable *Yin* restaurant instead (see p.121).

If you keep walking up Maoming Nan Lu you come to the Art Deco **Lyceum Theatre**, built in 1931 and once home to the British Amateur Dramatic Club. It now holds nightly acrobatic shows (see p.130).

Around Shaanxi Nan Lu

From Maoming Nan Lu, head west along Changle Lu, turn north up Shaanxi Nan Lu, and you'll see an incongruous Gothic fantasy up ahead – the **Hengshan Moller Villa**. It was built in 1936 by Eric Moller, and – rumour has it – designed by his twelve-year-old daughter. There's certainly something appealingly childlike about the tapering spires and striped brickwork. It's like a castle made of cake – perhaps she should have been allowed a hand in more of Shanghai's buildings. These days it's a pricey hotel (see p.108) and also home to the excellent on-site *Bonomi* café (see p.114).

From here, it's a short stroll north over Yan'an Zhong Lu to the sternly communist Exhibition Hall (see p.82) and the brash commercialism of Nanjing Xi Lu. Head south and west onto **Julu Lu** for a more relaxed ambience. With its strip of dive bars it's raucous at night but by day it's very civilized, with walled villas and plenty of restaurants. Some excellent examples of Palladian and Art Deco architecture survive in the private residences here and in nearby Changle Lu.

South on Xiangyang Bei Lu, the **Russian Orthodox Mission Church**, unmistakeable with its proud blue dome, is more evidence of the area's strong Russian connection. It's been used as a washing machine factory, a disco and a teahouse, but today it's empty. You can poke around outside but the interior is not open to the public. Nearby **Xiangyang Park** is busy with old folk playing cards. There aren't many parks in the Old French Concession so this one is much appreciated.

That building site just over Huaihai Zhong Lu was the famous Xiangyang Market, a huge mall of stores selling fakes, and you'll likely see tourists with guidebooks older than this one walking around looking bewildered. Put them right – point them towards the new fake market at 580 Nanjing Xi Lu (see p.82).

Along Fenyang Lu

Head south off busy Huaihai Zhong Lu and you quickly enter much quieter territory. Just past the refined Conservatory of Music, the **Arts and Crafts Museum** (daily 8.30am–4.30pm; ¥8) at 79 Fenyang Lu is housed in a charming Neoclassical building which in the 1950s was the residence of Shanghai's mayor. It's worth a poke about as there are some lavish pieces, though many display more craftsmanship than taste; it's all a bit fussily over-refined. There's plenty of embroidery, snuff bottles, kites, fans and paper cuts on display, and more for sale in the gift shop.

The **Taiyuan Villa**, a five-minute walk south of here at 160 Taiyuan Lu, is now an exclusive hotel (see p.109) with the look of a French château and an illustrious past; the American General Marshall, who arbitrated between Mao and Chiang Kaishek, lived here from 1945 to 1949, and it was one of Madame Mao's many residences. Even if you are not staying here you are free to wander the peaceful grounds.

West of Changshu Lu

West of Changshu Lu metro station you really get a good idea of what the French Concession is all about. Many of the villas here have been converted to embassy properties (the more sensitive are guarded by soldiers with fixed bayonets) and there are also plenty of upmarket, expat-oriented restaurants, a fair few beauty salons and oddly, not that many shops. It's more the place to soak up atmosphere on a sunny day than to take in sights.

Art Scene China and the Propaganda Poster Centre

Fuxing Xi Lu is a discreetly charming street, typical of the area, with a winning combination of artsiness, idiosyncratic low-rise buildings and coffee stops. **Art**

Scene China (daily except Mon 10.30am–6.30pm; ☎64370631, ⓦwww .artscenechina.com), an art gallery inside a restored villa, in an alley just off the southern side of the street, is always worth popping in on. Their stable of artists produces painterly, tasteful work that's neither trendy nor gaudy.

A pleasant ten-minute stroll away on Huashan Lu, the **Propaganda Poster Centre** (9.30am–4.30pm; ¥20; ☎62111845) is an abrupt change of tone, providing a fascinating glimpse into communist China – you will not come across a more vivid evocation of the bad old days of Marx and Mao. To find the place, present yourself to the security guard at the entrance to 868 Huashan Lu. He will give you a name card with a map on the back showing you which building in the complex beyond to head for – the centre is a basement flat in building 4. The walls are covered with Chinese socialist realist posters, over 3000 examples arranged chronologically from the 1950s to the 1970s, which the curator will talk you round, whether or not you understand his Chinese. There are, fortunately, English captions. With slogans like "The Soviet Union is the stronghold of world peace" and "Hail the over-fulfilment of steel production by ten million tons" and images of sturdy, lantern-jawed peasants and soldiers defeating big-nosed, green-skinned imperialists or riding tractors into a glorious future, the black-and-white world view of communism is dramatically realized. Note how the Soviet Union flips from friend to enemy and back again – it's all very *1984*. A few posters celebrate real achievements, such as the new freedom of girls to choose their husbands, but they are outnumbered by the grotesque lies, such as a picture of Tibetans welcoming the Chinese army. Never mind; it might be only a few decades ago but China has moved on so far it feels like centuries.

Take a look at the knick-knacks in the gift shop, such as an image of an ack-ack gunner on a teapot. Don't be tempted by these or by the posters on sale, priced at thousands of yuan; they're bound to be fakes. Only buy the postcards, at ¥10 each. The particular artistic style, influenced by Soviet socialist realism, advertising images and folk art, is not without merit, and many contemporary artists like to pastiche it, but with an ironic twist – peasants waving iPods instead of Mao's Little Red Book, say. It's even got a name – **McStruggle**. If that's your thing, you'll find examples in the galleries at Moganshan (see p.84) and T-shirts and bags decorated with McStruggle images at the Shirt Flag boutiques (see p.140).

Song Qingling's residence

About twenty minutes walk southwest from Hengshan Lu metro station, at 1843 Huaihai Xi Lu, is **Song Qingling's Former Residence** (daily 9–11am & 1–4.30pm; ¥8). As the wife of Sun Yatsen, Song Qingling was part of a bizarre family coterie – her sister Song Meiling was married to Chiang Kaishek and her brother, known as T.V. Soong, was finance minister to Chiang. Once again, the house is a charming step back into a residential Shanghai of the past, and although this time the trappings on display – including her official limousines parked in the garage – are largely post-1949, there is some lovely wood panelling and lacquerwork inside the house. Song Qingling lived here on and off from 1948 until her death in 1981.

5

Jing'an

Nanjing Xi Lu, the main artery of **Jing'an**, the district in the northwest of the centre, was once known to "Shanghailanders" – the Europeans who made their homes here – as Bubbling Well Road after a spring that used to gush at the far end of the street. Then, as now, it was one of the smartest addresses in the city, where Westerners' mock-Tudor mansions shelter behind high walls. Today the area is notable for its grand, exclusive **hotels** and ultra modern **malls**, but in amongst all the luxury it also offers some earthier and much cheaper attractions, in the form of the **fake market** and **Wujiang Lu Food Street**. Unexpectedly, and in counterpoint to the rampant commercialism that surrounds them, Jing'an is also host to two of the city's few notable places of worship: **Jing'an** and **Yufo temples**, both surprisingly busy with devotees. And lastly, in the north of the area close to Suzhou Creek, is the **Moganshan Art District**, an outpost of bohemianism that has become one of the city's highlights – with dozens of art galleries and studios to explore, you'll certainly find something to like.

Jing'an	静安	jìng ān
Nanjing Xi Lu	南京西路	nán jīng xī lù
Fengshine Plaza	风翔服饰礼品广场	fèng xiáng fú shì lǐ pǐn guǎng chǎng
Wujiang Lu Food Street	吴江路小吃街	wú jiāng lù xiǎo chī jiē
Plaza 66	恒隆广场	héng lóng guǎng chǎng
Westgate Mall	梅龙镇广场	méi lóng zhèn guǎng chǎng
CITIC Square	中信泰富广场	zhōng xìn tài fù guǎng chǎng
Shanghai Centre	上海商城	shàng hǎi shāng chéng
Exhibition Hall	展览馆	zhǎn lǎn guǎn
Jing'an Temple	静安寺	jìng ān sì
Jing'an Park	静安公园	jìng ān gōng yuán
Children's Palace	上海市少年宫	shàng hǎi shì shào nián gōng
Yufo (Jade Buddha) Temple	玉佛寺	yù fó sì
50 Moganshan Lu	莫干山路50号	mò gān shān lù wǔ shí hào
Art Scene Warehouse	艺术景仓库	yì shù jǐng cāng kù
Eastlink Gallery	东廊艺术	dōng láng yì shù
ShangART	香格纳画廊	xiāng gé nà huà láng
Zhang Minglou's studio	张明楼工作室	zhāng míng lóu gōng zuò shì
ArtSea gallery	艺思	yì sī
Bizart Centre	比翼艺术中心	bǐ yì yì shù zhōng xīn

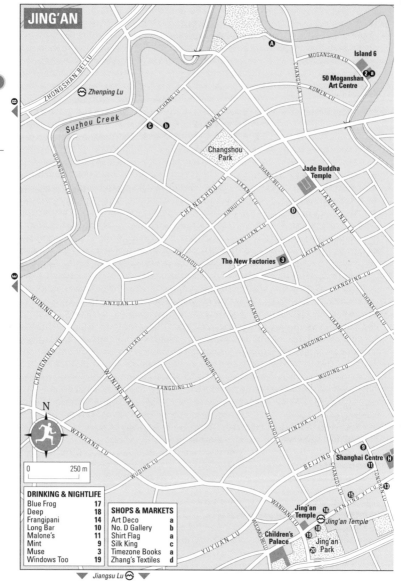

JING'AN

Island 6

MOGANSHAN LU

50 Moganshan
Art Centre

CHANGHUA LU

AOMEN LU

Zhenping Lu

ZHONGSHAN BEI LU

Suzhou Creek

GUANGFU LU

YICHANG LU

AOMEN LU

Changshou
Park

Jade Buddha
Temple

CHANGSHOU LU

XIKANG LU

SHANXI BEI LU

JIANGNING LU

XINHUI LU

ANYUAN LU

HAIFANG LU

JIAOZHOU LU

The New Factories 3

CHANGPING LU

SHANXI BEI LU

ANYUAN LU

CHANGDE LU

XIKANG LU

WUNING LU

KANGDING LU

CHANGNING LU

YUYAO LU

YANGPING LU

WUDING LU

WUNING NAN LU

KANGDING LU

JIAOZHOU LU

XINZHA LU

N

WANHANG LU

0   250 m

WUDING LU

BEIJING XI LU

Shanghai Centre H

Mint 9

CHANGDE LU

TONGREN LU

DRINKING & NIGHTLIFE		
Blue Frog	**17**	
Deep	**18**	**SHOPS & MARKETS**
Frangipani	**14**	Art Deco a
Long Bar	**10**	No. D Gallery b
Malone's	**11**	Shirt Flag a
Mint	**9**	Silk King c
Muse	**3**	Timezone Books a
Windows Too	**19**	Zhang's Textiles d

WANHANG LU

Jing'an
Temple   Jing'an Temple

MAOMING LU

Children's
Palace

YUYUAN LU

Jing'an
Park

NANJING XI LU

Nanjing Xi Lu

Wide Nanjing Xi Lu is one of Shanghai's busiest shopping streets, though with
a parade of giant malls it's rather less intimate than some of the other shopping

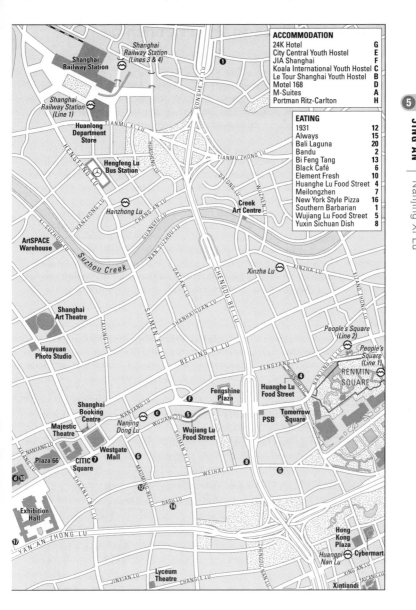

ACCOMMODATION

24K Hotel	G
City Central Youth Hostel	E
JIA Shanghai	F
Koala International Youth Hostel	C
Le Tour Shanghai Youth Hostel	B
Motel 168	D
M-Suites	A
Portman Ritz-Carlton	H

EATING

1931	12
Always	15
Bali Laguna	20
Bandu	2
Bi Feng Tang	13
Black Café	6
Element Fresh	10
Huanghe Lu Food Street	4
Meilongzhen	7
New York Style Pizza	16
Southern Barbarian	1
Wujiang Lu Food Street	5
Yuxin Sichuan Dish	8

areas; after all the unrelenting materialism you may be ready for the attractive temple at the street's western end. Bus #20 runs the length of the road and there are a couple of metro stops: Nanjing Xi Lu and Jing'an Temple, both on line #2.

Fengshine Plaza to the Friendship Exhibition Hall

Starting from Renmin Square and heading west, first stop for most visitors is **Fengshine Plaza** on the north side of the street at 580 Nanjing Xi Lu (daily 9am–8pm), where you can gauge China's true level of commitment to protecting intellectual property. The entire mall, all three storeys, is devoted to stalls selling fake goods – clothes, watches, software, bags and shoes (see p.137). Remember to bargain hard.

Across the road, an unassuming side street, **Wujiang Lu**, curls off Nanjing Xi then runs parallel to it, and is well worth exploration. Lined with cheap hole-in-the-wall restaurants, at meal times it's a slice of appealing picaresque chaos common to the rest of China but in short supply in glossy Shanghai. *Yang's* fried dumplings, at the western end, are some of the best in the city (see p.111).

Back on Nanjing Xi Lu, the north side of the street is given over to a string of **malls** – Westgate, CITIC Square and Plaza 66, kitschy buildings arranged in a row like souvenirs on a mantelpiece. They're all rather too heavily weighted towards luxury brands, with the result that there are generally more staff than shoppers. The last of the giants is the Shanghai Centre, which despite an underwhelming entrance through a car park, is one of the more interesting upscale places, host to the excellent *Element Fresh* café (see p.116) and the five-star *Portman Ritz-Carlton* hotel (see p.110). The Shanghai Centre Theatre here has nightly acrobatics shows (see p.130).

Directly over the road, and surely in a permanent sulk at the capitalist behemoths surrounding it, the **Shanghai Friendship Exhibition Hall** is a Stalinist wedding cake built to celebrate communism. It's worth examining for its colossal ornate entrance, decorated with columns patterned with red stars, and capped by a gilded spire. Constructed by the Russians in 1954, it was originally known as the Palace of Sino–Soviet Friendship and housed a permanent exhibition of industrial machinery from the Shanghai area – proof of the advances achieved after 1949. Now it's a vast and vulgar hall for trade

▲ Shanghai Friendship Exhibition Hall

fairs. Ironically, its most distinguished show in 2007 was the wildly popular "Millionaire's Fair", at which the city's new rich enjoyed browsing through yacht catalogues.

Jing'an Temple and around

Continuing down Nanjing Xi Lu brings you to the **Jing'an Temple** (daily 7.30am–5pm; ¥10), another building, hemmed in by skyscrapers, that doesn't seem quite comfortable in itself (perhaps aware that Shanghai's true places of worship are up the road, with names like Plaza 66). Building work first began on the temple in the third century, and its apparent obscurity today belies its past as the richest Buddhist foundation in the city. In the late nineteenth century it was headed by legendary abbot Khi Vehdu, who combined his religious duties with a gangster lifestyle; the abbot and his seven concubines were shadowed by White Russian bodyguards, each carrying a leather briefcase lined with bulletproof steel, to be used as a shield in case of attack. At the time of writing the temple was in an ugly state of reconstruction, but it should be considerably prettier by the time you read this. The main hall is currently a concrete bunker, holding a golden statue of the Laughing Buddha and figures of eighteen *arhats*; in the corner is a model of what the new hall will look like when it's finished. More effort seems to have gone into the shop in the western wall, which sells religious trinkets.

Over the road is attractive **Jing'an Park**, once Bubbling Well cemetery, which has a good pit stop in the form of the *Bali Laguna* restaurant (see p.121). One block southwest, at the corner of Wulumuqi Bei Lu and Yan'an Xi Lu, lies the grandiose yet slightly run-down **Children's Palace**. Originally known as Marble Hall, the sprawling estate was built in 1918 as a home for the Kadoories, a Sephardic Jewish family and one of the principal investors in pre-World War II Shanghai. The drab, worn exterior gives no clue to the chandeliered ballrooms of the mansion's grand interior. In its current function as a children's art centre, it hosts frequent singing and dancing performances on weekday afternoons and at weekends. The only official way to see them is by arranging a tour with CITS (see p.42), but you just might find the back gate along Nanjing Xi Lu ajar if you come here on your own.

Yufo Temple

Three kilometres north of the Jing'an Temple is the **Yufo Temple** (Jade Buddha Temple; daily 8am–5pm; ¥15) a much more interesting and attractive complex. The pretty temple buildings feel much more authentically temple-like than those at Jing'an, with flying eaves, complicated brackets and intricate roof and ceiling decorations. It's a lively place of worship, with great gusts of incense billowing from the central burner and worshippers kowtowing before effigies and tying red ribbons to the branches of trees, to decorative bells and to the stone lions on the railings.

The star attractions here, though, are the relics. Two **jade Buddhas** were brought here from Burma in 1882 and the temple was built to house them. The larger, at nearly two metres tall, sits in its own separate building in the north of the temple, and costs ¥10 to see. It was carved from a single block of milky-white jade and is encrusted with agate and emerald. The second statue, in the western

83

hall, is a little smaller, around a metre long, but easier to respond to. It shows a recumbent Buddha at the point of dying (or rather entering nirvana), with a languid expression on his face, like a man dropping off after a good meal.

The central **Great Treasure Hall** holds three huge figures of the past, present and future Buddhas, as well as the temple drum and bell. The gods of the twenty heavens, decorated with gold leaf, line the hall like guests at a celestial cocktail party, and a curvaceous copper Guanyin stands at the back. It's all something of a retreat from the material obsessions outside, but it's still Shanghai: religious trinkets, such as fake money for burning and Buddhas festooned with flashing lights, are for sale everywhere and the monks are doing a roaring trade flogging blessings. If you're at all peckish, check out the attached vegetarian restaurant, where a bowl of noodles costs ¥5 – go for the mushrooms.

Moganshan Arts District

A couple of kilometres northeast of the Yufo Temple, in an former industrial zone beside Suzhou Creek, the **Moganshan Arts District** is a complex of studios and galleries that makes up the city's biggest arts destination. In the early 1990s, attracted by cheap rents, artists began to take over the abandoned warehouse buildings at 50 Moganshan Lu and use them as studios. Then the art galleries moved in. Now the design studios and cafés and more commercial galleries are arriving as the district shoots inexorably upmarket. What makes it so fascinating for the moment is the way the area is both shabby and sophisticated, jumbling together paint-spattered artists, slick dealers, pretentious fashionistas and baffled locals. Most of the smaller galleries double as studios and there's something for all tastes, from cutting-edge video installations to chintzy kitsch, so expect to spend at least a morning poking around.

Getting here can be a bit of a problem as public transport is inconvenient: the nearest metro stop to Moganshan is Shanghai Station, a ten-minute walk away; otherwise you'll have to take a taxi. Most of the galleries (though not all) are closed on Mondays. If you're looking for a particular gallery, note that there's a map on the wall by the entrance. For more on the Chinese art scene, see p.133.

50 Moganshan Lu

There are more than thirty galleries at 50 Moganshan Lu, but most are small concerns selling work that's frankly rather derivative – lots of McStruggle (see p.78) and brightly coloured caricature figures. To see the best of Chinese art, you need to seek out the big hitters, who represent some true innovators. The best place to start is the cavernous **Art Scene Warehouse**, on the first floor of building 4, just beyond the main gate and on the left (daily except Mon 10.30am–6.30pm; ℡62774940, ⓦwww.artscenewarehouse.com). Not only will you find a representative selection of contemporary paintings, but the work is sympathetically displayed (which you can't say about all the galleries) in a minimalist white space. Look out for Xue Jiye's comically straining naked men and Shao Yinong's melancholy images of empty halls.

Next, take those unpromising looking stairs in the building next door (no. 6) to seek out **Eastlink**, on the fifth floor (daily 10am–5.30pm; ℡62769932, ⓦwww.eastlinkgallery.cn). The oldest gallery here, it maintains a repuation for sailing close to the wind, and represents controversial art scene figures such as

Ai Weiwei (who helped design Beijing's new Olympic stadium but is not shy to dismiss the whole event as propaganda for a brutal regime). Here you'll find Huang Yan's now iconic photos of Chinese traditional landscapes painted over human bodies.

Heading back out, go north to seek out **ShangART** (daily 10am–6pm; ☏63593923, ⓦwww.shangartgallery.com), housed in buildings 16 and 18. Though the work is not well displayed – it tends to be propped against the walls – the artists represented include big names such as Yang Fudong (see box, p.134) and Zhao Bandi, whose satirical photographs of himself with his toy panda captured the public imagination when they were used in an advertising campaign. While you're in the area, check out **Zhang Minlou's studio**, on the first floor of building 18; the artist has covered his walls with huge murals of figures and designs, referencing ancient Buddhist cave art.

Of the numerous photography galleries, half seem to show images of buildings in states of demolition – Shanghai's relentless development offers plenty of material to those heirs of romanticism who find ruins picturesque. The most highly reputed such gallery is **ArtSea**, on the second floor of building 9 (Wed–Sun 10am–6pm; ☏62278380). The **Bizart Centre**, on the fourth floor of building 7 (Mon–Sat 11am–6pm; ☏62775358, ⓦwww.biz-art.com), scores highest for credibility; it's a not-for-profit operation that promotes Chinese and foreign contemporary art, with an artist in residence programme. It doesn't represent artists, but works with them, putting on themed shows, and is always worth checking out.

You're probably all arted out now, so check out Timezone Books (see p.146), on the right of the entrance for the latest glossy art tomes, and have a coffee at the nearby *Bandu* café (see p.115).

Island 6

Inevitably, the scene is spreading, and more galleries are opening in the area. From 50 Moganshan Lu follow the street west, head north up the first alley, and you come to a striking warehouse building standing alone on an abandoned plot of land, against a backdrop of high rises – avant-garde venue **Island 6** (ⓦwww.island6.org). The work on display is (usually) less dramatic than the setting though.

6

Pudong

Pudong, the eastern bank of the Huangpu River, has been transformed in just a couple of decades from paddy fields into a glittering cityscape of giant boulevards and architectural showpieces. When Michael Winterbottom used it as the setting for his sci-fi flick *Code 46*, no computer-generated imagery was used – Pudong may not always be pretty but as an image of the future, it convinces.

Historically, the area was known as the wrong side of the Huangpu. Before 1949, it was populated by unemployed migrants and prostitutes, and characterized by murders and the most appalling living conditions in the city. It was here that bankrupt gamblers would *tiao huangpu*, commit suicide by drowning themselves in the river. Shanghai's top gangster, Du Yuesheng, more commonly known as "Big-eared Du", learned his trade growing up in this rough section of town. Under communist rule it continued its slide into shabby decay until in 1990, fifteen years after China's economic reforms started, it was finally decided to grant Pudong the status of Special Economic Zone (SEZ). This decision, more than any other, is fuelling Shanghai's dizzying economic advance. The maze of skyscrapers now stretches east as far as the eye can see.

The skyline may be iconic but critics say that it's only interesting from a distance. The bustling street life that so animates the rest of the city is striking for its absence – in between those fancy monoliths there are too many empty, windy boulevards – and it's the only part of the city that does not reward aimless

Getting to Pudong

The most entertaining way to cross from the west bank of the Huangpo to Pudong is to take the **Bund Tourist Tunnel** (capsules every minute; daily 8am–10.30pm; ¥30 one way, ¥40 return), the entrance to which is in the underpass at the north end of the Bund, opposite Beijing Dong Lu (see map, p.48). The capsule takes a couple of minutes to chug past psychedelic light displays, which have names such as "Heaven" and "Meteor Shower". It's something of a kitsch throwback and not what you'd expect in sophisticated Shanghai. A cheaper alternative is to take the **ferry** (every 15min; ¥0.8), which runs all day and night from a jetty opposite Yan'an Dong Lu at the south end of the Bund (not to be confused with the jetty for river cruises, further south). Ferries arrive at the south end of Binjiang Dadao (see p.88), a fifteen-minute walk from the Jinmao Tower.

From elsewhere west of the river, the **metro** is the quickest way to travel, whooshing passengers from People's Square to Lujiazui in less than three minutes, and all the way to the Science and Technology Museum in ten. **Bus** #3 runs from in front of the Shanghai Museum to the Jinmao Tower, but beware rush hour as the traffic in the tunnel gets badly snarled up.

Pudong	浦东	pǔ dōng
Bund Tourist Tunnel	外滩观光隧道	wài tān guān guāng suì dào
Lujiazui	陆家嘴	lù jiā zuǐ
Binjiang Dadao	滨江大道	bīn jiāng dà dào
Superbrand Mall	正大广场	zhèng dà guǎng chǎng
China Sex Culture Exhibition	中华性文化博物馆	zhōng huá xìng wén huà bó wù guǎn
Shanghai Aquarium	上海海洋水族馆	shàng hǎi hǎi yáng shuǐ zú guǎn
Natural World Insect Kingdom	大自然野生昆虫馆	dà zì rán yě shēng kūn chóng guǎn
Oriental Pearl Tower	东方明珠广播电视塔	dōng fāng míng zhū guǎng bō diàn shì tǎ
Shanghai History Museum	上海城市历史发展馆	shàng hǎi chéng shì lì shǐ fā zhǎn guǎn
Pearl Dock	明珠码头	míng zhū mǎ tóu
Jinmao Tower	金茂大厦	jīn mào dà shà
Jinmao Tower observation deck	金茂大厦88层观光厅	jīn mào dà shà bā shí bā céng guān guāng tīng
World Financial Centre	环球金融中心	huán qiú jīn róng zhōng xīn
Shiji Dadao	世纪大道	shì jì dà dào
Century Park	世纪公园	shì jì gōng yuán
Science and Technology Museum	上海科技馆	shàng hǎi kē jì guǎn
Oriental Arts Centre	上海东方艺术中心	shàng hǎi dōng fāng yì shù zhōng xīn
Zendai Museum of Modern Art	证大现代艺术馆	zhèng dà xiàn dài yì shù guǎn

wandering. That said, if you know where you're going a visit to Pudong can be very worthwhile. There are two areas that reward exploration. First is **Lujiazui**, the battery of skyscrapers just across the water from the Bund, which is home not just to the giant Jinmao and Pearl Orient towers, but to a couple of intriguing museums, including the China Sex Culture Exhibition. The second rewarding area to explore is spacious **Century Park**, 4km away; the rather more successful architectural experiments here include the Science and Technology Museum, the Oriental Arts Centre, and, further out, the Zendai Museum of Modern Art.

Lujiazui

In Lujiazui you'll find not just Shanghai's daftest edifice, the bulbous **Oriental Pearl Tower**, but also its most elegant, the **Jinmao Tower**; both offer sublime views across the city. In order to take advantage of the crowds of tourists who flock to the Pearl Tower, several **museums** have opened nearby, including the fun History Museum, and the intriguing China Sex Culture Exhibition. This is another area where it helps to plan where you're going to eat. For cheap eats head to the Superbrand Mall or the Jinmao Tower's basement food court; for something pricey and memorable you can't beat *Jade on 36*, in the *Pudong Shangri-La* (see p.122).

The riverside promenade

The riverside promenade, **Binjiang Dadao**, is a pleasant place for a stroll, close enough to the river to hear the slap of the water and much less crowded than the other side. There is outside seating at each of the name-brand **bars and cafés** (*Starbucks, Paulaner Bräuhaus, Häagen-Dazs*) along the strip, from which you can appreciate the glorious views of the full length of the Bund.

EATING & DRINKING			
Cloud Nine	C	Paulaner Bräuhaus	2
Jade on 36	B	Superbrand Mall	1
Jinmao Tower Food Court	C	Yi Café	B

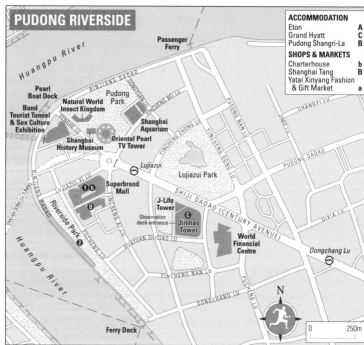

The China Sex Culture Exhibition

At the north end of the promenade, close to the exit from the Bund Tourist Tunnel, is the absorbing **China Sex Culture Exhibition** (daily 8am–10pm; ¥20), the private collection of a single-minded academic, Liu Dalin. As well the many rather quaint pornographic images and jade phalluses on show, exhibits include a "widow's pillow" – a headrest with a secret dildo compartment – a tool for expanding anuses, a knife used to turn men into eunuchs and a saddle with a wooden stump for punishing adulterous women. There are also graphic figurines from Africa and India and a well-endowed nude sculpture by artist Yu Qingcheng. Lengthy English captions touch on marriage customs, creation myths, sexual health and sexual symbolism – you may be surprised to discover what the common "double fish" icon, seen on everything from woodcuts to cigarette packets, actually stands for, and depictions of frogs and fish aren't as innocent as they might have seemed either. It's an unusual museum for China and corporate Pudong seems an incongruous place to put it – though perhaps its presence here is sly commentary on the subconscious motivations of the men who built the enormous erections outside.

Shanghai Aquarium and Natural World Insect Kingdom

In the immediate vicinity are two attractions that don't quite cut it for general visitors but are great if you have kids in tow. At the large **Shanghai Aquarium** at 158 Yincheng Bei Lu (daily 9am–6pm; ¥110, children ¥70; Ⓦwww .aquarium.sh.cn), there are sharks, penguins and seals as well as fish, and one section is devoted to endemic species such as the Chinese alligator and Chinese giant salamander. Particularly impressive is the aquarium's long viewing tunnel. The **Natural World Insect Kingdom** (daily 9am–5pm; ¥35, children ¥20), just around the corner on Fenghe Lu, is a little menagerie of creepy beasties. It's all fiercely tacky but surprisingly hands on – you can feed and handle some of the critters.

The Oriental Pearl Tower and History Museum

Like it or loathe it, the 457-metre-high **Oriental Pearl Tower** (daily 8am–9.30pm) has come to symbolize Shanghai, and its **viewing platforms** are now a required destination for every Chinese tourist. As a result, there's often quite a queue to get in. In fact, the Jinmao Tower (see p.90) observation platform is higher, classier and cheaper – though of course, viewing the city from inside the Pearl Tower does have one major advantage: for once, you can't see the gaudy thing. The pricing system is ridiculously complex: basically, go for the ¥70 ticket, which gets you to the highest bauble. There is a revolving restaurant in the middle globe but it's best avoided.

The **Shanghai History Museum** at the base of the tower (same hours; ¥35) is surprisingly decent; the majority of exhibits, which focus on the nineteenth century onwards, do a good job of evoking the old glory days, with convincing waxwork figures in dioramas of pharmacies, teahouses and the like. One of the old bronze lions from outside the HSBC building (see p.53) is on display, as well as a boundary stone from the International Settlement, and there's a detailed model of the Bund as it would have looked in the 1930s.

It's a short walk from here to the **Pearl Dock**, where you can join hordes of Chinese trippers on a boat tour down the Huangpu. A thirty-minute round trip costs ¥40; boats run every hour from 10am to 6pm.

Jinmao Tower and around

Shanghai's most attractive modern building, the **Jinmao Tower**, is an elegantly tapering postmodern take on Art Deco, built by the Chicago office of Skidmore, Owings and Merrill. All the proportions are based on the lucky number eight – the 88 floors are divided into sixteen segments, each of which is one-eighth shorter than the sixteen-storey base – but never mind the mathematics, the harmony is obvious at first glance. The roof wittily references a pagoda and, for once, doesn't look like a tacked-on afterthought. What look from a distance like filigree are actually decorative metal struts – they make the building appear eminently possible to climb, and indeed in 2001 it was scaled, apparently on a whim, by a visiting shoe salesman; hence the "no climbing" signs around the base. The tower's first 53 floors are offices; from there on up is the spectacular *Grand Hyatt* hotel (see p.110).

The **observation deck** on the 87th floor (daily 8am–10pm; ¥50) is accessible from the basement, via an entrance on the building's north side. An ear-popping lift whisks you up 340m to the top in a matter of seconds. The spectacle of the city spread out before you is of course sublime, but turn round for a giddying view down the building's glorious galleried atrium. Alternatively, for great views for free, go in the front door (on the eastern side) and up to the hotel lobby on the 54th floor where you can take advantage of the *Hyatt's* comfy, window-side chairs. To see the city in real style, though, come here at night for a cocktail at the hotel's swish *Cloud Nine* bar – it's not for the penny-pincher though (see p.126).

The **J-Life annex** on the northern side of the tower is a high-end shopping mall – all very pricey but it's good to know about the juice bar near the bottom of the escalators. On the eastern side, the **World Financial Centre** is a brutalist slab set to loom thuggishly over the trim Jinmao. At 492m, it will be, when finished, the world's second tallest building – though they're considering adding a spire to steal the title – and an observation deck is planned for the 100th floor. The tapering top was going to have a huge circular hole through it, but prickly locals protested that it made the apex look too much like the rising sun of the Japanese flag, so the hole was reshaped as an oblong.

Century Park and around

From Lujiazui, the eight-lane Shiji Dadao (Century Avenue) zooms for 4km to one of the city's largest and newest green expanses, **Century Park** (though it's not quite green enough as yet, as it will take a few years for all the new plants to mature). The area is being spruced with the 2010 Expo in mind, which is perhaps why there's an odd feeling here of being on a stage set that's waiting for its actors. It is, however, a very pleasant place to pass some time, with wide pavements and priority given to pedestrians over traffic, stretches of unbroken lawn and low-rise buildings conferring a great sense of space – it makes you realize how cramped the rest of the city is. There are also some striking new buildings – not high rises for once –foremost among which are the **Science and Technology Museum** and the **Oriental Arts Centre**.

The simplest way to get here is on the metro. Century Park has its own stop, which drops you at its southern edge, but a better approach is to get off at the Science and Technology Museum stop (labelled in English), just three stops east of Lujiazui – note that there's a huge fake market here too (see p.138). You'd be advised not to come here hungry, as there are few places to eat; the cheap canteen in the Science and Technology Museum subway stop is one option.

Century Park

From the Science and Technology Museum stop, it's a pleasant ten-minute stroll along a pedestrian walkway to the northern entrance to **Century Park** (daily 7am–6pm; ¥10). The granite path has lampposts shaped like birds in flight and offers great views of the Pudong skyline. Skaters and kite flyers congregate here, as both activities are banned in the city centre. The park, designed by a British firm, is spacious, the air is clean (well, cleaner) and it's possible to feel that you have escaped the city, at least on weekdays when it's not too crowded. You can hire a tandem bike (¥20 per hour) – sadly you're not allowed to ride your own bicycle – and pedalos are available to rent on the big central lake (¥25 per hour).

The Science and Technology Museum and the Oriental Arts Centre

The **Science and Technology Museum** (daily 9am–5pm; ¥60, students ¥45) is an absolutely enormous gleaming new building; rather too big perhaps, as the cavernous halls make some of the twelve exhibitions look threadbare. There isn't much English explanation or quite enough interactivity but the section on space exploration is good – a big topic in China right now, with the nation fully intending to get to the moon as soon as possible – with real spacesuits, models of spacecraft and the like. In the section on robots you can take on a robotic arm at archery and play a computer at go. The **cinemas** provide the most interest: the space theatre (showings every 40min; ¥40) shows astronomical films; the two IMAX domes in the basement (hourly 10.30am–4.30pm; ¥30/¥40) show cartoons; while the IWERKS dome on the first floor (every

▲ Strollers in Century Park

40min; ¥30) is an attempt to take the concept of immersive realism even further. The seats move, and there are water and wind effects – no Smell-O-Vision yet, but surely it's only a matter of time. The only distinctly Chinese example of science on display is a fantastic Ming dynasty azimuth in the courtyard. Held up by sculptured dragons it's a more successful blend of science and aesthetics than anything inside.

Just north of the museum, the **Oriental Arts Centre** (ⓦ www.shoac.com.cn) is a magnificent, glass-faced, flower-shaped building that houses a concert hall, opera theatre, exhibition space and performance hall – they form the petals. It was designed by French architect Paul Andreu, who also created the new opera house in Beijing. Locals complain that it's a white elephant – it cost more than a billion yuan, has huge maintenance costs and doesn't get a great deal of use. If you happen to be in the area, however, its worth a visit just to appreciate the elegant curves, puzzle at why they made the interior walls look like snakeskin, and to check out the third-floor exhibition of European music boxes.

The Zendai Museum of Modern Art

It's out of the way, but art buffs should seek out the **Zendai Museum of Modern Art** (daily except Tues 10am–8pm; ¥20, free on Sun; ☏ 50339801, ⓦ www.zendaiart.com), a half-hour stroll through the park and out of its north-eastern exit, at 28, Lane 199, Fangdian Lu. You'll know when you've arrived when you see the eye-catching red "love" sculpture outside. The Zendai MoMA is a privately run arts centre along the line of MoCA (see p.62), so expect similar work – a mix of the quite good and the hopelessly obscure. The museum also hosts frequent lectures and concerts.

North of Suzhou Creek

N orth from the Bund, you enter **Hongkou**, an area that, before World War II, was the Japanese quarter of the International Settlement. Since 1949 it has been largely taken over by housing developments, but though it may seem grey and undistinguished – you certainly won't find any celebrity restaurants – it's a charming, rather homely neighbourhood. The two obvious focuses of interest are the pretty **Duolun Culture Street** and nearby art gallery, and **Lu Xun Park**, around which are scattered several memorials dedicated to the political novelist Lu Xun. Both areas are within easy walking distance of each other so it's a good place to come on a sunny afternoon for a stroll, a mooch around the shops and a coffee. Tourists don't get out here much but it's popular with locals, and lively at weekends. If you like your scenic spots uncrowded, come during the week.

The easiest way to get here is to get the light rail line #3 to Dongbaoxing Lu or Hongkou Stadium. You'll probably have to change at Shanghai Railway Station; it's a five-minute walk (signposted) between the two stations, and note that your ticket, whatever it might say, is not valid for the continuing journey. Bus #21 runs to Duolun Lu from Sichuan Zhong Lu, behind the Bund.

Duolun Culture Street	多伦文化名人街	duō lún wén huà míng rén jiē
Mao Museum	毛泽东像章馆	máo zé dōng xiàng zhāng guǎn
Museum to the League of Left-wing Writers	中国左翼作家联盟会址纪念馆	zhōng guó zuǒ yì zuò jiā lián méng huì zhǐ jì niàn guǎn
Kong Residence	孔祥熙公寓	kǒng xiáng xī gōng yù
Duolun Museum of Modern Art	多伦现代美术馆	duō lún xiàn dài měi shù guǎn
Lu Xun Park	鲁迅公园	lǔ xùn gōng yuán
Lu Xun Memorial Hall	鲁迅纪念馆	lǔ xùn jì niàn guǎn
Lu Xun's Former Residence	鲁迅故居	lǔ xùn gù jū
Hongkou Stadium	虹口足球场	hóng kǒu zú qiú chǎng
Huashan Park	华山公园	huá shān gōng yuán
Ohel Moishe Synagogue	摩西会堂	mó xī huì táng

Duolun Culture Street

From the metro station, it's a couple of minutes walk east then north up an alley lined with hole-in-the-wall restaurants to pedestrianized **Duolun Culture Street**. This was once home to some of China's greatest writers, including Lu Xun (see box opposite), to whom so many statues have been dedicated that he seems practically to have been deified. One bronze effigy has him in static conver-

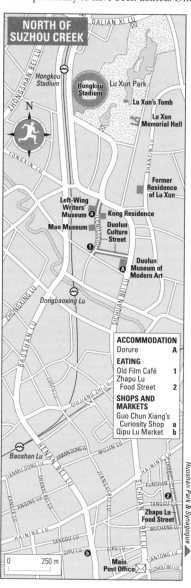

NORTH OF SUZHOU CREEK

Hongkou Stadium

Hongkou Stadium

Lu Xun Park

Lu Xun's Tomb

Lu Xun Memorial Hall

Former Residence of Lu Xun

Left-Wing Writers' Museum

Kong Residence

Mao Museum

Duolun Culture Street

Duolun Museum of Modern Art

Dongbaoxing Lu

Baoshan Lu

ACCOMMODATION
Dorure   A

EATING
Old Film Café   1
Zhapu Lu
   Food Street   2

SHOPS AND MARKETS
Guo Chun Xiang's
   Curiosity Shop   a
Qipu Lu Market   b

Zhapu Lu Food Street

Main Post Office

Huoshan Park & Synagogue

0   250 m

sation with another modernist writer, Guo Moruo; beside them is an empty seat for you to join the debate, which has inevitably become a favourite photo spot.

The *shikumen* houses (see p.74) lining the street have been converted to shops selling antiques, curios and art equipment. Don't miss no. 183, which now functions as a private **Mao Museum** (daily 9am–5pm; ¥2). Badges make up the bulk of the display – during the cult of personality, it was practically obligatory to wear devotion in the form of a tin badge – and they came in a great variety of shapes and sizes. The rarest, now worth thousands of yuan, are those produced in homage by communist African states. The owner's pampered lapdog commonly sleeps at the feet of a porcelain Mao, which makes for an amusing photo.

Head down lane 2 and you'll find the small **Museum to the League of Left-wing writers** (daily 9am–5pm; ¥5), which was set up here in 1930. Writers, sadly, don't make for compelling museums and the collection of oddments, books and photos is less interesting than the building itself, a fine example of a well-preserved *shikumen* house. Another is the grand former residence of Guomindang politician **H.H. Kong** at the northern end of the street; note the Middle Eastern influences evident in its window decorations. But probably the best thing about Duolun Lu is the *Old Film Café*, charmingly decorated with film posters (see p.116).

Lu Xun

Lu Xun (1881–1936) is regarded as the father of modern Chinese literature. Coming from humble origins in the nearby city of Shaoxing, he gave up a promising career in medicine to write books with the intention, he claimed, of curing the social ills of the nation. He used the demotic of the day, eschewing the sophisticated and obscure language of the literati so that ordinary people could read his books. His stories are short and punchy, something that can't be said about all Chinese classics.

Lu Xun's first significant work was *Diary of a Madman*, published in 1918. Taking its name from Gogol's short story of the same name, it was a satire of Confucian society. Three years later followed his most appealing and accessible book, *The True Story of Ah Q*, a tragicomic tale of a peasant who stumbles from disaster to disaster and justifies each to himself as a triumph – an allegory for the Confucian state. Ah Q ends up taking up the cause of revolution and is executed, as ignorant at the end as he was at the beginning.

Lu Xun's writing earned him the wrath of the ruling Guomindang and in 1926 he took refuge in Shanghai's International Settlement. The last ten years of his life were spent in his simple quarters in Hongkou. Since his death, the fact that he never joined the Communist Party has not stopped them from glorifying him as an icon of the Revolution.

Go back to the southern end of the street where it makes a right angle, and you'll find another stretch of curio shops. The weekend **street market** here is something of an oddity, catering to the Chinese hobbyist's appreciation for oddly shaped or coloured rocks. The stalls sell more pebbles and crystals than (it is safe to say) a person could possibly need. Some of the stallholders are grizzly types from Xinjiang in China's far northwest who profess bafflement at being able to charge good money for stones but aren't going to knock it. Pebbles valued for their colours are best viewed in a bowl of water – apparently all to do with balance, shape and harmony.

For rarefied aesthetic judgements of a different (but often equally obscure) nature, head 200m down to the **Duolun Museum of Modern Art**, an unattractive seven-storey monolith that broods at the end of the street (daily except Mon 10am–6pm; ¥10; Ⓦ www.duolunart.com). This is China's first state-run contemporary art museum – and that oxymoron alone should tell you that it was bound to run into trouble. After a couple of shows that the authorities deemed offensive, the gallery staff resigned en masse and were replaced by a more pliant crew. You won't see anything with a hint of the political here, and the privately run MoCA (see p.62) and Zendai (see p.92) are both rather better, but the place does pull in some big-name shows. Artists in residence have studios on the fifth floor, and visitors are welcome to come and chat. There's a good, if pricey bookshop and a schedule of performances and lectures.

Lu Xun Park and around

Lu Xun Park (daily 6am–7pm) is one of the best places for observing Shanghainese at their most leisured. Between 6 and 8am, the masses undergo their daily *tai ji* workout, while later in the day, amorous couples frolic on paddle boats in the park lagoon and old men teach their grandkids how to fly kites.

Jewish Shanghai

Many of the founders of international Shanghai were Sephardic Jews who fled the Middle East in the nineteenth century, families such as the Kadoories and the Sassoons (see p.52) amassing vast fortunes and empires. The Jewish presence increased during World War II, when more than ten thousand refugees from Europe arrived. As stateless persons, they were forced to live in a special enclosure in Hongkou, centred on **Huoshan Park** and nicknamed Little Vienna, where they lived cheek by jowl with the local Chinese.

After the war, most Jews left Shanghai, and the only record of their presence today are touches only the sharpest observer will pick up: a Star of David on an old window grille or nail holes where the mezuzoth hung. In the middle of Huoshan Park is a small memorial in Chinese, Hebrew and English, and just to its north a plaque marks the site of the American Jewish Joint Distribution Committee, which cared for the refugees. The **Ohel Moishe Synagogue** on Changyang Lu, just east of Huashan Park, is today rather dilapidated, and no longer used as a place of worship – though at least it's no longer an asylum for the insane, as it was in the 1970s. There's a pricey **museum** (¥50) on the third floor with a few photos and artefacts, and the curator will show you a short film. For a four-hour tour of Jewish Shanghai, contact Dvir Bar-Gal (☎1300 2146706, ⓦwww.shanghai-jews.com).

The park is also home to the pompous **Tomb of Lu Xun**, complete with a seated statue and an inscription in Mao's calligraphy, which was erected here in 1956 to commemorate the fact that Lu Xun had spent the last ten years of his life in this part of Shanghai. The building of the tomb went against Lu Xun's own wishes to be buried simply in a small grave in a western Shanghai cemetery. The novelist is further commemorated in the **Lu Xun Memorial Hall** (daily 9–11am & 1.30–4pm; ¥8), to the right of the main entrance to the park. Exhibits include original correspondence, among them letters and photographs from George Bernard Shaw.

A block southeast of the park on Shanyin Lu (Lane 132, House 9), **Lu Xun's Former Residence** (daily 9am–4pm; ¥8) is worth going out of your way to see. The sparsely furnished house, where Lu Xun and his wife and son lived from 1933 until his death in 1936, offers a fascinating glimpse into typical Japanese housing of the period – small, neat and tasteful.

Finally, you can't miss the hulking **Hongkou Stadium** on the west side of the park, which has its own line #3 metro stop. Shanghai Shenhua football team play here, with matches on Sundays between March and November (see box, p.30).

8

South and west: Xujiahui and beyond

S hanghai stretches westward for miles and miles, but it's not a zone that need bother the sightseer particularly. **Xujiahui**, on the edge of the Old French Concession, and **Hongqiao** beyond, are modern residential areas where the most talked-about landmark is the IKEA superstore. The suburbs are home to a great many expats, and services are geared towards fulfilling their needs. But as well as malls, freeways and gated communities there are a few places to visit, though sights are too distant from one another to walk between. The main attractions are the rambling old **Longhua Temple** in the southwest, and the **Wanguo Cemetery** and the **zoo** in the far west.

Xujiahui and Longhua

The **Xujiahui** subway pitches you right into the thick of things. You come out into the five-storey Grand Gateway mega-mall, then when you've found your way out, emerge at the giant intersection of Hongqiao Lu, Huashan Lu, Zhaojia-bang Lu and Caoxi Bei Lu, where you're confronted with another five giant malls (see box, p.136). It's easy to feel overwhelmed by a surfeit of neon and concrete, but fortunately just around the corner there's a rather nice cathedral, **St Ignatius**,

Xujiahui	徐家汇	*xú jiā huì*
St Ignatius Cathedral	圣依纳爵主教坐堂	*shèng yī nà jué zhǔ jiào zuò tang*
Longhua Cemetery of Martyrs	龙华烈士陵园	*lóng huá liè shì líng yuán*
Longhua Temple	龙华寺	*lóng huá sì*
Longwu Lu	龙吴路	*lóng wú lù*
Botanical Gardens	上海植物园	*shàng hǎi zhí wù yuán*
Honqiao Lu	虹桥路	*hóng qiáo lù*
Wanguo Cemetery	万国烈士陵园	*wàn guó liè shì líng yuán*
Shanghai Zoo	上海动物园	*shàng hǎi dòng wù yuán*
Cypress Hotel	龙柏饭店	*lóng bǎi fàn diàn*

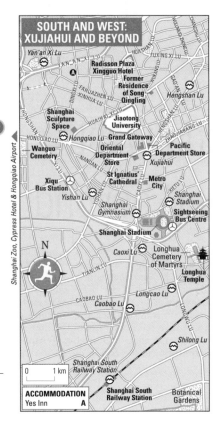

Yan'an Xi Lu

Radisson Plaza
Xingguo Hotel
Former
Residence
of Song
Qingling
Hengshan Lu

Shanghai
Sculpture
Space
Jiaotong
University

Hongqiao Lu   Grand Gateway

Wanguo
Cemetery
Oriental
Department
Store
Pacific
Department Store
Xujiahui

Xiqu
Bus Station
St Ignatius
Cathedral
Metro
City

Yishan Lu
Shanghai
Gymnasium
Shanghai
Stadium

Sightseeing
Bus Centre

Shanghai Stadium

N

Caoxi Lu
Longhua
Cemetery
of Martyrs
Longhua
Temple

Longcao Lu

Caobao Lu

Shilong Lu

Shanghai
South
Railway Station

0   1 km

ACCOMMODATION
Yes Inn   A

Shanghai South
Railway Station
Botanical
Gardens

Shanghai Zoo, Cypress Hotel & Hongqiao Airport

a pleasant interruption to any shopping trip. Afterwards, hop into a taxi (or take a bus) a couple of kilometres south to **Longhua Cemetery** – actually a rather charming park – and Temple.

St Ignatius Cathedral

It may be hard to imagine today, but Xujiahui is actually the site of Shanghai's oldest Western settlement: the Jesuits set up shop here in the seventeenth century. The only significant remnant from their sojourn is the red-brick, Gothic style Catholic cathedral, **St Ignatius**, built in 1910 on the grave of Paul Xu Guangqi, Matteo Ricci's personal assistant and first Jesuit convert. The cathedral was vandalized during the Cultural Revolution, its stained-glass windows smashed, and used as a granary. It reopened in 1979, when the spires were renovated; now the windows are being replaced with some that marry Christian and Chinese motifs. St Ignatius is one of the many places of public worship to have received a new lease of life as China's Christian population has boomed. The first service on weekdays starts at 6.30am, while Sunday services begin at 8am.

Longhua Cemetery and Temple

A couple of kilometres southeast of the St Ignatius Cathedral, **Longhua Cemetery of Martyrs** (daily 6.30am–4pm; cemetery ¥1, exhibition hall ¥5) memorializes those who died fighting for the cause of Chinese communism in the decades leading up to the final victory of 1949. Commemorative stone sculptures, many bearing a photo and a name, dot the park. The fresh flowers brought daily testify to the resonance these events maintain. Particularly remembered are those workers, activists and students massacred in Shanghai by Chiang Kaishek in the 1920s – the site of the cemetery is said to have been the main execution ground. In the centre is a glass-windowed, pyramid-shaped **exhibition hall** with a bombastic memorial to 250 communist martyrs who fought Chiang's forces. The cemetery is a short walk south from the terminus of bus #41, which you can catch from Huaihai Zhong Lu (close to Shaanxi Nan Lu), or from near the Shanghai Centre on Nanjing Xi Lu; alternatively take a taxi.

Right next to the Martyrs' Cemetery is the **Longhua Temple** (daily 5.30am–4pm; ¥10), the most active Buddhist site in the city and a centre for training monks. There has been a temple on the site since the third century, and though the present buildings are only around a century old, the design and layout are true to the original, comprising a complex of elegant multi-eaved halls. Pleasantly laid-back, the temple sees many more devotees than day-trippers. The temple is a must during Spring Festival (see p.29), when it hosts a huge and boisterous fair. At this time, the temple bell, in the tower to the right of the entrance, is banged 108 times, supposedly to ease the 108 "mundane worries" of Buddhist thought. You can whack it yourself, anytime, for ¥10.

The temple's stand-out feature is its tenth-century **pagoda**, an octagonal, forty-metre-high structure with seven brick storeys that are embellished with wooden balconies and red-lacquer pillars. Until the feverish construction of bank buildings along the Bund in the 1910s, it was the tallest edifice in Shanghai. After a long period of neglect (Red Guards saw it as a convenient structure to plaster with banners), an ambitious re-zoning project has spruced up the pagoda and created the tea gardens, greenery and shop stalls that now huddle around it.

▲ Longhua Temple

The Botanical Gardens

Taking bus #56 south down the main road, Longwu Lu, just to the west of the Longhua Temple site, will bring you to the **Botanical Gardens** (daily 7am–4pm; ¥15). More than nine thousand plants are on view in the gardens, including two pomegranate trees which are said to date from the reign of Emperor Qianlong in the eighteenth century; despite their antiquity they still bear fruit. Look out too for the orchid chamber, where more than a hundred different varieties are on show.

The western outskirts

Most visitors only head west of Xujiahui to get to Hongqiao airport but if you have time it's worth a trip out to Hongqiao Lu subway stop and nosing around the **Wanguo Cemetery**, **zoo** and the nearby **Cypress Hotel**, particularly if you have kids in tow – though pick a fine day.

Wanguo Cemetery

The pleasant and well-tended **Wanguo Cemetery** is a ten-minute walk west of Hongqiao Lu subway stop. There were once ten cemeteries for foreigners in Shanghai, but most of the tombstones of those interred in the city suffered ignoble fates – destroyed, used as foundation stones for buildings or sold in antique stores – and those that remain have been collected here, the only foreigners' cemetery left. The great Jewish families, the Kadoories and the Sassoons, are memorialized, as is "Friend of China" Talitha Gerlach, whose tomb stands out as it bears her photograph. Gerlach worked to improve the conditions of Chinese labourers and set up a night school for women. In 1987, she was awarded the first green card given by the communists to a foreigner in Shanghai. The cemetery's most celebrated occupant is Song Qingling (see p.78), who has her own mausoleum and, next to it, a small exhibition on her life.

Shanghai Zoo and Cypress Hotel

A couple of kilometres west of Wanguo Cemetery along Hongqiao Lu, shortly before the airport, is **Shanghai Zoo** (daily 6.30am–4.30pm; ¥20), the grounds of which until 1949 were one of Shanghai's most exclusive golf courses. The zoo is a massive affair with more than two thousand animals and birds caged in conditions which, while not entirely wholesome, are better than in most Chinese zoos. The stars, inevitably, are the giant pandas, though check out the animal-shaped topiary too.

Next door, at 2409 Hongqiao Lu, stands the **Cypress Hotel**, a mansion that once served as home to the Sassoons. Though it's too far out to recommend staying in, it's worth a look around, as the grounds are tranquil and some of the buildings rather grand. The living room originally boasted a fireplace large enough to roast an ox, but Victor Sassoon (see p.52), who used this mansion as a weekend residence, only allowed for the design of two small bedrooms because he wanted to avoid potential overnight guests. The house has since served as a Japanese naval HQ, a casino and as the private villa of the Gang of Four.

The easiest way to get the zoo and hotel is to take the subway to Hongqiao Lu, then grab a taxi.

Listings

Listings

Accommodation

ccommodation in Shanghai is plentiful, and sometimes stylish, with prices that are higher than elsewhere in China but still much cheaper than you'll find in a large Western city. A double room in one of the **grand old-world hotels** that form so integral a part of Shanghai's history will cost at least US$120 per night these days, and for comfort and elegance have been overtaken by new arrivals. The concept of chic **boutique hotels** has only just taken hold, but has been enthusiastically embraced. As yet though, there are not quite enough small, characterful, affordable places – honourable exceptions are listed below.

If you want to be near the centre of the action, go for somewhere between **People's Square** and **the Bund**, where there are options for all budgets. It might be noisy but as soon as you walk out the front door you'll know you're in the real Shanghai. For style and panache, head to the more genteel **Old French Concession**, where there are plenty of mid-range hotels, housed in attractive buildings and grounds and close to upmarket dining and nightlife. To the north, the upscale accommodation in the commercial district of **Jing'an** puts you at the heart of modern, international Shanghai, with plenty of places to eat, drink and shop nearby. For the latest in corporate chic, **Pudong** has the fanciest options, but really, the area is rather dull.

At all but the cheapest hotels, **rack rates** should not be taken seriously; it's almost always possible to bargain the rate down – in off season by as much as two-thirds. The biggest discounts are available **online**, and if you don't have a reservation, it's quite possible that you'll end up paying less for your room on

---

Accommodation price codes

The accommodation in this book has been categorized according to the **price codes** below, representing the cost of the **cheapest en-suite double room**. Some upmarket establishments have high-season (April–Sept) and low-season (Oct–March) rates, in which case the price code represents the cost in high season. In those places where the cheapest rooms are not representative of the general standard, a range of codes are given. Single rooms are uncommon, but where available will generally cost around two-thirds of the price of a double.

Note that in the upscale establishments, a ten or fifteen percent service charge is added to the bill; this is included in the price code. In cheaper hotels with **dormitories**, prices for a bed are given in yuan.

❶ up to ¥150	❹ ¥350–500	❼ ¥900–1300
❷ ¥150–250	❺ ¥500–700	❽ ¥1300–1600
❸ ¥250–350	❻ ¥700–900	❾ Over ¥1600

the Internet than by going to reception. Sites such as Ⓦwww.sinohotel.com and Ⓦwww.asia-hotels.com don't usually have a booking fee but do require that you pay a percentage of the fee up front by credit card.

Reception staff will always speak passable English except at the cheap business hotels, which don't see much foreign custom. **Checking in** involves filling in a form and paying a deposit. Remember to grab a few hotel business cards – these are vital when you want to let taxi drivers know where you're staying. And don't just show them the matchbox from the hotel bar – an apocryphal American tourist did that and found himself taken to a suburban match factory. Whatever type of place you are staying, you can rely on the plastic slippers and thermos of hot water that the attendant will refill for you any time.

Note that it's common practice for prostitutes to phone around hotel rooms at all hours of the night, so disconnect the phone. Even the cheapest places generally offer free wireless or free **Internet** and will book train and plane tickets for a small commission.

For information on finding long-term accommodation, see p.38.

Youth hostels and budget hotels

Many travellers arrive in Shanghai assuming there is only one real budget option in the entire city: the *Pujiang*. Well, not any more – it's gone upmarket. In its place a host of good options have opened up. In the **youth hostels** you can expect free Internet, a self-service kitchen, air-conditioning in the room and a cheap bar. Though you might find some aspects of your stay a little rough around the edges, standards are higher than anywhere else in China and if the staff aren't always completely professional they usually make up for it with friendliness. Anywhere calling itself a hostel will offer a discount (¥10 or so) with a Hostelling International card; you can also pick up a card on the premises (¥50). The hostels we list offer more rooms than dorms so even if you do not identify with the backpacking hordes they're still worth considering. All hostels can be booked in advance on Ⓦwww.hostelbookers.com.

An alternative budget option is the new **motel-style chains** such as *24K* or *Motel 168* which are presently blasting the much loathed dingy two-star Chinese hotel into deserved oblivion – at last, you don't have to tolerate cigarette burns on the carpets and mould on the walls. The hotel restaurant won't be up to much and there are no extras such as health centres or pools, but rooms are clean and spacious and very good value at less than ¥200 a night. Not all the staff will speak English but they'll point to you to others who do.

24K Hotel
24K国际连锁酒店
24k guó jì lián suǒ jiǔ diàn
155 Weihai Lu ☏51181222 **& 555 Fuzhou Lu** ☏51503588; Ⓦwww.24khotels.com. **See maps, pp.80–81 & p.48.** This chain of new business hotels has a winning formula that's making it very popular: chirpy design, spacious and clean rooms, and it's much cheaper than the competition. Most are a little too far out to be convenient but these two branches are very central, both located on busy roads not far from People's Square, and walkable from the metro. Some English is spoken

and there's even a machine that dispenses medicines in the lobby. You should go out to eat, but if you're just looking for somewhere comfortable to crash, this is one to consider. ❸

Captain Hostel
船长青年酒店
chuán zhǎng qīng nián jiǔ diàn
37 Fuzhou Lu ☏63235053, Ⓦwww .captainhostel.com.cn. **See map, p.51.** Doubles at this place just off the Bund are pricey, and it's most of interest for its clean, cheap dorms. The hostel has a nautical theme, which is carried through with admirable

thoroughness – rooms are made to look like cabins, with portholes for windows, and staff are dressed in sailor suits (though it hasn't made them any jollier). It also has a good bar – the *Captain Bar* – on the sixth floor, with great views of Pudong (see p.124). Unusually, dorms are same-sex and Chinese and foreign guests are billeted together. Be warned that the cleaning staff will barge in and get on with it whether you're out of bed or not. Internet access is ¥10/hr, bike rental ¥2/hr (guests only), and there's free use of the washing machine. To reach it, go to Huangpi Nan Lu metro station and walk south or get bus #64 from the train station. Dorm beds ¥70, rooms ❺.

City Central Youth Hostel
万里路国际青年旅舍
wàn lǐ lù guó jì lǚ shè
300 Wuning Lu, near Zhongshan Bei Lu ☎52905577. **See map, pp.80–81.** This giant, no-nonsense hostel, painted a striking blue and orange, boasts the city's cheapest rooms and dorms. It's clean, and staff are efficient and English-speaking and there's a busy bar-cum-restaurant. It's just 300m north of Caoyang Lu metro station, in the west of town, but can be tricky to find the first time. Follow the subway line north until you reach the crossroads with Wuning Lu, cross over and on your right you'll see an archway. Walk through it and you'll see the hostel sign. Dorms ¥40, rooms with shared bathrooms ❶.

Koala International Youth Hostel
考拉国际青年旅舍
kǎo lā guó jì qīng nián lǚ shè
1447 Xikang Lu ☎62769430. **See map, pp.80–81.** Budget Chinese hotels can disintegrate rapidly; at least for the moment, this new one is fantastic value, with large rooms, enthusiastic staff and a range of facilities – such as microwaves and fridges in the rooms – that you would expect from a much pricier place. It's a little bit far from the action, though in a quiet neighbourhood next to Suzhou Creek, a 10min walk from Zhenping Lu subway stop (line #3), on the route of bus #24. Four-bed dorms ¥100, rooms ❷.

Le Tour Shanghai Youth Hostel
乐途上海国际青年旅舍
lè tú shàng gǎi guó jì qīng nián lǚ shè
136 Bailan Lu, near Kaixuan Bei Lu ☎52510800. **See map, pp.80–81.** Friendly staff and good facilities make this worth considering

despite its rather peripheral location a few minutes' walk from Caoyang Lu subway station, in the northwest of the city. The rooms with shared bathrooms are some of the cheapest private rooms in the city, and there are lockers and laundry. Four- and six-bed dorms ¥80; rooms with shared bathroom ❶; rooms with private bath ❷.

Mingtown Etour Hostel
上海明堂新易途国际青年旅馆
shàng hǎi míng táng xīn yì tú guó jì qīng nián lǚ guǎn
57 Jiangyin Lu ☎63277766. **See map, p.58.** This is the best of the cheapies, being very well located – tucked in the alleyway behind Tomorrow Square, right beside Renmin Park – yet quiet and surprisingly affordable. A dark corridor opens into a relaxing courtyard featuring a pond with goldfish and a cat. The cheap bar-restaurant here has a free pool table and shows films at night. There's also a self-service laundry. Rooms vary in size, so ask to see a few – one or two have balconies – and bathrooms are shared between two or three rooms. From People's Square metro, walk five minutes to Tomorrow Square and look for the blue hostel sign in the alley immediately south. Dorms ¥45, doubles ❷.

Mingtown Hikers Hostel
明堂上海旅行者国际青年旅馆
míng táng shàng hǎi lǚ xíng zhé guó jì qīng nián lǚ guǎn
450 Jiangxi Zhong Lu ☎63297889. **See map, p.48.** Very well located just west of the Bund (nearest metro stop: Nanjing Dong Lu), this cheap and cheerful hostel books up quickly. It's sociable, so can be noisy, and the rooms with bathrooms are not a good deal as they're rather dark, but the other options are good for the price. Four- and six-bed dorms ¥45; rooms with shared bathrooms ❶; rooms with their own bathrooms ❷.

Motel 168
莫泰连锁旅店
mò tài lián suǒ lǚ diàn
678 Anyuan Lu, in the northwest of the city, 7min walk north of the Yufo Temple, on bus route #19 from the Bund; 1119 Yan'an Xi Lu, by Fanyu Lu, 5min walk from Jiangsu Lu metro station; all reservations ☎63168168. See maps, pp.80–81 & 70–71. There are a dozen or so branches of this functional American-style motel all over Shanghai – we've listed the two most centrally located. Standard rooms are ¥168 but you can also upgrade to a more

spacious room for ¥268. Services are basic but the rooms are cheap and clean, with a bright colour scheme, and staff speak some English. They do offer rooms by the hour, though – the place isn't sleazy but you might not want your kids to stay. ❷–❸.

Yes Inn
悦思酒店
yuè sī jiǔ diàn
711 Ding Xi Lu ☎62826070, ⓦwww.yesinn .com. See map, p.98. Though billing itself as a boutique hostel for backpackers, this is really just a downmarket business hotel with more beds in the room than usual and some odd design touches, such as chequerboard floor tiles and a bold colour

scheme. Staff could be friendlier but the dorms are pretty comfortable, with TVs and DVD players. It's on the route of bus #806, a 10min walk from Yan'an Xi Lu subway station. Dorms ¥88, rooms ❸.

YMCA Hotel
青年会宾馆
qīng nián huì bīn guǎn
123 Xizang Nan Lu ☎63261040, ⓦwww .ymcahotel.com. See map, p.64. It has seen better days and the four-bed dorms may be on the pricey side (you can do better elsewhere), but this bright, practical, no-frills place is central, and the private rooms are cheap considering the location. Dorms ¥100, rooms ❹–❺.

Mid-range and upmarket hotels

Shanghai's **mid-range hotels** (❹–❻) are usually well equipped and comfortable, though they tend to be rather anonymous. There are some exceptions, however, in the form of the charming converted mansions of the Old French Concession. You can expect an en-suite bathroom, a business centre, WiFi (for which you will have to pay a small surcharge), a booking service for onward transport, and the larger ones will have a gym and sauna. Breakfast apart, meals are better eaten out than in the hotel restaurant as hotel food at this level is never much good.

Moving up the scale, there are plenty of **upmarket places** (❼–❾) and more are being thrown up all the time. They're comparable to their counterparts elsewhere in the world, offering all the facilities you might expect, with gyms, saunas and swimming pools. The choice in this bracket comes down to whether you want to be right in the heart of the neon jungle, or if you want views of it from your window – few places manage both.

Even if a room in one of these establishments is beyond your budget, you can still avail yourself of their lavish facilities, including restaurants that are often pretty good and, by Western standards, not expensive. You may find the finer nuances of service lacking, particularly in older places – the Chinese hospitality industry is experiencing a steep learning curve, which means that the staff and services in newer places are much, much better. An annoyance at this level is the high extra charges for services that are free in cheaper places, such as wireless Internet (sometimes as much as ¥100 a day); hoick your laptop to a nearby café instead.

The Bund and Nanjing Dong Lu

Broadway Mansions
上海大厦
shàng hǎi dà shà
20 Suzhou Bei Lu ☎63246260, ⓦwww .broadwaymansions.com. See map, p.51. This huge, ugly, 1930s lump on the north bank of the Suzhou Creek was originally a residential block, but now offers rooms rather larger

than those at the *Peace* and with superb views along the length of the Bund (room rates increase the higher you go). Some rooms are drab, others have been newly renovated, so check out a few. Like all the other old hotels it leaves something to be desired in terms of style and service. ❼

Le Royale Méridien
世贸皇家艾美酒店
shì mào huáng jiā ài měi jiǔ diàn

789 Nanjing Dong Lu ☎33189999, ⓦwww
.starwoodhotels.com. See map, p.48. The
excellent location, five-star services and the
discreet style of this new high-end venue at
the Renmin Park end of Nanjing Dong Lu
makes it set to give its competitors a scare.
Owned by Starwood, it perhaps has the edge
on the group's other Shanghai property, the
Westin. The building is one of the city centre's
landmarks, with 66 floors and what look like
antennae on the roof. The rather cavernous
reception, which has something of a Bond
villain's secret base about it, is on the 11th
floor. Ask for a room as high up as possible
to take full advantage of the views from the
wall to ceiling windows. ❾

Metropole
新城饭店
xīn chéng fàn diàn
180 Jiangxi Lu ☎63213030, ⓦwww.metropole
hotel-sh.com/l-en.htm. See map, p.48. Just off
the Bund and dating from 1931, this is one of
the more affordable of the older hotels, but it
also suffers from uninspired renovation and
old-fashioned service. There's a great Art
Deco lobby and exterior, but the rooms are
plain. Go for as high a room as possible as
the street is quite noisy. High prices in the
business centre are a rip-off – go elsewhere
to use the Internet or receive faxes. ❻

Peace Hotel
和平饭店
hé píng fàn diàn
Junction of the Bund and Nanjing Dong Lu
☎63216888, ⓦwww.shanghaipeacehotel.com.
See map, p.51. As the *Cathay Hotel*, this was
the most famous hotel in Shanghai, with a
list of illustrious guests that included Charlie
Chaplin and Noel Coward (see p.52). These
days, though, its glories have faded, the
rooms – despite the prices (doubles start at
¥880) – are poky and cluttered with chintz,
and the service is definitely not up to it.
Come to visit the Art Deco lobby and *Jazz
Bar* (see p.125) but don't stay. ❼–❾

Pujiang
浦江饭店
pǔ jiāng fàn diàn
15 Huangpu Lu ☎63246388, ⓦwww
.pujianghotel.com. See map, p.51. Formerly the
Astor Hotel and dating back to 1846, this
pleasingly old-fashioned place, just north of
the Bund across Waibadu Bridge, has the
feel of a Victorian school, with creaky
wooden floors and high ceilings. Portraits of
past guests such as Einstein and Charlie

Chaplin line the walls; they too may have
wondered why the lift was so slow – never
mind, the staircase is magnificent. Rooms
are surprisingly large but they vary so ask to
see a few. The views aren't great and the
restaurant should be avoided, but overall
this is the best of Shanghai's historic hotels;
think of it as a batty maiden aunt with some
good stories and forgive its eccentricities. ❺

Seagull
海鸥饭店
hǎi ōu fàn diàn
60 Huangpu Lu ☎63251500, ⓦwww
.seagull-hotel.com. See map, p.51. Gull
statuary, pink-uniformed staff and a chintzy
lobby give this place an air of campness,
but it does offer recently refurbished rooms
with great views of the Huangpu for less
than you'd pay elsewhere. The area is not
very exciting but you're only a five-minute
walk across the bridge to the Bund. ❼

Westin
威斯汀大酒店
wēi sī tīng dà fàn diàn
88 Henan Zhong Lu ☎63351888, ⓦwww
.westin.com/shanghai. See map, p.48. Chinese
luxury hotels usually try to impress with either
a water feature or palm trees in the lobby;
the over-the-top *Westin* goes for both. So is
it the best? Well no, but it's not bad. It scores
for having good on-site restaurants such as
the *Stage* (see p.116) and a nice little bakery
(see p.113), for the Banyan Tree spa (see
p.31), and for its location behind the Bund,
but loses a few points for the Vegas
ambience and the lack of views from most of
the rooms. Decor is modern with a few flash
touches such as rainforest showerheads and
mood lighting. ❾

People's Square

See the map on p.58 for the location of the
two places reviewed here.

JW Marriott
明天广场JW万怡酒店
míng tiān guǎng chǎng JW wàn yí jiǔ diàn
Tomorrow Square, 399 Nanjing Xi Lu
☎53594969, ⓦwww.marriott.com. Housed in
the top floors of one of Shanghai's most
uncompromising landmarks (something like
an upraised claw), this swanky venue boasts
more than 200 serviced apartments for
stressed executives, who will at least always
be able to find their way home. With its
excellent location and magnificent views it's
one of the best of the top-end destinations,

though not if you suffer vertigo or dislike ear-popping lifts – the lobby is on the 38th floor. Request an east-facing room for views of the liveliest scenes. Windows are huge and have deep sills for sitting and gazing. ⑨

Radisson New World
新世界丽笙大酒店
xīn shì jiè lì shēng dà jiǔ diàn
88 Nanjing Xi Lu ☎63599999, Ⓦwww.radisson .com. This swish new venue offers in general a slick upscale experience, though the lobby, with its gold lighting, is a bit too much. Has all the facilities you could expect, including spa, gym and pool, and a great location at the end of Nanjing Xi Lu, though eclectic design features give the impression that it doesn't seem quite to have worked out an identity yet. That UFO on the roof is actually a revolving restaurant, though the view is more distinguished than the food. ⑧

The Old French Concession

Establishments reviewed here are marked on the map on pp.70–71, except where noted.

🏃 88 Xintiandi
88 新天地
bā shí bā xīn tiān dì
380 Huangpi Nan Lu ☎53838833, Ⓦwww.88intiandi.com. See map, p.73. Handily close to Huangpi Nan Lu metro, this fifty-room boutique hotel, Shanghai's first, is at the edge of the yuppie fantasyland that is the Xintiandi complex. With half the city's destination restaurants on your doorstep you won't have to go far to eat, though each room has a little kitchen attached so you can do your own cooking if you (rather perversely) want to. Carved wood, screens and curtains jazz up a design that isn't quite far enough away from the standard business hotel model – still, it's got a lot more character than most Shanghai hotels. The best rooms have a view of the small lake to the east and the no-smoking floors are a nice touch. There's also a pool and guests can use the adjacent spa and fitness centre. Note that it can get noisy outside at weekends. Pricey, but worth it. ⑧

Donghu
东湖宾馆
dōng hú bīn guǎn
70 Donghu Lu, one block north of Huaihai Zhong Lu ☎64158158, Ⓦwww.donghuhotel.com. Seven buildings in total make up the *Donghu*, in a sprawling complex separated by Donghu Lu. The villas on the south side have a chequered past; they served as an opium warehouse

and the centre of gangland operations in the 1920s and 1930s. Today, rooms in this section are sedate and spacious with big bathrooms – the best are in building one, where all the furniture is in traditional Chinese style. The rooms in the new buildings on the north side of the street are much less interesting, but cheaper. Its good location and pleasant gardens make this one of the best hotels in its price range. ⑤–⑦

🏃 Hengshan Moller Villa
衡山马勒墅饭店
héng shān mǎ lè shù fàn diàn
30 Shaanxi Nan Lu ☎62478881, Ⓦwww .mollervilla.com. Describing itself as a boutique heritage hotel, the main villa here is a gorgeous Scandinavian gothic fantasy (see p.76), built in the 1930s and set in lovely, quiet grounds. You have a choice of where to stay – the main villa's rooms have balconies, wood panelling and fireplaces, but they're pricey, and there are only a couple of singles, which you'll have to book long in advance. Rooms in the new three-storey block just behind are clean and modern, of much less interest but considerably cheaper. Breakfast is served in the villa, and there's a great branch of the *Bonomi* café on site. ⑥–⑧

Jinjiang
锦江之星
jǐn jiāng zhī xīng
59 Maoming Nan Lu ☎62582582, Ⓦwww .jinjianghotels.com. This vast place with many wings, built in the 1930s, is one of Shanghai's most historic addresses (see p.75). Perhaps it's a trifle old-fashioned, and has been overtaken by slick new competitors, but it's well located, just north of Shaanxi Nan Lu subway, off busy Huaihai Zhong Lu. Rooms in the main, Georgian-style Cathay building to the north are a little ordinary for the price; the best are in the Grosvenor building and the recently renovated south building. ⑦–⑨

Mansion Hotel
上海首席公馆酒店
shàng hǎi shǒu xí gōng guǎn jiǔ diàn
82 Xinle Lu ☎54039888. This painstakingly reconstructed 1920s mansion, discreetly tucked away from the street amongst manicured gardens, has the feel of an elite private members club – in fact it was once home to notorious gangster Du Yuesheng (see p.179). The building is magnificent but they've tried too hard with the lobby and corridor furnishings, cramming unrelated antiques into every corner. Still, the thirty

guestrooms are impressive, light and airy, with dark wooden furnishings. All have Jacuzzis. ❾

The Nine
9 Lane 355, Jianguo Xi Lu, by Taiyuan Lu ☎64719950. This small boutique hotel in an old villa cultivates an air of exclusivity; there's not even a sign – look for the sturdy gates. There are only five rooms, all bedecked with antiques, and fine meals are served at the long table. It's intimate and classy; guests are made to feel as if they are weekending at a country house. Phone reservations long in advance are essential. ❽

Okura Garden
上海花园饭店
shàng hǎi huā yuán fàn diàn
58 Maoming Nan Lu ☎64151111, ⓦwww .gardenhotelshanghai.com. The grounds are lovely at this Japanese-run mansion, and the lobby, which used to be the Cercle Sportif French Club, has some great Art Deco detailing. Rooms, though, are in that nondescript new monolith looming at the back. All have been newly renovated and have multi-function toilets with a bidet attachment and seat warmer. ❾

Old House Inn
上海老时光餐厅酒吧
shàng hǎi lǎo shí guāng cān tīng jiǔ bā
16 Lane 351, Huashan Lu, by Changshu Lu ☎62486118, ⓦwww.oldhouse.cn. A small, atmospheric guesthouse in a sympathetically restored *shikumen* house, set in a leafy courtyard. The dozen rooms are all chic and comfortable, with four-poster beds, retro furnishings and dark wooden floors. The corridors are authentically poky, and it's a bit ramshackle in places and chilly in winter, but if you're looking for affordable character, this is the place to stay. The incongruously hip attached restaurant is of high quality but can get noisy at weekends. The bar here makes up for the fact that the hotel has no common area. Reservations essential. ❻

▲ Old House Inn

Ruijin Hotel
瑞金宾馆
ruì jīn bīn guǎn
118 Ruijin Er Lu (main entrance on Fuxing Lu) ☎64725222, ⓦwww.ruijinhotelsh.com. This Tudor-style villa complex, a couple of blocks south of Huaihai Zhong Lu, is set in manicured gardens, complete with lawn tennis courts. It was once the home of the editor of the *North China Daily News* in the 1920s; as a hotel, it's hosted both Ho Chi Minh and Nixon. The villas, none higher than four storeys, are cosy and exclusive; ask to stay in Building One, where Mao used to stay, as it has the finest Art Deco touches – in the lampshades, balustrades and window decorations – and is in the best nick. The lavish *Face Bar* (see p.125) and *Lan Na Thai* restaurant above it are an additional bonus. The only downside is the occasionally lacklustre service, the usual complaint for any Chinese establishment run by the government; but it's still recommended. ❼–❾

Taiyuan Villa
太原别墅
tài yuán bié shù
106 Taiyuan Lu, by Yongjia Lu ☎64716688. If you don't mind a 10min walk to the nearest subway, Changshu Lu, this historic villa (see p.77), set on a quiet street in lovely grounds, is certainly one of the best places to stay in this price range. In the turreted old block the period charm is enhanced by dark-wood panelling and antique furniture in the rooms. A new block holds serviced apartments – comfortable and nicely furnished, but much less interesting than the villa. Facilities are limited – there's no business centre or gym – so it's best suited for the short stay tourist who values character and quiet. ❼

Jing'an

See the map on pp.80–81 for the location of the places reviewed here.

JIA Shanghai
JIA酒店
jiā jiǔ diàn
931 Nanjing Xi Lu ☎62179000, ⓦwww .jiashanghai.com. In a good position on Nanjing Xi Lu, this is a brand-new branch of the Hong Kong boutique hotel chain and is already causing quite a stir among the smart set. Its 55 rooms are housed in a rather dashing building from the 1920s, with big balconies and Art Deco touches. Phillipe Starck had a hand in the classy interior

design, a familiar Shanghai east–west fusion style, light and airy, and the second floor restaurant is managed by Italian celebrity chef Salvatore Cuomo. There are two penthouse suites, a gym and spa, and every room has a small kitchen. The rooftop bar will no doubt become one of the city's hotspots soon. The overall feel is like a private members club for fashionistas. ❾

M-Suites

一号码头精品酒店

yī hào mǎ tóu jīng pǐn jiǔ diàn

88 Yi Chang Lu ☎51558399, ⓦwww.msuites
.com.cn. Part of the leisure complex, Pier One – which will either be a roaring success or a ghost town by the time your read this – this is the most boutiquey of the new small hotels. It's in the far north of Jing'an, by Suzhou Creek, close to hip hangout Moganshan art district, and set in spacious gardens so that the proles in this grimy industrial area are out of sight. Most of the 24 rooms overlook the river and have been designed in a funkily ostentatious style. ❼–❾

Portman Ritz-Carlton

波特曼丽嘉酒店

bō tè màn lì jiā jiǔ diàn

1376 Nanjing Xi Lu ☎62798888, ⓦwww
.ritzcarlton.com. With 600 rooms on 50 floors, this is the mother ship of business hotels. The underwhelming entrance resembles an underground car park but leads to a luxurious foyer. Rooms are crisply modern with Chinese motifs in the fittings and wooden sliding panel doors. There's a health club, two swimming pools, tennis and squash courts and a gym, and expat complex the Shanghai Centre next door has good cafés (including a branch of *Element Fresh*, see p.114), bars and restaurants. It's a good choice if you want to be at the centre of the action and don't need a view. Big discounts off the rack rate are generally available at reception. ❾

Pudong

These hotels are marked on the map on p.88.

Eton

裕景大饭店

yù jǐng dà fàn diàn

69 Dongfang Lu ☎38789888, ⓦwww
.theetonhotel.com. It's quite far out in Pudong, but this new luxury venue is stylish (think corporate boutique chic) and offers lavish facilities – there's even a flat-screen TV in the bathroom – at cheaper rates than its competitors. ❽

Grand Hyatt

上海金茂凯悦大酒店

shàng hǎi jīn mào kǎi yuè dà jiǔ diàn

Jinmao Tower, 88 Shiji Dadao ☎50491234, ⓦwww.shanghai.hyatt.com. Taking up the top floors of the magnificent Jinmao Tower, the *Hyatt* is the world's tallest hotel, with, correspondingly, the world's longest laundry chute and its highest bar, *Cloud Nine* (see p.126). Rooms are undistinguished but, with floor to ceiling windows, are all about the view, so pay a little extra to go as high as you can (get one overlooking the Bund, preferably on a corner) and reserve long in advance. Spacious bathrooms, all glass and mirrors, are designed so that you can even get your fix on the clouds from the tub. There's no doubt, the place is fantastic – great design, lots of lucky numbers (see p.90) as well as awesome views – but, it has to be said, the area is hardly interesting. Never mind, you might not want to leave the hotel anyway. ❾

🏃 **Pudong Shangri-La**

浦东香格里拉大酒店

pǔ dōng xiāng gé lǐ lā dà jiǔ diàn

33 Fucheng Lu ☎68828888, ⓦwww.shangri
-la.com/shanghai. The other monster hotel in Pudong, with almost a thousand rooms, is popular with upscale business travellers for comfort, convenience and of course, the views through its huge windows. Classy, with discreet Chinese motifs in the decor, it's not overly corporate, which makes up for the time it takes to get across the river. It's worth upgrading for a Bund view. Spacious rooms are rather better than competitor the *Hyatt* and liveried staff provide more polished service. It's also home to the fabulous *Jade on 36* restaurant, and *Yí Café* (boh reviewed on p.122). ❾

North of Suzhou Creek

Dorure

都伦国际大酒店

dū lún guó jì dà jiǔ diàn

1885 Sichuan Bei Lu ☎56969999, ⓦwww
.dorurehotel.com. See map, p.94. This smart new international business hotel, located at the end of charming Duolun Lu Culture Street, is one of the best mid-range options; it's well designed with a vivid colour scheme and subdued lighting, and staff are keen. Though it's a little far from the centre of town, the Dongbaoxing Lu subway stop is a seven-minute walk away. ❺

Eating

ood is one of the true attractions of China; eating might not be the reason you came, but it will be one thing you remember. And Shanghai can make a convincing claim to be China's culinary hotspot. Upmarket restaurants starring celebrity chefs are opening every few months – and they may be good for splashing out – but what any visitor here can really appreciate is the diversity and superb quality of everyday, white-collar eateries. It's all a little more expensive than in the rest of China, but still a bargain – it's not difficult to get a good meal for around ¥50 a head.

Street food

Wujiang Lu (吴江路小吃街; *wú jiāng lù xiǎo chī jiē*), an alley off Nanjing Xi Lu, is the best place for street snack food, with an earthy atmosphere that's common in the rest of China but rare in central Shanghai. *Yang's Fried Dumplings* (小杨生煎馆; *xiǎo yáng shēng jiān guǎn*) at no. 54, near the eastern end of the alley, is a tiny takeaway shop with a huge reputation – you won't miss it because of the long queue for their *shengjian bao* dumplings (four for ¥3). Other stalls sell stinky tofu (*chou dofu*; ¥2 for a skewer), which tastes a little better than it smells, chicken wings and drumsticks (¥10 for four), the ubiquitous squid-on-a-stick and oysters (best avoided). There are also some small sit-down places, and vendors won't generally overcharge foreigners.

North of the Suzhou Creek, and just a few minutes' walk west of the *Pujiang Hotel*, runs **Zhapu Lu** (乍浦路美食街; *zhà pǔ lù měi shí jiē*) – at night it is entirely neon-lit and easily recognizable. There are a large number of Shanghainese restaurants along here – you can't go wrong if you pick a busy one and steer clear of the seafood – and the alleys to the west are full of vendors selling corn on the cob, kebabs, hand-sliced noodles and the like.

Yunnan Lu (云南路; *yún nán lù*), which leads south from Nanjing Dong Lu a block to the east of Renmin Park, is perhaps the most interesting of the food streets, though these days it's more of a restaurant row, with the ingredients, including snakes and toads, on display on the pavement. Finally, **Huanghe Lu** (黄河路; *huáng hé lù*), due north of Renmin Park – in particular the section north of Beijing Xi Lu – contains another large concentration of restaurants and vendors, many of them open 24 hours.

For an unusual gastronomic experience, head to the wholesale **seafood market** at 920 Tongchuan Lu (铜川路水产市场; *tóng chuān lù shuǐ chǎn shì chǎng*) in the far north of the city. You buy live seafood – there's a huge selection on offer, including turtles and sea snakes – then take the squirming bundle to a restaurant at the side, where it's cooked for you by weight. It's a warts-and-all kind of place, noisy and smelly, but memorable, and you won't get fresher fish. It's also the cheapest place in the city for a crab feast. The market is a little way out, so you'll have to take a taxi (around ¥25).

You'll be able to find all of China's many regional **cuisines** (see *China's regional cuisines* colour section) somewhere – Sichuan and Cantonese are perennially popular. Japanese and Korean food is widely available and Thai and Indian are growing increasingly accepted. If you're looking for Western food, you've come to the right Chinese city, with a great deal of restaurants catering for expats; all the big internationals are here too. The Shanghainese are faddish and food goes in and out of fashion like everything else; at the moment it's sandwich bars, raw food and "destination" restaurants. Note that a lot of the best places are chains, with several locations, many of them inside plazas and malls.

For the latest in dining – and bitchy user **reviews** of over-hyped restaurants – check ⓦwww.smartshanghai.com. Note that you can even forego the whole tiresome business of leaving your room altogether; for a small delivery fee, Sherpa's (ⓣ62096209, ⓦwww.sherpa.com.cn) will **deliver** from a host of different restaurants around town. And finally, note that while street food is generally okay – after all, it's cooked in front of you – you should try to avoid drinking tap **water**, as it's full of heavy metals.

Dining etiquette

Most places will have a **menu** in English, though it might be a handwritten scrap of greasy paper – anyway, just about everywhere has picture menus these days. Cold appetizers are served first, main courses arrive a few minutes later, then the meal is finished off with soup and perhaps some fruit. Note that **rice** generally arrives about halfway through the meal, and is eaten to fill you up rather than be mixed with your dishes. If you want it brought earlier, you have to ask for it – say *mi fan*. **Tea** is free except at more upscale places; if you want your teapot refilled, upend the lid. It's common at business banquets to drink **baijiu**, the pungent Chinese booze that tastes like lighter fluid, in toasts, during which you are expected to *gan bei* – swallow it all in one ghastly, throat-searing gulp. You won't get away with saying that you just like a little in moderation, so it might be a good idea on such occasions to pretend that you don't drink at all.

As for **table manners** – well, earthy peasant values are out of fashion, so don't spit on the floor; apart from that, pretty much anything goes. It's impolite to show your teeth, so if you want to use a toothpick, cover your mouth with the other hand. Slurping your soup is normal, even rather polite. You don't have to eat with chopsticks; all restaurants have knives (*daozi*) and forks (*chazi*). Tofu dishes are eaten with a spoon.

If you want the waitress's attention, call *fuwuyuan*, and if you want the **bill** ask for the *maidan*. In restaurants, the Chinese don't usually share the bill, so don't offer to pay your share, as the notion may cause embarrassment to your hosts. Instead, diners contest for the honour of paying it, with the most respected winning. You should make some effort to stake your claim but, as a visiting guest, you can pretty much guarantee that you won't get to pay a jiao. If it makes you uncomfortable, insist that next time dinner is on you.

Supermarkets

If you're **self-catering**, it's worth knowing about City Shop (daily 10am–10pm), which sells Western and Chinese groceries, and has branches in the basement of Times Square (93 Huaihai Zhong Lu) and on the first floor of the Shanghai Centre (1376 Nanjing Xi Lu), and Parkson Supermarket (daily 10am–10pm) in the basement at 918 Huaihai Lu.

China's regional cuisines

The Chinese obsess about food: the Mandarin for "how are you?" – *ni chi fan ma* – literally translates as "have you eaten yet?" Accordingly, they have created one of the world's great cuisines. It's much more complex than you might suspect from its manifestations overseas, with each region boasting its own delicious specialities. All kinds of Chinese food are available somewhere in cosmopolitan Shanghai, including of course the city's own distinctive variety; here's a short guide to regional cuisines, and where to try them.

▲ Street food

Shanghai cuisine

Shanghai cuisine is sweet, light and oily. Much of the cooking involves adding ginger, sugar and sweet rice wine, but spice is used sparingly. Dishes are generally served in small portions; this might cause derision in other parts of China but it's very handy for visitors who want to sample a good variety of dishes.

Fish and shrimp are considered basic to any respectable meal, not surprising perhaps bearing in mind the city's proximity to the sea; eel and crab may appear too. Fish and seafood are often lightly cooked (steamed mandarin fish is especially good), or even served raw; "drunken shrimps", for instance, simply comprises live shrimps drowning in wine.

For Chinese and pinyin translation of the dishes covered here, and many others, see pp.194–201 of the Language section.

Meat dishes are well represented too. Sweet and sour spare ribs are given a zesty tang by the heavy sauce; you might be shocked to discover how much sugar goes into it. One unmissable local treat is beggars' chicken, in which the whole bird is wrapped in lotus leaves, sealed with clay and oven-cooked. Like many popular dishes, there's a

Hairy crabs

Between October and December look out for the local speciality **hairy crabs** (mitten crabs in the West), a grey freshwater crustacean that's harvested in its breeding season. Prise the shell off and you'll find delicious white meat inside, and, if it's a female, maybe the highly prized orange roe. Hairy crabs are eaten with a sauce of soy, ginger and vinegar, and, because they are thought to be cooling to the body, usually accompanied with warmed Shaoxing wine.

Where to try Shanghai cuisine

- **Yin** (right) Upmarket and very foreigner friendly, this is a great place to try out a range of local dishes, including beggars' chicken. See p.121.
- **Yang's Fried Dumplings** Line up with the locals for the finest *shengjianbao* in town. See p.111.
- **Wang Baohe** The place for a crab banquet. See p.116.
- **Xiao Shaoxing** Where locals in the know get their drunken chicken. See p.118.
- **Nan Xiang** Unassuming dumpling restaurant on every tourist's to-do list. See p.117.
- **Shanghai Ren Jia** The Chinese like their restaurants *renao* (hot and noisy). Try those drunken shrimps if you're brave enough. See p.117.
- **Lao Zhenxing** Simple, unpretentious and always busy; this place keeps them coming with classic Shanghai dishes. See p.116.

story behind it: it's said that a thief stole a chicken and prepared a fire to cook it. When the emperor's guards passed by, he hid the chicken by covering it with mud and then threw it in the fire. When the guards had gone he was rewarded with the tastiest dish he'd ever had.

Every meal will feature so-called "cold" dishes, eaten as appetizers at room temperature; try crispy eel or "drunken chicken" (chicken marinated in rice wine). More of an acquired taste is *pidan dofu* – bright green, jelly-like eggs that have been preserved for months in lime and clay – served with tofu.

Finally, don't overlook the humble dumpling. *Xiaolongbao* are delicious small buns filled with pork and a gelatinous soup – careful though, as they're steaming hot inside – and served with a sauce made with ginger and vinegar. Also try *shengjianbao*, a steamed bun with a crispy base and topped with chives and sesame.

Sichuan cuisine

Sichuan, in China's far west, is renowned for its heavy use of **chillis** and lip-tingling pepper, though plenty of other flavours, such as orange peel, ginger and spring onions, are used. Classic dishes include hot spiced bean curd (*mapo doufu*), stir-fried chicken with peanuts and chillis (*gongbao jiding*); and fish with pickled vegetables (*suan cai yu*). Try them all out at *Yuxin Sichuan Dish* (see p.121), or, if you'd rather go easy on the spice, at *South Beauty 881* (see p.120).

▲ Dim sum

Cantonese cuisine

The joke that the Chinese will eat anything with four legs except a table and anything in the sea except submarines is a reference to Cantonese cuisine, from China's south. Snake liver, civet cat and guinea pig are among the more unusual dishes here, strange even to other Chinese, but more conventionally there are plenty of lightly seasoned fresh fish and vegetable dishes. A meal of **dim sum** (*dianxin* in Mandarin) comprises tiny flavoured buns, dumplings and pancakes and is often eaten in Shanghai as lunch (in Guangdong province it's breakfast). There's no shortage of restaurants in Shanghai to try it; two great places are the chic *Crystal Jade* (see p.118) and the cheap and cheerful *Bi Feng Tang* (see p.118 & p.121).

Northern cuisine

The cuisine of northern China is hale and hearty, with steamed buns and noodles as staples. Dishes tend to be heavily seasoned, with liberal use of vinegar and garlic. **Beijing duck** is the most famous dish, best sampled at *Quanjude* (see p.117). Other classic northern dishes such as **jiaozi** (small dumplings) can be sampled at *Dongbei Ren* (see p.119), and the classic winter warmer, **hotpot**, where diners dip raw ingredients into a heated stock in the centre of the table, is the speciality at *Hot Pot King* (see p.119).

► Hotpot

Tipping is never expected, which may be one reason why service standards aren't quite up to international levels, but some of the pricier places, and most hotel restaurants, add a fifteen percent **service charge**.

Fast food, cafés and breakfast

For **fast food**, *McDonald's*, *KFC* and their ilk are everywhere like a rash; rather better – and certainly healthier – is the Asian fast-food noodle chain *Ajisen* (味千拉面; *wèi qiān lā miàn*); there are convenient branches at 327 Nanjing Dong Lu, 518 Huaihai Zhong Lu, and in the basement of Raffles Mall. Every mall and shopping centre has a cluster of fast-food restaurants, either in the basement or on the top floor. A good one is in the basement of Raffles Mall on Fuzhou Lu. **Street food** is not as prevalent here as elsewhere in China, but there are a few places worth trying – see the box on p.111 for more details.

Unlike many other Chinese, the Shanghainese are famous for their sweet tooth, a tradition that dates back to the period of the International Settlement. They are indulged by **bakeries and pastry shops** across the city; try Nanjing Dong Lu or the bakery at the *Westin* (see p.107).

Café culture has really taken off in Shanghai, and every mall and shopping street now boasts a *Starbucks*, or representatives of the better but pricier Italian chain *Bonomi*, or the Taiwanese *Manabe*. As any tourist itinerary here involves lots of fairly unstructured wandering around, visitors might find themselves spending more time than they thought people watching over a cappuccino.

Finally, many visitors find the Chinese **breakfast** of glutinous rice and fried dough sticks unpalatable; fortunately, there are plenty of places for a good Western breakfast – best are *Wagas* (see p.115), *Zentral* (see p.114) and *Element Fresh* (see p.114).

Places are generally open every day, but there are no standard **opening times** so we have included these in the reviews below.

The Bund and Nanjing Dong Lu

 Bonomi
波诺米咖啡店
bō nuò mǐ kā fēi diàn
**Room 226, 12 Zhongshan Dong Yi Lu.
8am–10pm.** On the second floor of the former HSBC Building, this stylish little Italian café feels like a secret club, and has a lovely tiled terrace too. Whisper "café" to the doorman, head up two sets of stairs and follow the sign. The coffee is good though the sandwiches are pricey.

Westin Bakery
Bund Centre, 88 Henan Zhong Lu. 9am–7pm.
Tucked at the back of the over-the-top *Westin* hotel lobby (see p.107), this good-value bakery deserves a mention for being understated (in contrast to the hotel). Tasty cakes, tarts and coffees are served – treat yourself to a lychee vodka truffle (¥7).

People's Square

Barbarossa
芭芭露莎
bā bā lù shā
231 Nanjing Xi Lu, inside People's Park. 11am–late. This mellow, onion-domed Arabian fantasy is beautifully situated by the lotus pond in Renmin Park, and makes a great pit

▲ Barbarossa

stop for anyone doing the sights in People's Square. It also functions as a bar and a restaurant but we're calling it a café as that's what it does best. Relax over a drink, smoke a hookah and admire the view of the skyscrapers over the treetops, but don't eat here as the food is overpriced.

Element Fresh
新元素
xīn yuán sù
Unit 2, 2nd Floor, Headquarters Building, 168 Xizang Zhong Lu. Ⓦ www.elementfresh.com. 7am–7pm. This handy branch of the popular chain (see p.113), inside an office block south of Fuzhou Lu, is a good place for a light lunch. They also do free delivery.

The Old City and around

Delifrance
德意法兰西
dé yì fǎ lán xī
Basement of the Times Square mall, 381 Huaihai Zhong Lu. 8am–10pm. Cheap and tasty coffee and pastries from a Hong Kong chain, in a faux Parisian café. Another good place for breakfast.

Zentral
膳趣健康膳食
shàn qù jiàn kāng shàn shí
567 Huangpi Nan Lu, corner of Fuxing Zhong Lu. Ⓦ www.zentral.com.cn. 8am–10pm. Health food restaurant behind Xintiandi, with rather better fare than you'll get there and none of the froufrou. Dishes are light, low on salt and cheap, with good burgers (¥38) and smoothies, including a hangover special (¥35). Good Western breakfast menu. Free delivery.

The Old French Concession

Arch
玖间酒吧
jiǔ jiān jiǔ bā
439 Wukang Lu, on the corner with Huaihai Zhong Lu. 10.30am–2am. Situated in a striking flatiron building at the western end of the Old French Concession, this stylish café is well loved by the media set – you'll hear more *ciaos* than *ni haos*. Good burgers (¥40), cheesecake (¥25) and smoothies (¥35), and the tenderloin steak has a rare reputation (¥70). Design magazines lie around and there's free wireless Internet. It's more like a bar at night, with a good range of European beers.

Art Deco Garden Café
瑞金宾馆三号楼
ruì jīn bīn guǎn sān hào lóu
Building 3, Ruijin Hotel, 118 Ruijin Er Lu. 8.30am–1am. A refined venue in the garden of the *Ruijin Hotel* (see p.109), light and airy with big bay windows. Though there's not much that's Art Deco about it, it does have agreeable outdoor seating by a lawn. Coffee ¥25.

Bonomi
波诺米咖啡店
bō nuò mǐ kā fēi diàn
Hengshan Moller Villa, 30 Shaanxi Nan Lu, just north of Julu Lu. 8am–10pm. This branch of the excellent Italian chain (see p.113) has a lovely terrace. You won't mind paying ¥25 for a coffee with a view like this, of lush gardens and Gothic towers (see p.76) that seems straight out of a fairy tale.

Boonna I and II
布那咖啡店
bù nà kā fēi diàn
88 Xinle Lu; 57 Fuxing Xi Lu. 9am–1am. Artsy, laid-back little cafés with free WiFi. Writing a business plan on an Apple Mac is not mandatory but would certainly help you fit in with this international hipster crowd. The paintings and photos are all for sale. Afternoon tea is ¥28 and the tuna melt sandwich ¥38. One of the best Old French Concession pit stops.

Citizen Bar and Café
天台餐厅
tiān tái cān tīng
222 Jinxian Lu Ⓣ 62581620. 11am–1am. A great Continental-style café tucked away in an elegantly gentrified neighbourhood. It's very popular with French expats – perhaps because of the good coffee, free WiFi and the limitless potential for people watching from the balcony. It's a good brunch place too, with a wide choice of bar snacks, and a very civilized venue for a pre-dinner cocktail or a slice of apple pie.

Ginger Café
金格咖啡
jīn gé kā fēi
299 Fuxing Xi Lu (between Huashan Lu and Gaoyou Lu). 9am–11pm. An amiable place hidden away at the edge of the Old French Concession, with home-made cakes and plenty of books for whiling away an afternoon. There's free WiFi and – uniquely for Shanghai – it's all non-smoking.

Evenings here are very civilized too, making it a good place for a date. Two cocktails and a tapas sampler cost ¥78.

Kommune
公社酒吧

gōng shè jiǔ bā

Building 7, 210 Taikang Lu. 9am–10pm. Hip café located at the heart of Taikang Lu Art Street – head north up the alley, take the first left and it's just there. Very popular with the designer set, especially for weekend brunch when the courtyard outside fills up. Deli sandwiches from ¥38.

La Casbah
卡西巴咖啡

kǎ xī bā

1554 Huaihai Zhong Lu, opposite the library. 8am–10pm. A tiny café, patronized by students and English teachers, that deserves celebrating for offering a decent coffee for ¥10. Also worthy of mention are the tuna melt sandwiches, cheesecake and scrambled egg breakfasts (¥25). The noticeboard is a good place to look for flats, nannies or teachers.

Manabe
真锅咖啡厅

zhēn guō kā fēi tīng

85 Huating Lu, just off Huaihai Zhong Lu. 24hr. The food at this coffee-shop chain is undistinguished, but their breakfast deal – ¥25 for pancakes and a coffee – is worthy of note, and there is an extensive range of teas.

Old China Hand Reading Room
汉源书屋

hàn yuán shū wū

27 Shaoxing Lu, by Shaanxi Nan Lu ☏**64732526. 10am–midnight.** Bookish but not fusty, this is the place to come for leisured reflection. There's a huge collection of tomes to peruse or buy, many printed by the café press, which specializes in coffee table books about French Concession architecture. Period furniture, big picture windows and – what's that eerie quality? Oh, silence. Afternoon coffee with a scoop of ice cream and biscuits is ¥45. No meals.

Urban Tribe
城市山民

chéng shì shān mín

133 Fuxing Xi Lu. 9.30am–10pm. It's a boutique selling pricey knick-knacks really, but there's a nice bamboo garden at the back. Coffee served in a cute handmade cup costs ¥20.

Vienna Café
维也纳咖啡馆

wéi yě nà kā fēi guǎn

25 Shaoxing Lu, near Ruijin Er Lu. 8am–8pm. Popular and rather charming Austrian-style café, almost managing that fin-de-siècle vibe. You can't fault their strudel or Kaiser-schmarrn – pancake served with apple sauce. Free WiFi.

Wagas
沃歌斯

wò gē sī

Shop G107, Hong Kong World Plaza, 300 Huaihai Zhong Lu. 7.30am–11pm. Good-looking yet wholesome food, decor and staff at this New York-style deli. Order the Western breakfast before 10am and it's half-price – only ¥27 – with coffee only an extra ¥10. There are also smoothies and frappés for ¥30, and wraps and sandwiches for just a little more. It's also a good place for dinner – after 6pm, their tasty bowls of pasta are half-price at ¥28. At lunchtimes though it's rather too busy.

Whisk
威斯忌

wēi sī jì

1250 Huaihai Zhong Lu, near Changshu Lu subway stop. 8.30am–11.30pm. Minimalist decor and a chocolate-themed menu. They do meals, but they're undistinguished – come for the speciality hot chocolate or one of the many varieties of velvety chocolate cake naughtiness. Free WiFi – just try not to get chocolate all over your laptop.

Xianzonglin
仙踪林

xiān zōng lín

671 Huaihai Zhong Lu. 10am–10pm. A Taiwanese chain café that specializes in bubble tea – that's the sweet stuff with gooey balls in it. The huge drinks list includes plenty of oddities such as blueberry tea. Sip while you sit on a swing – teenagers would love it.

Jing'an

Always
奥维斯饭店

ào wéi sī fàn diàn

1528 Nanjing Xi Lu. 10.30am–midnight. This long-running diner is very popular, largely thanks to the cheap lunchtime special (served 11.30am–5pm): for just ¥20 you get a Western meal, such as burger with fries, and unlimited coffee.

Bandu
半度音乐

bàn dù yīn yuè

50 Moganshan Lu. 11am–11pm. The best of

the Moganshan Art District cafés, this intimate hideaway hosts performances of Chinese folk music every Saturday at 8pm.

Element Fresh

新元素

xīn yuán sù

Shanghai Centre (east side), 1376 Nanjing Xi Lu ⓦwww.elementfresh.com. 7am–11pm. This airy, informal bistro is the best place in town for a Western breakfast (note that they're open early) – there are plenty of options both hearty and healthy, none of which will cost you more than ¥60 (which includes limitless coffee). It's also well liked for its deli-style sandwiches, smoothies,

health drinks and cheap coffee (only ¥15). Free delivery.

North of Suzhou Creek

Old Film Café

老电影咖啡吧

lǎo diàn yǐng kā fēi bā

123 Duolun Lu ⓣ56964763. 10am–1am. If you're in the area, this charming old house, full of period detail and wallpapered with old film ads, is the place for refreshment. Film buffs will be excited by the possibility of screening the fine collection of old Chinese and Russian films – just ask the owner.

Restaurants

Restaurants are more expensive in Shanghai than elsewhere in China, although **prices** remain reasonable by international standards; most dishes at Chinese restaurants are priced at around ¥30, and even many upmarket Western restaurants have meal specials that come to less than ¥90 (¥88 is a popular set menu price, 8s being lucky). Prices per head, given in the reviews, cover a couple of dishes and tea. Phone numbers are given for those venues where **reservations** are advisable. The Chinese like to eat early, sitting down for lunch at noon and dinner at 6pm, but **restaurant hours** are long – usually 11am–2pm and 5–10pm; exceptions to this general rule are noted below. Anywhere with a bar, or any expat place, will usually be open later.

The Bund and Nanjing Dong Lu

This strip of real estate along the Bund must contain some of the world's most over-hyped, over-designed and over-rated restaurants. *Sens & Bund*, *Jean Georges*, *Laris*, *New Heights* – they all arrived to massive publicity, boast great views of the Bund, have been lavishly designed but, ultimately, they're not as good as they're cracked up to be. Only eat at one of these "destination" restaurants if you are on an expense account, you've been here for ages and you really miss Continental-style fine dining, or you want to spot Chinese celebrities.

Lao Zhenxing

老振兴餐馆

lǎo zhèn xìng cān guǎn

556 Fuzhou Lu. This unassuming restaurant is perennially popular for its light, non-greasy Shanghai cuisine. It's good for seafood and famous for its herring; try "squirrel fish" and a selection of dumplings. Around ¥50 per person.

M on the Bund

米氏西餐厅

mǐ shì xī cān tīng

Floor 7, Five on the Bund, entrance on Guangdong Lu ⓣ63509988. *M on the Bund* is worth it for the extraordinary view overlooking the Bund alone. Service could be better, and some complain that as a fine dining experience it isn't all that great, but the Mediterranean-style cuisine is some of the classiest (and most expensive) food in town, and the set lunch (¥118) is good value. If you're going to splash out, try grilled salmon and finish with pavlova.

The Stage, Westin

Level 1, Bund Centre, 88 Henan Zhong Lu, near Guangdong Lu ⓣ63350577. 6am–midnight. The "it" place for a buffet brunch, served from 11am to 2.30pm – ¥200 (plus fifteen percent service charge) for as much as you can eat and drink, including champagne and caviar. Come hungry and not too hung over, and pig out.

Wang Baohe

王宝和酒家

wáng bǎo hé jiǔ jiā

603 Fuzhou Lu ☎63223673. *Wang Baohe* bills itself as the "king of crabs and ancestor of wine". It's been around for more than 200 years, so it must be doing something right, and is famous for its hairy crab set meals, which start at ¥200 per person.

Whampoa Club

黄浦会

huáng pǔ huì

5th Floor, Three on the Bund ☎63213737. Posh nosh from celebrity chef Jereme Leung in what looks like an art gallery. The cuisine is broadly Shanghainese, with a twist. Go for the signature slow-cooked Australian abalone or – if you don't mind spending more than you would on a hundred bowls of noodles and still feeling hungry at the end of it – the five-course tasting menu (¥550). Reserve for a riverside view.

Yuanlu Huizhuan Shousi

元绿回转寿司

yuán lù huí zhuǎn shòu sī

Zhongshan Yi Lu (The Bund), at the corner of Beijing Dong Lu. Convenient, bright and friendly Japanese restaurant with sushi on a conveyor belt; each plate is priced between ¥9 and ¥18.

People's Square

As well as the restaurants below, check out *Element Fresh* (see p.114) and *Barbarossa* (see p.113).

Godly

功德林

gōng dé lín

445 Nanjing Xi Lu. A vegetarian restaurant with a temple-themed decor, specializing in fake meat dishes. It's all rather hit and miss: try the meatballs, roast duck, crab and ham, but avoid anything meant to taste like fish or pork, and be wary of ordering just vegetables as they'll turn up too oily. Staff could be livelier. Around ¥60 per head.

Kathleen's 5

赛马餐饮

sài mǎ cān yǐn wǔ

5th Floor, Shanghai Art Museum, 325 Nanjing Xi Lu ☎63272221. In a great location – an elegant glass box on top of the Shanghai Art Museum – with views over People's Square. The Western food is not quite as inspiring but the three-course lunch sets (¥140) are decent value, as is the afternoon tea set (¥50). Try the crab meat tower (which includes avocado and mango) as a starter and follow with the cod or lamb. Good for a date.

The Old City and around

The Yu Yuan area has traditionally been an excellent place for **snacks** – *xiaolongbao* and the like – eaten in unpretentious surroundings. Now that the area is so firmly on the Chinese tourist itinerary places get very busy and you'll pay a bit more than in the rest of the city. For quick bites, check out the satay, noodle and corn-on-the-cob stands lining the street bordering the western side of Yuyuan Bazaar.

EBI Sushi

和风海老日本料理

hé fēng hǎi lǎo rì běn liào lǐ

Basement, Times Square, 111 Huaihai Zhong Lu. This elegant little Japanese restaurant has nicely understated decor. Either pick one of the red booths or plonk yourself down by the conveyor belt. A sushi set meal is good value at ¥65.

Lu Bo Lang

绿波廊

lù bō láng

115–131 Yuyuan Lu, just south of the Huxing Ting Tea House. Tourist-friendly venue, tricked out with chinoiserie, with good enough, if rather pricey, *dim sum* and the like.

Nan Xiang

南翔馒头店

nán xiáng mán tóu diàn

85 Yuyuan Lu. A famous dumpling place that's on the "must-do" list for Chinese tourists. The ground floor is for proles to munch your standard pork and crab; the higher you go, the fancier the decor and the dumplings become. Most customers are here for takeaway – eat in and there's a minimum spend of ¥60 per person.

Quanjude

全聚德烤鸭店

quán jù dé

4th Floor, 786 Huaihai Zhong Lu ☎54045799. A Beijing duck chain restaurant. A whole duck, which will feed three, is ¥160. Smear it with sauce and wrap it in a pancake, and then finish with duck soup. You can even have a side order of duck tongues.

Shanghai Ren Jia

上海人家

shàng hǎi rén jiā

41 Yunnan Nan Lu ☎63513060. Huge, bustling chain restaurant, with interesting twists on standard Shanghainese fare. It's best to come in a large group so you can order and share multiple dishes. Roasted pig's trotter (¥58) is the house speciality, and they also serve "drunken shrimp" which comes to the table live and soaked in booze – you pull off its head and eat it while it twitches.

Xiao Shaoxing

小绍兴饭店

xiǎo shào xìng

Yunnan Nan Lu (east side), immediately north of Jinling Zhong Lu. Old-fashioned Chinese style dining – big tables, bright and noisy and the waitresses expect you to call for their attention – so hardly suitable for a date, but it's fun for a group. It's famous in Shanghai for its "drunken chicken", which will set you back ¥80; other dishes are much cheaper. Adventurous diners might wish to sample the blood soup or chicken feet.

Xiaxie

Huaihai Zhong Lu, opposite Huaihai Park, just west of Times Square. Open 24hr. Some say you've not really done Shanghai until you've put on plastic gloves and a bib and ripped apart a tray of crayfish. If you want to test this dubious contention, this is as good a place as any. It's a fun way to end a night out, an equivalent to the British greasy kebab. ¥30 per person.

The Old French Concession

This is the area where most expatriates eat and correspondingly where prices begin to approach international levels. Menus are in English, and English will be spoken, too. In **Xintiandi**, an olde-worlde complex of upscale bars, restaurants and cafés (see pp.70–74), you're spoilt for choice but you won't see much change from a ¥100 bill.

1221

1221 Yan'an Xi Lu, by Pan Yu Lu. ☎62136585. It's a little out of the way, a 10min walk east of Yan'an Xi Lu subway stop, but this is one of the city's best and most creative Shanghainese restaurants, attracting a mix of locals and expatriates. Decor is modern and minimalist so don't expect an evocation of old Shanghai in anything but the food. The drunken chicken and *xiang su ya* (fragrant crispy duck) are excellent, as are the onion cakes. It's a good choice for vegetarians too. Reserve.

Bi Feng Tang

避风塘

bì fēng táng

175 Changle Lu. 24hr. Useful branch of this Cantonese chain (see p.121), rather less raucous than the other branches and a popular way to end off a night out in the Old French Concession.

Charmant

小城故事

xiǎo chéng gù shì

1414 Huaihai Zhong Lu. 11.30am–4am. *Charmant* is a great place to know about – convenient and cheap, it functions as much as a café as a restaurant, and is open till the early hours, so it makes a handy last spot after a night on the tiles. Slip into a window booth and linger over a peanut smoothie, which is nicer than it sounds. For meals, the Taiwanese style pork or tofu are recommended.

Chun

春

chūn

124 Jinxian Lu ☎62560301. This is like having dinner in someone's front room: there's no sign outside, only four tables and no menu – you just turn up and eat what's put in front of you. Needless to say, the Shanghai dishes on offer are superb and, don't worry, it's all pretty cheap. You'll certainly have to reserve, and there's no English spoken.

Crystal Jade

翡翠酒家

fěi cuì jiǔ jiā

Unit 12A–B, 2nd Floor, No. 7 Building, South Block, Xintiandi ☎63858752; B110 Hong Kong Plaza, 300 Huaihai Zhong Lu. Great Hong Kong food, sophisticated looks and down-to-earth prices (around ¥80 per head) make this *the* place to eat in Xintiandi, and the finest in town for *dim sum*. Even being tucked away at the back of the upper

▲ Crystal Jade

floor of a shopping centre doesn't dent its popularity – reservations are a must. Try the barbecued pork and leave room for mango pudding. Solitary diners are made to feel comfortable at the long central table. The second branch in the Hong Kong Plaza is not as swanky, but is also less busy, so if it's a weekend night and you haven't booked, go there.

Dongbei Ren
东北人
dōng běi rén

1 Shaanxi Nan Lu, by Yan'an Zhong Lu. ☏52289898. Hale and hearty and no la-di-da stuff, the way those sturdy *dongbei ren* – northeasterners – like it. It's all meat and potatoes, like standard Scottish fare; must be something to do with the cold. Try the dumplings, lamb skewers and braised pork shank. ¥60 a head.

Fu 1039
福一零三九
fú yī líng sān jiǔ

Lane 1039, Yu Yuan Lu ☏52371878. Located in a well-restored 1930s mansion, this is one of those places that looks like it's going to be fearsomely expensive but isn't. Attracting local foodies in the know, it clearly doesn't feel the need to brag – you can't see it from the street and there's not even a sign; to find it, head up the lane at 1039 Yuyuan Lu (close to the Jiangsu Lu subway station) for about 100m then turn left. The cuisine is sweet and mild Shanghainese, and includes dishes such as steamed carp drizzled with shaoxing wine and sautéed chicken with mango. Not much English is spoken.

Fulin Xuan
福临轩饭店
fú lín xuān fàn diàn

37 Sinan Lu, two blocks south of Huaihai Zhong Lu. Typically massive Cantonese place with an English menu and a good reputation among locals. The abalone and shark's fin are almost as good as in Hong Kong, and the beef with black pepper and Hong Kong-style claypot rice are also recommended.

Grape
葡萄园
pú táo yuán

55A Xinle Lu, close to Xiangyang Bei Lu. Unchallenging decor and some English-speaking staff make this Shanghainese place popular with expats, but it's good enough to draw the local crowd too. Try

lamb with leek or duck pancakes and make room for a few of their savoury cold dishes. ¥100 a head.

Guyi Hunan
古意湘味浓
gǔ yì xiāng wèi nóng

89 Fumin Lu, near Julu Lu ☏62495628. This stylish place is the best in the city to sample Hunan cuisine – known for being hot and spicy and for its liberal use of garlic, shallots and smoked meat. Reserve in advance and bring a few people to get a good range of dishes. Go for the spare ribs, fish with beans and scallions or tangerine-peel beef, which tastes better than you might expect. About ¥80 per head.

Hot Pot King
来福楼
lái fú lóu

2nd Floor, 146 Huaihai Zhong Lu, by Fuxing Xi Lu ☏64736380. 11am–4am. An accessible place to sample a local favourite, thanks to the English menus, understanding staff and tasteful decor. Order lamb, glass noodles, mushrooms and tofu (plus whatever else you choose) and chuck them into the pot in the middle of the table. Perfect for winter evenings. ¥70 per person.

KABB
凯博西餐厅
kǎi bó xī cān tīng

181 Taicang Lu, 5 Xintiandi Bei Li ☏33070798 7am–1am. This casual American-style diner is one of Xintiandi's more relaxed places. Portions are huge and it's especially good value at breakfast and lunchtime. About ¥100 per person.

Lapis Lazuli
藏龙坊
cáng lóng fǎng

9 Dongping Lu, near Hengshan Lu ☏64731021. Very stylish hideaway (if a little dark), with an intimate garden terrace that makes it a great place for a date on a summer evening. The Continental food is reasonably priced; try the seafood risotto and leave space for one of their quality desserts. About ¥100 per head; cocktails around ¥60.

Mesa
梅萨
méi sà

748 Julu Lu, near Fumin Lu ☏62899108. 10am–late. Fine dining, Western style, in a classy converted factory. Try the carpaccio of beef or seared duck breast but leave room for the dessert tasting platter. Service could be a tad better but they're trying. The weekend buffet brunch (served 11.30am–5pm) is good value at ¥150; otherwise it's ¥300 per person in the evenings. The bar upstairs, *Manifesto* (see p.125) is handy.

Shen Yue Xuan

申粤轩

shēn yuè xuān

849 Huashan Lu ☏ **62511166.** The best Cantonese place in Shanghai, situated in an old mansion, and serving scrumptious *dim sum* at lunchtime. In warmer weather you can dine alfresco in the garden, a rarity for a Cantonese restaurant. Dinner for two comes to around ¥120 per head, drinks included.

Shintori

新都里无二店

xīn dū lǐ wú ér diàn

803 Julu Lu ☏ **54045252.** Take someone you want to impress to this nouvelle Japanese trendsetter: the buffet will set you back around ¥300. Entertaining presentation will give you something to talk about, though you'd better order a lot or you'll be bitching about the small portions. Finish with green tea tiramisu (¥60).

Shu Di La Zi Yu Guan

蜀地辣子鱼馆

shǔ dì là zi yú guǎn

187 Anfu Lu, on the corner with Wulumuqi Zhong Lu. Never mind the tacky decor – concentrate on the excellent, inexpensive Sichuan and Hunanese cuisine. A big pot of Sichuan spicy fish is a must, but also recommended are bamboo fragrant chicken (*zhu xiang ji*) and old fave, *mala doufu* – spicy tofu.

Simply Thai

天泰餐厅

tiān tài cān tīng

5-C Dongping Lu ☏ **64459551.** The best of the city's Thai joints, with an eclectic range of good-quality dishes and a smart but informal setting with a leafy courtyard. Try the stir-fried asparagus and fish cakes. There also a branch in Xintiandi but it's not nearly as good.

South Beauty 881

俏江南

qiào jiāng nán

881 Yan'an Zhong Lu, opposite the Exhibition Hall ☏ **62475878.** Upmarket Sichuan food in what looks like an English country house. Speciality of the house is beef in boiling oil, cooked at your table. Linger afterwards for

drinks in the fantastic bar, and imagine yourself starring in a Merchant Ivory production. There's even a cigar room. ¥200 per person but watch out for hidden extras though, like the charge for a glass of water.

T8

House 8, North Block, Xintiandi, Taicang Lu ☏ **63558999.** Fine Continental-style dining, courtesy of an Australian chef, in an elegant reconstruction of a courtyard house. Reserve, and ask for one of the booths at the back. Try the pie with coriander bisque or the braised lamb shank pie. Fabulous desserts include a chocolate addiction platter. ¥400 a head.

Tony's

多利餐厅

duō lì cān tīng

16 Wulumuqi Nan Lu. Decent, foreigner-friendly Sichuan food at a reasonable price make this a good place to experiment with China's spiciest cuisine (though if you develop a taste, try *Yuxin*, opposite). The emphasis is on hale and hearty and the menu shows how spicy each dish is.

Vedas

维达斯饭店

wéi dá sī fàn diàn

550 Jianguo Lu, near Wulumuqi Nan Lu ☏ **64458100. 11.30am–2.30pm & 6–11.30pm.** An unpretentious little restaurant that knows its stuff: tasty Indian food, reasonably priced at around ¥100 per person, and no compromises for wimpy palettes.

Xinjishi (Jesse Restaurant)

新吉士餐厅

xīn jí shì cān tīng

41 Tianping Lu ☏ **62829260; Shop 9, North block, Xintiandi, 181 Taicang Lu** ☏ **63364746.** The decor is a bit tatty at the tiny original branch on Tianping Lu but there's nothing at all wrong with the tasty home-style cooking. Dishes are from all over the country, but go for the red cooked pork and other local faves. Reservations are required. The new branch at Xintiandi, with its traditional styling, looks better, but the food is not quite as good.

Ye Shanghai

夜上海

yè shàng hǎi

House 6, North Block, Xintiandi, 338 Huangpi Nan Lu ☏ **63111323.** Shanghai cuisine in an upmarket pastiche of colonial grandeur – so lots of red lanterns and dark wood. Go for drunken chicken, prawns with chilli sauce or one of the many crab dishes. A good introduction to local flavours. Around ¥200 per person.

 Yin
音

yīn

59 Maoming Nan Lu ☎ 54665070. Hardwood floors and screens create an intimate atmosphere, and the food is similarly tasteful, well thought through and understated. No MSG is used and all dishes – Shanghai staples – are light and not oily, making it a great place to sample local cuisine; drunken chicken and eggplant pancakes are particular highlights. There's no sign; head for the alley parallel to Maoming Nan Lu, and you'll see its grand wooden doors opposite the back of Shanghai Tang. Set menu is ¥100 per person.

Jing'an

Jing'an is a good area for international cuisine, and though you won't find any romantic converted villas there are some surprisingly intimate venues.

1931

112 Maoming Nan Lu, just south of Weihai Lu ☎ 64725264. This civilized little place rather resembles a nineteenth-century front room. The food is a good mix of Shanghainese, Japanese and Southeast Asian cuisines, served in reasonably priced, good-sized portions. Reservations required. ¥150 per person.

Bali Laguna
巴厘岛
bā lǐ dǎo

189 Huashan Lu, inside Jing'an Park, near Yan'an Zhong Lu ☎ 62486970. A classy, popular Indonesian restaurant beautifully situated in quiet Jing'an Park – look at the trees and realize what you're missing. Good place for a date. Try the seafood curry (¥88), served inside a pineapple. ¥140 per person.

 Bi Feng Tang
避风塘
bì fēng táng

1333 Nanjing Xi Lu, by Tongren Lu. 24hr. This cheap Cantonese fast-food diner makes a tasty last spot on a night out (though beware the merciless lighting). There are many branches around town; this one is handy for business travellers at the *Portman* and revellers from Tongren Lu (indeed, it seems to be at its busiest around midnight).

There's a picture menu and you can't go far wrong with any of their numerous tasty *dim sum* and dumpling options. Finish off with custard tarts.

Black Café
黑暗餐厅
hēi àn cān tīng

65 Maoming Bei Lu, near Yan'an Zhong Lu ☎ 52286575. The gimmick here is that you eat your meal in complete darkness – you're helped to a table and left to feel your way around. Don't wear your best clothes. Anyway it's novel, and the food's not bad. Set Western meal is ¥168.

Meilongzhen
梅龙镇酒家
méi lóng zhèn

22, Lane 1081, Nanjing Xi Lu ☎ 62535353. A Shanghai restaurant with a dash of Sichuan spiciness; it's very popular, so reserve. Go for twice-cooked pork, and drink "eight-treasure" tea – check out the long spouted kettles – finishing off with a sugar-roasted banana. It's tucked behind Nanjing Xi Lu, but you can't miss the colourful arched doorway. ¥90 per person.

New York Style Pizza
Inside Jing'an Plaza, Huashan Lu, near Nanjing Xi Lu. 10am–midnight. An undemanding diner that does the best pizzas in town; ¥10 a slice, ¥70 for the whole goddamn thing. Good for post-booze munchies.

 Southern Barbarian
南蛮子
nán mán zi

1449 Qiujiang Lu, near Gonghe Xi Lu, 1.5km from Shanghai Railway Station ☎ 13621 797634. Excellent food from Yunnan, in southwest China, in a cosy little modern bistro. Try fried goat's cheese and wild mushrooms, or so-called "crossing the bridge" (chicken broth) noodles, and then the barbecued chicken wings and potato pancake. ¥50 per person.

 Yuxin Sichuan Dish
渝信川菜
yú xìn chuān cài

3rd Floor, 333 Chengdu Bei Lu ☎ 52980438. Super-spicy Sichuan food in a no-nonsense dining hall. Very popular with families and the white-collar crowd, so reservation is recommended. Go for the *kou shui ji* (saliva chicken) and *sha guo yu* (fish pot), with which you can work on developing a face as red as the peppers. Little English is spoken but there's a picture menu.

Pudong

Pudong is rather soulless, and the most notable restaurants are those attached to the swanky hotels. For cheap eats, try the Superbrand Mall or the basement food court of the Jinmao Tower (see p.90).

Jade on 36

翡翠36餐厅

fěi cuì sān shí liù cān tīng

36th floor, Tower 2, Pudong Shangri-La, 33 Fucheng Lu ☏68828888.

Celebrity chef Paul Pairet's gimmicky food contrasts with the grandiloquence of the venue, which has an amazing view of the Bund. There are lots of foams and sorbets, and odd combinations abound – a foie gras lollipop and a sardine mousse, for example. All very entertaining if you can afford it, and it's certainly one of the better of the destination restaurants. There are only set menus, which start at ¥480.

Yi Café

一咖啡

yī kā fēi

L2, Tower 2, Pudong Shangri-La, 33 Fucheng Lu ☏68828888. 6am–1am.

This slickly designed place is the best of the hotel buffets and is especially popular for Sunday brunch. All-you-can-eat and, with ten show kitchens, there's an enormous choice – for ¥268 plus fifteen percent service charge. Arrive hungry.

Drinking and nightlife

S hanghai's cosmopolitan denizens are famous for their thirst for novelty, love of style and dedication to the good times; the city's always been good at putting on a do. Today you'll find plenty of parallels with the glory days of "taxi girls" (see box, p.76), flower houses and anything-but-innocent "tea dances". So far as China goes, this is party central. There's something for all tastes, from spit-and-sawdust dives to exclusive cocktail **bars**, cheesy mega discos to slick DJ **clubs**. That said, the scene is nothing if not capricious. Places go in and out of fashion and open and close with the seasons. The ones listed below have all proved themselves to have some degree of staying power so should still be there by the time you read this. For bang up-to-date information on the nightlife scene, check out Ⓦ www.smartshanghai .com or an expat listings magazine (see p.43).

Bars

There are a number of bar districts in Shanghai, and it's well worth taking in more than one over the course of the evening. Too long at a Maoming Nan Lu dive bar will makes your skin crawl, but the posiness of an urbane Bund venue could grow equally tiring; both in the same evening, on the other hand, would make for a night of dynamic contrasts. The best nights in the city tend to involve a bit of bar hopping; and just remember how cheap taxis are.

Bright Lights, Big City

Shanghai at night, between dusk and about 10pm, is lit up like a pinball game. The city sucks up so much of China's energy that the national grid can't take it, and power cuts are endured in the sticks. The best places to appreciate the awesome spectacle are:

Cloud Nine bar (see p.126). The cocktails are expensive, but the view makes it just worth it.

Huangpu River night cruise (see p.54). It's touristy but it's cool. Just don't expect too much from the buffet.

Yuyuan (see p.64). This olde-worlde Chinatown takes on a whole new aspect when the neon comes on. Fun, if ridiculous.

Attica (see p.127). This hot new club has great views of Pudong from its roof terrace, and even from one of its dancefloors.

Nanjing Dong Lu (see p.55). You might not want to buy anything here, but the lights are spectacular.

Marriott Hotel lobby (see p.107). Be discreet; if too many people start turning up, they'll probably star charging. An awesome view of People's Square.

Where to drink

The biggest range of watering holes can be found in the **Old French Concession**. Xintiandi is upmarket, perhaps just a little too respectable, but a good place for a civilized drink if you can afford it. At the opposite end of the scale, Julu Lu is a strip of dive bars growing long in the tooth, as typified by gritty *Goodfellas*. Southeast of here, the bar strip of Maoming Nan Lu is perpetually under threat of closure for lowering the tone around what its otherwise an exclusive area. Heading south down the street you can expect to run a gamut of bar girls shrieking "You come my bar!", though there are a couple of cultured alternatives. To the west, Hengshan Lu is a more diffuse zone, stretching for several kilometres, with bars catering to most tastes but veering towards the expat friendly just-like-home pastiche.

In **Jing'an**, Tongren Lu provides an updated version of Maoming Nan Lu, with a few decent venues along an otherwise shameless parade, while **the Bund** is the fastest rising new area; here, an air of exclusivity is reflected in the prices.

Opening hours and prices

Bar **hours** are flexible; a bar tends to close when its last barfly has lurched off – though all places open till at least midnight, and on the weekends much later. We've listed phone numbers and/or websites for places that can be hard to find, or anywhere that has **live music**.

Though Chinese beer can be cheaper than bottled water in shops, bar **prices** can come as something of a shock; even in the shabbiest dive, a small bottle of Tsingtao will cost upwards of ¥25. In the swankiest venues it will be more than ¥50, and for a cocktail you won't get much change from a ¥100 note. But just about everywhere has a happy hour (two drinks for the price of one), and

these are generally long – sometimes 5–8pm. Wednesday is often ladies' night, with many places offering free drinks for women before midnight. Look out too for **open bar** nights – all you can drink for around ¥100 – advertised in expat magazines. Only the swankiest venues have cover charges, and they usually include one free drink.

If you're horny and dumb enough to follow one of the ubiquitous touts promising to take you to a "**lady bar**", then you deserve the subsequent shakedown. Anyway, it's not as if there's a shortage of "independent female contractors" in the regular dive bars.

Finally, remember that some of the venues listed under cafés and restaurants work very well after dark as bars, notably *Arch*, *Citizen Bar and Café* (both p.114), *Lapis Lazuli* (see p.119), *South Beauty 881* (see p.120) and *Barbarossa* (see p.113).

The Bund and Nanjing Dong Lu

Bar Rouge

7F, No. 18 The Bund. Staff are snobbish, clientele are pretentious, but the terrace has unrivalled views over the Bund. Cover is ¥50 on weekends and you won't get much change from a red bill for a drink, but go for one, check out the view, and then hit somewhere less posey.

Captain Bar

6th Floor, 37 Fuzhou Lu, by Sichuan Zhong Lu. This relaxed venue is one of the few in the area where you won't feel the need to dress up. Never mind the unremarkable interior, it's all about the terrace, with its fabulous view of Pudong. It sits atop a backpacker hostel (see p.104), though most guests are put off by the prices – draught beer ¥40.

Glamour Bar
魅力酒吧
mèi lì jiǔ bā

6th Floor, M on the Bund, 20 Guangdong Lu, by Zhongshan Dong Yi Lu ⓦ www.m-theglamourbar .com. Pink, frivolous and fabulous, this is Shanghai's destination *du jour* for poseurs. Good view of the Bund though, and there's a schedule of cultural events such as book launches and readings. Cocktails from ¥65; go for the mojito.

I Love Shanghai
我爱上海
wǒ ài shàng hǎi

155 Zhongshan Dong Yi Lu, at the intersection with Jinling Dong Lu. The decor is undistinguished at this friendly Bund bar, but it's also cheaper and has less attitude than any of the more glamorous venues over the road, making it popular with foreign students, teachers and backpackers. Tuesday is ladies' night; Saturday is a ¥100 open bar. Beers from ¥30.

Peace Hotel Jazz Bar

Junction of The Bund and Nanjing Dong Lu. A cavernous pub inside the north building of the *Peace Hotel*, famous for its eight-piece dance band whose original members played here in the 1930s, suffered persecution during the Cultural Revolution, then re-emerged in the twilight of their years to fame and fortune. Their younger successors now play stately instrumental versions of Fats Domino and Elvis Presley standards, while portly tourists swirl to the nostalgic rhythms and sip cocktails amid the original 1930s decor. Cover charge ¥60.

The Old French Concession

Blue Frog
蓝蛙
lán wā

207 Maoming Nan Lu, by Fuxing Zhong Lu. A cultivated frog among the sleazy toads of Maoming Lu (so no overfriendly bar girls) that won't leave you feeling the need for a shower. Offers a good Western food list, an intimate upstairs lounge and a talkative crowd.

British Bulldog

1 Wulumuqi Nan Lu, near Hengshan Lu. A pastiche British boozer, all wood and brass, with McEwans on draught and bangers and mash on the menu. The kitchen stays open till 2am.

Cotton Club
棉花俱乐部
mián huā jù lè bù

1416 Huaihai Zhong Lu, near Fuxing Xi Lu ☎64377110. A long running, relaxed jazz club with none of that bristling Shanghai attitude. Music gets going at 9.30pm, a bit later at weekends.

Face Bar

Building Four, Ruijin Hotel, 118 Ruijin Er Lu. The most civilized bar in Shanghai, largely thanks to the venue, a lovely old villa in the manicured grounds of the *Ruijin Hotel*. It's quiet, the lighting is low, the decor is opium den chic and the crowd is smart, casual and loaded. Cocktails ¥65, happy hour 5–8pm. A great place to take a date on a summer evening.

▲ Cocktails at the Face Bar

Goodfellas
高乐酒吧
gāo lè jiǔ bā

907 Julu Lu. Grungey expat dive bar that's lively on weekends. Beers around ¥35, with a happy hour from 6.30 to 10pm.

JZ Club
爵士
jué shì

46 Fuxing Xi Lu, near Yongfu Lu ⊛ www.jzclub.cn. A popular venue, dark but not smoky, with live jazz every night from 10pm. Drinks are pricey (starting at ¥45) but there's no cover.

Manifesto
梅萨
méi sà

748 Julu Lu, near Fumin Lu. Urbane lounge bar, sister to the *Mesa* restaurant next door – you can order their tapas if you're peckish. Go for the chocolate martini (¥60).

Mural

摩砚

mó yàn

**697 Yongjia Lu, near Hengshan Lu Ⓦwww
.muralbar.com.** Cheap and cheery basement
venue, incongruously decorated like a
Buddhist cave, popular for its ¥100 open
bar on Friday nights.

O'Malley's Irish Pub

欧玛莉餐厅

ōu mǎ lì cān tīng

**42 Taojiang Lu, near Wulumuqi Nan Lu Ⓦwww
.omalleys-shanghai.com.** A respectable Irish
pub with a pleasant garden, good for live
sport screenings; a bit pricey at ¥65 for a
Guinness.

Paulaner Bräuhaus

宝莱纳

bǎo lái nà

House 19-20, North Block, Xintiandi, Taicang Lu.
A giant beer hall, featuring greeters in leder-
hosen and a Filipino band, that runs its own
microbrewery and offers German food. It's
not cheap, with the smallest lager costing
¥68 (a litre is ¥105), but gets packed every
night with the Chinese white-collar set.

Yongfu Elite

雍福会

yōng fú huì

200 Yongfu Lu, by Hunan Lu. A private
member's club now open to the public, this
fabulously opulent villa has vintage everything; heaven forbid that you spill a drink.
Sip cocktails (which start at ¥60) on the
veranda under the gaze of the garden's
huge Buddha statue, and feel like a film star.

Zapatas

**5 Hengshan Lu, near Dongping Lu Ⓦwww
.zapatas-shanghai.com.** No self-respecting
Mexican anarchist would be seen dead in
the company of the lascivious frat house
crowd here, who come the revolution will be
first against the wall. Never mind, it's a
heaving party on Monday and Wednesday
nights, when ladies are offered free margar-
itas before midnight. Enter through the
garden of *Sasha's*, the nearby restaurant.

Jing'an

Blue Frog

蓝蛙

lán wā

86 Tongren Lu. This is a polished neighbourhood bar on an otherwise unprepossessing
row, with a good Western food menu and
more than a hundred shots on offer. For a
quiet drink with no view of the tawdry street
life, head upstairs.

Long Bar

长廊酒吧

cháng láng jiǔ bā

2F, Shanghai Centre, 1376 Nanjing Xi Lu. Comfy
expat bar for networking and post-work
drinks, where you can watch sport on TV.
Pizzas are "buy one get one free" on
Mondays. Beers from ¥35.

Malone's

马龙

mǎ lóng

**255 Tongren Lu, near Nanjing Xi Lu Ⓦwww
.malones.com.cn.** Sports bar popular with the
expat business crowd and famous for its
burgers. House band plays reliable crowd
pleasers every night.

Windows Too

**J104, Jingan Temple Plaza, 1699 Nanjing Xi Lu,
by Huashan Lu.** Packs them in nightly thanks
to a revolutionary idea – affordable beer, at
¥10 a bottle. It's popular with those at the
bottom of the Shanghai foreigner food chain
– students, teachers and backpackers –
and those who'll deign to talk to them.
Commercial hip-hop on the decks, and a
¥50 cover on the weekend. No posing, no
attitude, no class.

Pudong

Cloud Nine

**88th floor, Grand Hyatt Hotel, Jinmao Tower, 88
Shiji Dadao Ⓣ50491234.** The highest bar in
the world, on the 87th floor of the *Grand
Hyatt* in the Jinmao Tower (see p.110).
Inside it's all rather dark and metallic, but
never mind, the view is astonishing. Be
smart, pick a cloudless day, and arrive soon
after opening time (6pm) to bag one of the
coveted window-side tables facing the
Bund. Minimum spend is ¥120 per person,
and cocktails start at ¥80.

Paulaner Bräuhaus

宝莱纳

bǎo lái nà

Binjiang Dadao, near Shangri-La Hotel. Another
branch of the German-style pub chain (see
above) with pricey Paulaner beer from its
own microbrewery. Good views of the Bund
make it worth considering.

Clubs

The dancing scene in Shanghai will be eerily familiar to anyone who's been clubbing in any Western capital – you won't hear much in the way of local sounds – but at least the door **prices** are much cheaper, and never more than ¥100. One Chinese innovation is the addition of **karaoke** booths at the back; another, much less welcome, is the annoying practice of having to pay to sit at a table – a waitress will soon shoo you off if you blanch at the (often ridiculous) price. There isn't really a club zone – though they tend to be near the bar clusters – with the one exception being **Fuxing Park**, which hosts several of the more upscale venues.

Most places have international **DJs** and plenty of famous faces have popped in for a spin of the decks. Wednesday is ladies' night, Thursday is hip-hop night and of course the weekends are massive. Most places open at around 9pm, get going after midnight, and close at 4am or later. Venues move in and out of fashion; at the time of writing the hottest party spot was *Attica*. Note that there are also dancefloors in *Windows Too* and *Zapatas*, reviewed in Bars.

The Bund and Nanjing Dong Lu

Attica
爱齐多
ài qí duō
11F, 15 Zhongshan Dong Er Lu, near Jinling Dong Lu ⓦwww.attica-shanghai.com. The trendiest club in town, with an awesome view of Pudong from the terrace for when the dancefloors (one house/techno, one R&B) get too sweaty. ¥100 cover gets you one drink at the bar; women get in free before midnight. Doesn't really get going till 1am, then it's party central till 5am.

The Old French Concession

Bonbon
2F Yunhai Tower, 1329 Huaihai Zhong Lu ⓦwww.clubbonbon.com. The home of clubbing franchise Godskitchen, gaudy megaclub *Bonbon* is packed with a young crowd even on weekdays – it's particularly popular on Tuesdays, when they often host international guest DJs, and it's hip-hop on Thursdays. Cover is ¥40–100, with a ¥100 open bar most nights.

California
兰桂坊
lán guì fǎng
2A Gaolan Lu, inside Fuxing Park ⓦwww .lankwaifong.com. Mon–Thurs & Sun 8pm–2am, Fri & Sat 9pm–late. So red inside it's like being inside a liver; not inappropriately then, it's a meat market. This house club is more upscale than most and popular with both locals and expats. It's in upscale entertainment complex Park 97.

Guandi
官邸
guān dǐ
2 Gaolan Lu, inside Fuxing Park. Brash hip-hop

Gay and lesbian Shanghai

These days, China is fairly relaxed about homosexuality; at least it's no longer on the official list of psychiatric diseases. Shanghai is the Chinese city most accepting of alternative lifestyles, though anyone used to the scene in a Western capital will find things tamer here; venues are still somewhat low-key.

The best **gay club** in town is *Deep* at 1649 Nanjing Xi Lu, inside Jing'an Park (深度俱乐部; *shēn dù jù lè bù*; ⓦwww.clubdeep.cn). International DJs keep the music eclectic and there are male model **shows**. Just outside Fuxing Park at 18 Gaolan Lu, *Pinkhome* (ⓦwww.barhome.com) is a stylish venue, the envy of many of a straighter bar, with decent music and reasonably priced drinks. *Eddy's* on Tianping Lu, just off Huaihai Lu (ⓦwww.eddys-bar.com), with no dancefloor and rather oppressively dark decor, draws an older crowd. Finally, *Frangipani* (凡居潘林咖啡; *fán jū pān lín kā fēi*) at 399 Dagu Lu, near Shimen Yi Lu (ⓦwww.frangipanibar.com), is a promising new arrival that's also a charming café during the day; there's a lesbian night on Tuesday and an open bar on Thursdays.

venue, popular on Thursdays and rammed every weekend. Attracts a posey local crowd. ¥60 cover on weekends.

Rojam

罗杰

luó jié

4F Hong Kong Plaza, 283 Huaihai Zhong Lu, near Songshan Lu Ⓦ**www.rojam.com.** Mega-disco for an enthusiastic young and local crowd. There are two dancefloors, usually playing hip-hop and trance, and karaoke rooms at the back. ¥50–70.

Jing'an

Mint

2F, 333 Tongren Lu, near Beijing Xi Lu Ⓦ**www .mintclub.com.cn.** Popular, pocket-sized,

lounge-style house music venue, hosting international guest DJs on the weekends. Happy hour 6–8pm, but it doesn't really get going till after midnight, then it's jumping till 6am. ¥50 on weekends.

Muse

同乐坊

tóng lè fāng

68 Yuyao Lu, New Factories, near Xikang Lu Ⓦ**www.museshanghai.com.** Promising new place inside a huge new leisure complex. There's a lively atmosphere but, is it too far out to last? Open till 2am on weekdays, 4am on weekends. ¥70.

Entertainment and art

Shanghai might be a hotbed of materialism but these days culture is increasingly emphasized as a vital part of the city's appeal. Most visitors take in an **acrobatics show** and perhaps an **opera** but equally worthy of note are the flourishing **contemporary art** and **music** worlds, and international-standard **dance** and **drama** scenes. Furthermore, a host of new and very impressive government-funded **arts venues** have opened, from the lovely Oriental Arts Centre in Pudong (see p.92) to the Duolun Museum of Modern Art in Hongkou (see p.95), and there are ambitious plans for dozens more.

The **Shanghai Arts Festival** (Ⓦwww.artsbird.com) is held from mid-October to mid-November; though you'd be forgiven for not noticing it, arts programming does much better during this period, with a lot of visiting shows.

Drama and dance

Most Shanghai **theatre** is light-hearted fare about the trials of urban dating life, in Chinese of course, though some troupes occasionally put on shows in English. **Dance** is popular, but it's almost always the conservative end of the spectrum. If you're into modern dance, look out for the work of choreographer Jinxing, China's most high profile transsexual and one of the scene's few innovators.

The big draws at the moment are imported big-hitting musicals and big-name ballets – worth investigating as they are cheaper than they would be at home. The city is even planning its own version of Broadway along Huashan and Anfu Lu.

Information and tickets

For **listings** of big cultural spectaculars such as visiting ballet troupes check the *China Daily*, but for the lowdown on punk gigs, underground art shows and the like get an up-to-date expat magazine such as *City Weekend* or check the website Ⓦwww.smartshanghai.com. The schedules of all the most popular venues can be found on the websites of the Shanghai Cultural Information and Booking Centre (Ⓦwww.culture.sh.cn/english; reservations on ☏62172426) and China Ticket Online (Ⓦshdx.piao.com.cn/en_piao; ☏63744968). At both, **tickets** can be booked over the phone and delivered to your hotel or home (at no extra charge provided you book more than three days before the performance). You can also buy tickets from the booking centre behind the Westgate Mall on Nanjing Xi Lu, or at box offices. Few venues have the facility to take credit card bookings.

Chinese opera

Chinese opera is a unique combination of song, dance, acrobatics and mime. It's highly stylized, with every aspect of the performance, from costumes and make-up to movements, imbued with a specific symbolic meaning, Colour is very significant, red for example signifying loyalty and blue cruelty. Plots feature straightforward goodies and baddies, often concerning young lovers who are forbidden to marry, supernatural interventions and so on. The main barrier to appreciation for the uninitiated is the percussive din of the accompanying orchestra. These days, with the fan base growing increasingly elderly, in a bid to appeal to a younger audience shows have been shortened from four hours to an hour or two, and include plenty of slapstick and martial arts.

There are hundreds of regional variations, such as Yue opera from nearby Zhejiang province, Kun opera from Jiangsu and the local form, Hu. One of the few places in Shanghai where you can hear these is the **Yifu Theatre** at 701 Fuzhou Lu (天蟾逸夫 舞台; *tiān chán yì fū wu3 tái*; ☏63225075), just east of People's Square. There's a different show every night of the week and a brisk English summary at the start explains the plot. Performances start at 7.15pm, and tickets, which can be bought on the day, cost from ¥30 to ¥300. There are also some afternoon performances.

Majestic Theatre
美琪大剧院
měi qí dà jù yuàn
66 Jiangning Lu, near Nanjing Xi Lu ☏62174409. When it was built in 1941 this was one of Asia's best theatres. Today, musicals are the main fare, but the programme is interspersed with some English language drama.

Shanghai Art Theatre
艺海剧院
yì hǎi jù yuàn
466 Jiangning Lu, near Kangding Lu ☏64278199. This airy modern complex tends to show classical Chinese opera and rather rusty old Chinese dramas.

Shanghai Dramatic Arts Centre
上海话剧艺术中心
shàng hǎi huà jù yì shù zhōng xīn

288 Anfu Lu ☏51695229. Slick productions in a modern auditorium; performances are usually of classics or crowd pleasers. Western plays are accompanied by English subtitles on an electronic screen.

Shanghai Grand Theatre
上海大剧院
shàng hǎi dà jù yuàn
300 Renmin Dadao ☏63273094, ⓦ www .shgtheatre.com. Popular contemporary dramas, operas and classical ballet are all staged at this lovely venue, which also plays host to most of the visiting musicals. Regular performances by the in-house Shanghai Symphony Orchestra (see opposite).

Acrobatics

Acrobatics have a long tradition in China and **acrobatic shows** are a guaranteed crowd pleaser. The style may be vaudeville but the stunts are spectacular – a dozen people stacked on one bicycle and the like. Performances have a little bit of everything: plate spinners, hoop divers, a comedy turn, jugglers and all sorts of feats of gymnastics. Many of the performers will have been trained for their roles since childhood in specialist schools.

Lyceum Theatre
兰心大戏院
lán xīn dà xì yuàn
57 Maoming Nan Lu ☏62565544. Acrobats in spangly costumes are guaranteed to draw some oohs and aahs; the juggler is rubbish

though. Daily performance at 7.30pm; tickets ¥150–250.

Shanghai Centre Theatre
上海商城剧院
shàng hǎi shāng chéng jù yuàn
1376 Nanjing Xi Lu, by Xikang Lu ☏62798948.

▲ Acrobats at the Shanghai Centre Theatre

Plenty of cunning stunts (and no animals). Performances start daily at 7.30pm and finish at 9pm; tickets ¥100–200.

Shanghai Circus World
上海马戏城
shàng hǎi mǎ xì chéng
2266 Gonghe Xi Lu ☏66527750, ⓦwww
.era-shanghai.com. **Shanghai Circus World
metro (line #1).** Avoid the beast house, which hosts wince-inducing animal turns, and head for the gold-coloured central dome, which hosts "ERA, the Intersection of Time". Never mind the daft name, the shows here are good old-fashioned spectaculars, with audiovisual trickery enhancing the awe-inspiring acrobatic cavortings. Performances daily at 7.30pm; tickets ¥50–580.

Live music

Shanghai's music scene is not yet the rival to Beijing's but it's only a matter of time as more venues open, new talent is trained in the impressive music schools, more international artists make appearances – and more disaffected kids buy electric guitars.

For **classical music**, in addition to the venues listed below, there's a classical concert on the first Sunday of every month in the *Jinjiang* hotel at 2pm (¥50). Concerts are also held at the Shanghai Grand Theatre – check the website.

Jazz devotees should avoid the septuagenarians at the *Peace Hotel* and head up to Fuxing Xi Lu for the *JZ Club* or nearby *Cotton Club* (both p.125). There's plenty of **hip-hop** around, but it's all about fashion and posing and the scene has yet to produce any music of note.

The **indie music** scene is not nearly as good as Beijing's, but it's there, and it is worth dipping a toe into. Try and catch indie popsters Flying Fruit or folk-punk rockers Top Floor Circus, who play regularly at *4live* (see p.132). The best underground venue, though, showcasing the latest live acts for the delectation of the Converse-and-black-nail-varnish crowd, is *Yuyintang (育音堂; yǜ yīn táng)*. Thanks to disapproving authorities, it's always having to change venue; check ⓦwww.yuyintang.com for the latest.

Classical music

Jinmao Concert Hall
金茂音乐厅
jīn mào yīn yuè tīng
1st Floor, annex of Jinmao Tower, 88 Shiji Dadao
☏50472612. Small venue for recitals, with reasonably priced tickets (from ¥60).

Oriental Arts Centre
上海东方艺术中心
shàng hǎi dōng fāng yì shù zhōng xīn
425 Dingxiang Lu, near Shiji Dadao ☏68541234. There's no doubt that this fantastic 40,000-square-metre behemoth (see p.92) is one of Asia's most important concert venues, with superb acoustics, though despite hosting a little bit of everything it's struggling to fill its schedule. At night the ceiling sparkles and changes colour according to the tunes being played.

Shanghai Concert Hall
上海音乐厅
shàng hǎi yīn yuè tīng
523 Yan'an Zhong Lu near Xizang Zhong Lu
☏63862836. This lovely old building was moved at tremendous cost sixty metres east in 2003, in order to get it away from the din of Yan'an Lu. Today it's the city's premier venue for classical music. Tickets from ¥80.

Shanghai Symphony Orchestra Hall
上海交响乐团演奏厅
shàng hǎi jiāo xiǎng yuè tuán yǎn zòu tīng
105 Hunan Lu ☎64372735. Home to the Shanghai Symphony Orchestra, who are very good, if rather conservative in their repertoire.

Rock and pop music

4live
8–10 Jianguo Zhong Lu, off Sinan Lu
☎74244008, ⦿www.4liveunderground.com.
Formerly a mediocre dance club, this place has reinvented itself as the saviour of live rock music in Shanghai – and as such is worthy of support (the last rescuer of Shanghai's indie soul ended up hosting pillowfight

parties – we'll see how long this one lasts). Local bands play during the week and there are guest bands from further afield on weekends. The crowd is young and fashionable but not posey, and the acoustics and layout are excellent. Tickets are usually around ¥30–50, a beer is ¥15.

Shanghai Stadium
上海体育场
shàng hǎi tǐ yù chǎng
666 Tianyaoqiao Lu ☎64266666, ext 2567.
Shanghai Stadium metro. Venue for mega gigs by visiting bands such as the Rolling Stones and Korean superstar Rain as well as homegrown idols. Tickets are cheaper than they would be in the West, usually around ¥120.

Shanghai cinema

China's first ever moving picture was shown in Shanghai, at a teahouse variety show, and the nation's first cinema was built here twelve years later. By the 1930s film had caught on both with the foreign population and with the locals and a number of studios had opened. Eschewing the formalism and abstractions of Chinese drama, film-makers, influenced by the May Fourth Movement, sought to make naturalistic films which challenged imperialism and social conservatism.

One classic from the era, *Sister Flower* (1933), tells the story of twin sisters separated at birth, one of whom ends up in Shanghai while the other remains a poor villager. *Spring Silk Worm*, from the same year, portrays grim decline in Zhejiang province, and points the finger at Japanese colonialism. The most celebrated film of the time was *The Goddess* (1934), about the struggle of a prostitute to have her son educated; it features a stand-out performance from the tragic beauty Ruan Lingyu, China's Garbo, who killed herself a year later.

When the Japanese invaded in 1937 Shanghai's studios were closed, and film-making talent fled. Despite the turmoil, the Shanghai film-makers made one last great work, the epic *Spring River Flows East*, telling the story of a family torn apart by the conflict.

When the Communists took over things didn't get any easier. Officially derided as bourgeois, they managed to release one privately funded film in *The Life of Wu Xun* (1949), the story of a nineteenth-century philanthropist. Mao damned it as revisionist and closed the studios. From then on Chinese film-makers were only allowed to shoot dry government propaganda.

All these old classics, and others of the time, can be seen at the *Old Film Café* (see p.116), or you can buy them on DVD from the Foreign Language Bookstore (see p.145) or from the shop in the Shanghai Grand Theatre (see p.130).

Though the studios have yet to return, a new film school has opened and the city has once more begun to be depicted in contemporary Chinese cinema, most notably in Lou Ye's tragic love story *Suzhou Creek* (2002). The inherent theatricality of Shanghai has been used as an exotic backdrop by **foreign film-makers**; parts of *Mission Impossible III* were set here, and Michael Winterbottom filmed sci-fi action flick *Code 46* in Pudong – though neither film is any good, the city comes out looking great.

The decadent prewar days have a perennial appeal to film-makers, it would seem, providing the setting for the stilted Merchant Ivory boreathon *The White Countess* (2004), Steven Spielberg's excellent *Empire of the Sun* (1987) and Zhang Yimou's *Shanghai Triad* (1995), which set the standard for the "lipstick and *qipao*" genre. Wong Kar Wai's *The Lady of Shanghai*, to be released in 2008, looks like being another worthy addition to that canon.

Film

Twenty foreign films are passed for domestic Chinese consumption every year by notoriously prickly censors. There are plenty of cinemas to see them in but generally all films are dubbed into Mandarin; exceptions are noted below.

For **art-house** flicks, in addition to the possibilities below there are irregular screenings of art films at the DDM Warehouse (see p.134) and every Thursday night at *Arch* café (see p.114). Maria's Choice is a club for cineastes that arranges private screenings of indie foreign and Chinese films with English subtitles. They gather once a month at the Kodak Cinema in Xujiahui; email for a schedule (€mariaschoice-subscribe@topica.com). In mid-June the city hosts the Shanghai International Film Festival (W www.siff.com), when there is much more varied fare on offer.

Broadband International Cineplex
6th Floor, Times Square, 99 Huaihai Lu
℡63910363, W www.swy99.com. Multiplex showing Chinese releases. Tickets ¥50 and up.

Cathay Theatre
国泰电影院
guó tài diàn yǐng yuàn
870 Huaihai Zhong Lu ℡54040415, W www
.guotaifilm.com. Grand, rather creaky, old venue with much cheaper tickets than the multiplexes (from ¥15) for much smaller seats.

IMAX
Science and Technology Museum ℡68622000,
W www.sstm.org.cn. Daily science spectacu-lars – they were screening films about comets at the time of writing (see p.91).

Kodak Cinema
5th Floor, Metro City, 1111 Zhaojiabang Lu,
Xujiahui ℡01758472. Hosts monthly cine club Maria's Choice (see above).

Paradise Warner International City
永华电影城
yǒng huá diàn yǐng chéng
6th Floor, Grand Gateway, 1 Hongqiao Lu,
Xujiahui ℡64076622, W www.paradisewarner
.com. Shows foreign films in their original languages, alongside Chinese releases (in Mandarin Chinese only). Tickets from ¥50.

Shanghai Film Art Centre
上海影院中心
shàng hǎi yǐng yuàn zhōng xīn
160 Xinhua Lu, near Panyu Lu ℡62804088,
W www.filmcenter.com.cn. The only vaguely art-house cinema, which has at least some non-mainstream content. Tickets from ¥45.

UME International Cineplex
国际影城
guó jì yǐng chéng
5th Floor, South Block, Xintiandi ℡63733333 (an English schedule follows the Chinese when you call), W www.ume.com. Original-language films; tickets from ¥50.

Art

Of all the arts, the most thriving scene, and certainly the most accessible to the visitor, is **contemporary art**. Chinese art is hot, and is being snapped up by international dealers, though it remains to be seen, when the dust clears, how worthwhile this hyped-up work will turn out to be: much is a sophisticated form of chinoiserie, selling an image of China for foreign consumption. Still, there's plenty of good stuff out there, and for once the government is not meddling.

A cluster of new **art museums** – the Duolun (see p.95), MoCA (see p.62) and Zendai (see p.92) are stimulating the scene, and the **Shanghai Biennale**, held every even-numbered year between September and November and centring on the Art Museum (see p.61), gets bigger every time (W www.shanghaibiennale .com). But the first stop for the artily inclined has to be **50 Moganshan Lu**, a derelict suburban textile factory that was first taken over by artists in the 1990s because rents were cheap, and has now become one of the city's premier tourist attractions. For a detailed account of the best of its many galleries, see p.84.

As China has opened up, artists have rapidly discovered and imitated Western forms, from surrealism to Dada to Pop, but the best have absorbed international trends and made from them something that is distinctly Chinese. It's not easy in this foment of activity to pick out names, but artists to look out for include **Qing Qing**, who makes wall pieces of Chinese dresses embedded with dried flowers, razor blades and the like.

Documentary realism is a strong strain in Chinese art, with artists given leeway to bring up, albeit obliquely, issues that are banned from discussion in the press; pollution, corruption and the destruction of the urban environment are common themes. Artists who exemplify this include **Yang Fudong**, notable for his wistful images of city life and migrant workers, and **Cui Xiuwen**, whose work includes film of women in a toilet at a karaoke bar.

Just as strong is a contrasting tendancy towards outrageous **sensationalism**, though again it's all about pushing the limits. **Wu Gaozhong** drew attention for a performance piece in which he climbed into the belly of a slaughtered cow, but his recent work, involving giant props implanted with boar hair, is rather more subtle, with a creepy beauty. And it's always worth looking out for a show curated by *enfant terrible* **Gu Zhenqing**, who has a reputation for gleefully courting controversy.

In addition to Moganshan and the art museums mentioned on p.133, the galleries below are well worth checking out.

ArtSPACE Warehouse
艺术空间仓库yì
shù kōng jiān cāng kù
78 Changping Lu, near Xi Suzhou Lu ☎52286776, ⓦwww.1918artspace.com. Daily except Mon 10.30am–6.30pm. See map, pp.80–81. Small and chic gallery in the north of the city showing contemporary Chinese art.

Art Scene China
艺术景画廊
yì shù jǐng huà láng
8, Lane 37 Fuxing Xi Lu ☎64370631, ⓦwww .artscenechina.com. Daily except Mon 10.30am–7.30pm. See map, pp.70–71. Classy and well-executed works from a highly reputed stable of artists are on show at this lovely restored courtyard house in the Old French Concession (see also p.77).

Creek Art Centre
上海体育场
shàng hǎi tǐ yù chǎng
423 Guangfu Lu, near Datong Lu ☎63804150, ⓦwww.creekart.cn. Wed–Sun noon–8pm. See map, pp.80–81. This seven-storey art centre overlooking Suzhou Creek was originally a flour factory. Today, it's an enormous exhibition space for contemporary art, with intelligently themed exhibitions.

DDM Warehouse
东大名创库
dōng dà míng chuàng kù
3rd Floor, 713 Daming Dong Lu, near Gaoyang Lu ☎35013213, ⓦwww.ddmwarehouse.org. Daily except Mon 11am–7pm. See Central Shanghai colour map. A rough-and-ready space showing trendy, conceptual work.

Deke Erh Centre
东强艺术中心
dōng qiáng yì shù zhōng xīn
Building 2, 210 Taikang Lu Art Street ☎64150675, ⓦwww.han-yuan.com. Daily 10am–6pm. See map, pp.70–71. Modernish *objets d'art* and some interesting photographs, all fairly affordable.

Shanghai Gallery of Art
外滩三号沪申画廊
wài tān sān hào hù shēn huà láng
3rd Floor, Three on the Bund, Zhongshan Dong Yi Lu ☎63215757, ⓦwww.threeonthebund.com. Daily 11am–11pm. See map, p.51. An impressive space in a beautiful and upscale building, just above the Armani flagship, that is yet to realize its full potential – so far, it's hosted only timid shows of established big hitters.

Shanghai Sculpture Space
上海城市雕塑艺术中心
shàng hǎi chéng shì diāo sù yì shù zhōng xīn
570 Huaihai Xi Lu ☎62807844, ⓦwww .sss570.com. Daily except Mon 10am–4pm. See map, p.98. This charming sculpture gallery, more than two thousand square metres in size, occupies an old steel factory. There's a permanent display of quirky and uneven work.

Shopping

Shanghai is excellent for shopping, with something for all tastes, whether you like getting stuck into teeming markets or swaggering about with the glitterati. And with the yuan artificially pegged at a low rate, for foreign visitors it's all great value too.

The Shanghainese love **luxury goods**, and it's not uncommon to find young women spending several months' salary on a handbag – it's advertising status in a society that only recently lost traditional forms of hierarchical display. But all those glitzy brand names that give the streets their sheen are not good value at all; high-end goods and international brands are generally twenty percent more expensive than they would be in the West. Ignore them, and instead plunge into the fascinating world of the **backstreet boutiques and markets**, where you can get just about anything you could think of for less than you thought possible. It's a rare visitor who doesn't end up having to buy another bag to keep all his new goodies in.

Serious shoppers should first get themselves to the Foreign Language Bookstore or Garden Books (see p.146), both of which sell a little white **book** with no English title, published by Shanghai Creative Bazaar. It's full of photos from fifty of the city's most interesting shops, with interviews with their owners, a blurb on each and all addresses listed in Chinese.

Shops and markets generally open from 10am to 8pm, later in malls; those with significantly different **opening hours** are listed. First checking out prices and goods online can save a lot of time, so useful **websites** have been listed.

You can exchange goods with a receipt except in small shops. Technically, you cannot take items out of China that are over 200 years old, but you'd be hard-pushed to find anything that old in Shanghai anyway. Only in the most high-end shops will be you able to use a credit card.

What to buy

Shanghai's **best buys** are: international brand designer clothes from factory outlet stores such as Hot Wind, where the original label has been snipped off; low-end electronics such as digital camera and mobile phone memory sticks; tailored clothes and made-to-order shoes; designer originals by local designers; fake name-brand labels; DVDs and CDs; and quirky homeware such as handmade porcelain.

As for **souvenirs**, well chopsticks, kites, fans, signature chops, tea and teapots are the perennial favourites, but for some other ideas see p.143.

Where to shop

For souvenirs the first place to head for is **Yuyuan Bazaar**, where you can get all the perennial favourites. **Nanjing Dong Lu** used to be known as the golden mile but these days, with stores full of cheap clothes, it's pretty prosaic. At least it's pedestrianized. Most foreign visitors will be more impressed with the retail opportunities offered around the corner on **the Bund**, where luxury brand names have opened showpiece stores – though all but the absurdly wealthy will have to make do with window-shopping. Pricey luxury goods are also available in the malls of **Nanjing Xi Lu** or yuppie playground **Xintiandi**.

The most chic area to shop is the **Old French Concession**; central Huaihai Zhong Lu itself is full of familiar brands, but the streets off it, such as Nanchang Lu, Shaanxi Nan Lu and Maoming Lu, are full of fascinating little boutiques, making this the place to forage for fashionable gear. For local crafts, and anything that's a bit more creative, head to Taikang Lu Art Street (lane 210 off Taikang Lu).

For stores geared to local tastes, check out **Xujiahui**; as soon as you exit the subway you're bang in the middle of a dense concentration of retail outlets – the Grand Gateway Plaza, Pacific Department Store, Metro City and the Oriental Department Store – aimed at the burgeoning middle classes. This is a good place to come for electronic equipment and affordable fashion.

Carrefour, at 268 Shuicheng Nan Lu in the southwest of the city, is a huge Western superstore. It's the place to go for those hard to find items such as nappies; they also sell very cheap bikes (around ¥200).

Bargaining

In malls and high street stores, prices are fixed, but there is always leeway for **bargaining** in small shops and markets. In touristy places such as fake markets or Yuyuan haggling is essential, as vendors can start at ten or even fifty times what they'll accept.

Always bargain good-naturedly, as confrontational behaviour will make the seller clam up. Feign complete disinterest in the object even if you've fallen in love with it. The seller (a girl, usually) will tap a price into a calculator. You then tap your best price in and she acts as if you just shot her puppy. After a little more discussion, walk away ruefully shaking your head, and she'll chase after you and gives you a "last price". Then you start negotiating again.

The best way to get a reasonable price is to decide how much you want to pay for a thing and then keep obstinately repeating that figure, rather than getting drawn into incremental increases. Remember that in places like fake markets you are likely to see the same thing for sale in the next store along, so having got a price from one place, take it to another and ask if they will beat it.

Fakes

Quite a lot in China is not what it seems – ninety percent of the world's counterfeit goods originate here. There are several **fake markets** catering largely to foreigners, though if you are buying anything antique or in a market you had better assume it is a fake. This doesn't mean that it won't work, and equally, not everything is a copy – sometimes the fakes are the real thing (particularly in the case of jeans and trainers), made in the same factory, just without the correct paperwork. However, you'd be wise to steer clear of dodgy electronics and medicines (look for spelling mistakes in the small print on the packaging or instructions), and fake designer clothes will fall apart or shrink in the wash.

In the markets, as well as the gear on display (mostly clothes and bags), at the back of every stall is a secret hidey-hole where the more sensitive items (generally watches and DVDs) are stored. You'll have to **bargain** harder here than anywhere else in the city; the pushy vendors commonly start at ten or twenty times the real price and it pays to shop around as plenty of people are selling the same thing. As a rough guide, a man's watch costs between ¥100 and ¥200, a woman's watch ¥50–100; Converse trainers can be had for ¥70, other brands for a little more. Handbags range from ¥80 to ¥130, a bit more for suitcases and backpacks. You can pick up fake computer games and software for ¥50 or so (Microsoft Vista copies were available the week it came out), and DVDs for ¥7. All clothes should cost less than ¥100, and sunglasses, belts and Mont Blanc pens are all around ¥25. There's also golf gear on sale, and some stalls just hawk souvenirs.

Imitation nation

In Shanghai, it's not just the "antique" snuff bottles at Dongtai Lu market that are **fake** – you can buy counterfeit phones, medicine, computers, even cars. The government does little to crack down, and though token efforts are occasionally made, in fact there is little incentive to enforce intellectual property rights: the easy availability of, for example, pirate software and machinery acts as a kind of unofficial subsidy for Chinese businesses, and copying is seen as a short cut to mastering new technologies. But as China develops, piracy will become harmful to its interests, as it removes any incentive to innovate – there's no point when any new invention is instantly copied – and creative industries such as film will continue to struggle to get off the ground as counterfeiters eat up all the profits. Still, to many visitors the lure of fakes, whether a designer label bag, watch or a few DVDs, is irresistible.

Note that according to the **customs laws** of Western countries, you are only allowed to import one dubious item per brand; so one fake Armani watch is fine, but a dozen will be impounded. Fake DVDs will be confiscated if you leave them in the original packaging, so store them in a DVD wallet.

Fake markets

Fengshine Plaza
风翔服饰礼品广场
fèng xiáng fú shì lǐ pǐn guǎng chǎng
580 Nanjing Xi Lu (People's Square subway). Daily 10am–8pm. See map, pp.80–81. The most convenient fake market, with three storeys of dodgy shops.

Qipu Lu Market
七浦路和河南北路
qī pǔ lù hé hé nán běi lù
183 Qipu Lu, just off Henan Bei Lu, northeast of the Bund. Daily 10am–8pm. See map, p.94. A sprinkling of stores sell local fashion among all the counterfeits at this, the most popular market.

Yatai Xinyang Fashion & Gift Market
亚太新阳服饰礼品市场
yà tài xīn yáng fú shì lǐ pǐn shì chǎng
Science and Technology Museum subway station (entrance close to the ticketing machines). See map, p.88. This is the biggest fake market, though it has rather a claustrophobic feel.

Antiques

There's no shortage of **antique markets** selling opium pipes, Cultural Revolution alarm clocks, carved screens, Mao's Little Red Book, silk paintings – but never mind what the vendor tells you, always assume you're buying a modern copy. Still, it's all fairly cheap. The Dongtai Lu market is the best place for this stuff, but barter hard. A few genuine antiques are available at the antique stores, but again most of their stock is reproduction.

▲ "Antiques", Dongtai Lu Market

Dongtai Lu Market
东台路古玩市场
dōng tái lù gǔ wán shì chǎng
Dongtai Lu. Huangpi Nan Lu subway. See map, p.64. Scores of small stores sell all manner of portable knick-knacks along this street, though nothing is genuine. It's at its biggest at weekends. Bargain hard, as starting prices are commonly twenty times what something is worth.

Guo Chun Xiang's Curiosity Shop
郭纯享家庭集报馆
guō chún xiǎng jiā tíng jí bào guǎn
179–181 Duolun Lu, near Sichuan Bei Lu. See map, p.94. Guo has an excellent showroom full of early twentieth-century knick-knacks and antiques.

Henry Antique Warehouse
亨利古典家具店
hēng lì gǔ diǎn jiā jù diàn
3/F, Building 2, 359 Hongzhong Lu ⓦwww .h-antique.com. Daily 9am–6pm. The English-speaking staff at this huge space show off antique Chinese furniture and furnishings; a carved Chinese bed costs around ¥13,000. Overseas shipping provided. It's in the southern outskirts of the city, so you'll have to take a taxi.

Zhang's Textiles
花张
huā zhāng
Shanghai Centre, 202A Nanjing Xi Lu ⓦwww .zhangstextiles.com. Genuine framed Qing Dynasty embroidery, jade bracelets, silk pillows and silk pillow boxes. It's not cheap, though, at hundreds of thousands of yuan for a piece.

Clothes and shoes

Sartorial elegance is something of a local obsession, and there's an old Chinese joke that Shanghai men would rather have oil for their hair than their wok. So you're spoilt for choice if you're looking for some gladrags. Name brands and chain stores will cost the same as at home or more but there's a surfeit of great local shops and **designers**, and getting something **tailor-made** is a bargain.

Always try prospective purchases on as a Chinese extra-large size is equivalent to a Western medium. Shops don't usually stock anything much bigger than that, and no shoes bigger than a (male) British size ten (US size 10.5), so if you're looking for larger sizes you'll have to get something custom-made or head for one of the fake markets.

If you're after **high street fashions**, try Raffles Mall, Nanjing Dong Lu or Huaihai Lu; if you just want something cheap and smart looking head for a Giordano or a Uniqlo (there are branches of both at the eastern end of Nanjing Dong Lu).

For **kids' clothes**, as well as the recommendations below check out the underground Nihong Children's Clothing Market, on Pu'an Lu at the junction with Jinling Lu (霓虹儿童广场; *ní hóng ér tóng guǎng chǎng*; Huangpi Nan Lu subway stop; daily 9.30–8pm; see map, p.64). There are hundreds of stalls, a playground where you can leave the little darlings (¥15) and you can get a fancy dress costume and a sweater for your dog while you're at it.

Designer clothes

If you want to see international designer clothes in showpiece stores head to Plaza 66 (see p.136) or the Bund. Alternatively, if you're after real designer gear for a steal, make for the discount and factory outlet stores (see p.141). But Shanghai has produced some great local designers, who deserve support. For stylish one-off fashions, browse the boutiques on Taikang Lu Art Street, Maoming Nan Lu and Shaanxi Nan Lu.

 Cha Gang
茶缸
chá gāng
House 1, Lane 299, Fuxing Lu ⓦwww.zuczug .com. See map, pp.70–71. Wang Yigang's unique but restrained unisex fashions and

accessories, sold in a space that resembles an art gallery, are deservedly popular, though they're not cheap at around ¥800 for a top.

 Insh

200 Taikang Lu ⊛ **www.insh.com.cn. See map, pp.70–71.** Creative and affordable clothes, from a talented local designer, Helen Lee. Traditional designs are given a modern twist to create distinctive street wear. A T-shirt costs about ¥200; nice bags too.

La Vie

Courtyard 7, Lane 210, Taikang Lu ☎ **64453585. See map, pp.70–71.** A very mixed collection of women's clothes, by local and Hong Kong designers, that's worth rooting around for the odd gem. Prices start at around ¥300 for a top.

Rouge Baiser

299 Fuxing Xi Lu. See map, pp.70–71. Stylish children's clothing, with embroidered lotus flowers and the like. Also embroidered tunics, bedspreads and pyjamas.

Shanghai Tang

上海滩

shàng hǎi tān

59 Maoming Nan Lu; 15 Xintiandi North Block, Lane 181, Taicang Lu; Shangri-La Hotel, 33 Fucheng Lu, Pudong. Daily 10am–10pm. See maps, pp.70–71, p.83 & p.88. This is the only international Chinese luxury brand, offering a colourful collection of chinoiserie such as silk pyjamas with embroidered dragons and the like. Home accessories and gifts are also on sale. Never mind that all their designers are foreign, and it's fearsomely overpriced; it's a lovely place to gawp.

Shiatzy Chen

夏姿陈

xià zī chén

9 Zhongshan Dong Yi Lu ⊛ **www.shiatzychen .com. See map, p.51.** Pleated skirts, tailored shirts and lavish evening gowns by Taiwanese designer Shiatzy Chen combine East and West with a dash of Hollywood glamour.

Shirt Flag

衫旗帜

shān qí zhì

Room 8, No. 7, Lane 210, Taikang Lu; 1st Floor, Building 17, 50 Moganshan Lu. Daily 11am–10pm. See maps, pp.70–71 & pp.80–81. Retro-Cultural Revolution chic, casual wear and bags; so-called McStruggle images, such as lantern-jawed workers waving iPods rather

than Little Red Books, predominate. The bags are cool and it's not too expensive, at ¥160 for a T-shirt.

 Younik

2nd Floor, Bund 18 ⊛ **www.bund18.com. See map, p.51.** A shiny boutique selling high-end clothes by Chinese designers. Look for Jenny Ji, who combines embroidered textiles with modern shapes, and Shanghai Trio (see p.142).

Tailors and cobblers

Getting some clothes or shoes made up is a recommended Shanghai experience, as it will cost so much less than at home and the artisans are skilled (provided you're clear about exactly what you are after) and quick. Either head to the South Bund Fabric Market and barter, or play it safe and spend more at one of the established brands listed below. If you're looking for a tailored *qipao* – that elegant slit dress – your best bet is to head to one of the dozen or so specialist stores on Maoming Nan Lu, just south of Huaihai Lu.

Dave's Custom Tailoring

上海不列颠西服

shàng hǎi bú liè diān xī fú

288 Wuyuan Lu ☎ **54040001,** ⊛ **www.tailordave .com. See map, pp.70–71.** The men's dress shirts and wool suits made here are certainly not the cheapest in town (suits start at ¥3500) but English-speaking staff make it popular with businessmen. Items require ten days and two fittings to complete.

Silk King

真丝大王

zhēn sī dà wáng

588 Nanjing Dong Lu; 819 Nanjing Xi Lu; 588 Huaihai Zhong Lu; 1226 Huaihai Zhong Lu. Daily 9.30am–10pm. See maps, p.48, pp.80–81 and pp.70–71. The top silk retailers in Shanghai, they can tailor you a silk or wool suit or a *qipao* in as little as 24 hours. Silk starts around ¥100 per metre, while cashmere is almost 10 times that.

 South Bund Fabric Market

南外滩轻纺面料市场

nán wài tān qīng fǎng miàn liào shì chǎng

399 Lujiabang Lu. Daily 10am–7pm. See map, p.64. Never mind the run-down area, this market is great, with a huge choice of textiles – from denim and corduroy to bouclé and gold lamé – that can be bargained down to ¥20–50 per metre, a little more for silk or cashmere (be wary with silk though as some of it is fake). In addition, most shops also have an on-site tailor, though few will speak English (one that does is Eric Chang at no. 310). Come with a good idea of what you want – a photo from a fashion magazine will do, but you'll get much better results if you ask them to directly copy something you give them; if you're interested in a man's suit they'll show you a catalogue of styles. Don't be talked into buying more material than you need: a man's suit requires about 5m of material, a shirt about 1.5m. Prices vary, but expect to pay roughly ¥80 for a linen shirt, ¥100 for wool trousers, and ¥220 for a man's lined corduroy blazer. If you've bartered sharply, the total price for a man's wool suit with a spare pair of trousers will be around ¥600 – less than half what you'd pay in a local shop. It will take them around a week to make.

Suzhou Cobblers
苏州鞋匠
sū zhōu xié jiàng
Room 101, 17 Fuzhou Lu Ⓦ www.suzhou -cobblers.com. See map, p.51. Hand-embroidered slippers, bags and hand-knitted children's clothing in charming traditional designs. A pair of embroidered slippers is around ¥500.

Yanye Shoe Studio
言业制鞋
yán yè zhì xié
893 Huashan Lu, near Fuxing Xi Lu. See map, pp.70–71. Made-to-order shoes, very reasonably priced, starting at ¥400 or so. Choose the material from a range of leathers and plastics, and details such as depth of heel and finish. You'll have to wait twenty days before they're finished.

Discounts and factory overstock

Forget the bad-quality counterfeit designer gear in the fake markets – if you know where to look, you can get the real thing for not much more. Just about all the world's textile production has moved to China, and it's common practice for Chinese factories to make a little more than was ordered and sell the **overstock** out the back door. This grey market gear makes its way, together with **factory seconds**, to backstreet stores, which sell it on at not much over cost price. Sometimes the label is cut or defaced, as a legal requirement, but never in such a way that it's not easy to work out.

These shops will be unpromising from the outside, quite possibly won't have a name, and will usually carry their own lines in the window, with the good stuff hung rather negligently on a rail at the back. The place to start is at **Ruijin Er Lu**, at the intersection with Huaihai Zhong Lu. Head south down the street then turn onto Nanchang Lu; look in any clothes shop that's busy on the way. A second concentration of these stores is on **Fuxing Zhong Lu**, east of Baoqing Lu. There's not much in the way of men's clothes, but try your luck at the nameless store at 1236 Fuxing Zhong Lu, which at the time of writing was selling Zegna and Armani suits for ¥300.

Hot Wind
热风
rè fēng
128 Fujian Zhong Lu; 358 Huaihai Zhong Lu; 127 Ruijin Yi Lu; 106 Ruijin Yi Lu; 4th floor, 408A Grand Gateway; 100 Xiangyang Bei Lu; 25 Caobao Lu; 890 Changning Lu; Ⓦ www.hotwind .net. Named perhaps for the feeling that passes through a fashionista on discovering these little gold mines. Hot Wind takes factory overstock, whacks their own label on top of the original and sells it on for ¥150 or so. Your job then, is to scrape their labels off with a nail or find the secondary label on the hem, and discover who really made it – you can turn up some great bargains. Good shoes too, but it's impossible to get the labels off. The most convenient store is the one on Huaihai Zhong Lu: go to Huangpi Nan Lu metro station and you'll find it opposite exit 3 (see map, pp.70–71).

Knicks-knacks, jewellery and accessories

Shanghai does curios, accessories and knick-knacks much better than it does antiques, with something of a craft renaissance going on. There is also some very well-designed mass-market homeware and porcelain that's well worth investigating.

The place to start looking is **Taikang Lu Art Street**. Notable stores here, in addition to those listed below, include: the Tian Zi Fang Leather workshop at no. 15, lane 210, which sells bags and belts; Cholon at 108, no. 3, which sells Vietnamese homeware; Hari Rabu at House 6, which has a Shanghai take on Indonesian curios; and Jooi Design at Studio 201 of the International Artist Factory, which has some great cushion covers and embroidered evening bags.

Stores are marked on the Old French Concession map (pp.70–71), unless where noted.

Annabel Lee

安梨家居

ān lí jiā jū

Unit 3, North Block, Xintiandi, Lane 18, Taicang Lu ⓦ www.annabel-lee.com. See map, p.73. Tiny, chic boutique selling cashmere scarves and blankets, silk underwear and pricey souvenirs such as tissue holders.

Blue Shanghai White

海晨

hǎi chén

Unit 103, 17 Fuzhou Lu. See map, p.51. Porcelain made and painted by the owner, Hai Chen. Vases and teapots from ¥300.

Brocade Country

锦绣坊

jǐn xiù fáng

616 Julu Lu. Hand-stitched tapestries (from ¥150) collected by owner Liu Xiao Lan in Miao villages. The Miao tribe are famous for their intricate embroidery and handcrafted silver ornaments that decorate their traditional dress – clothing that may take a woman many years to complete.

Christine Tsui's Fashion Club

24 Xinle Lu, near Shaanxi Lu. The owner designs many of the wares here, and tries to fuse old and new. It doesn't always work but with reasonable prices like these (¥200 for a handbag), no one is complaining.

Ellie Britzke

Lane 137, Jianguo Zhong Lu, Taikang Lu Art St. Affordable handmade jewellery.

Harvest Studio

盈稼坊工作室

yíng jià fáng gōng zuò shì

Room 118, No. 3, Lane 210, Taikang Lu Art St. Hand-embroidered clothing, soft furnishings, notebooks and wallets by eight resident Miao tribeswomen (see above). Also offers embroidery classes.

Lan Yin Hua Bu Guan

蓝印花布馆

lán yìn huā bù guǎn

637 Changle Lu. Boutique selling handmade bags, waistcoats, tablecloths and the like made from a traditionally produced blue-and-white batik-style nankeen fabric.

Madame Mao's Dowry

毛太设计

máo tài shè jì

207 Fumin Lu. Cultural Revolution kitsch for the home, with Mao geegaws and knick-knacks aplenty. Remember that none of this is original.

Paddy Field

稻 家居

dào jiā jū

30 Hunan Lu. This design emporium sells Southeast Asian-inspired homeware made from stone, leather and mother of pearl. Will also create custom furniture in about three weeks, and ship internationally.

Platane

127 Yongfu Lu, near Fuxing Xi Lu. Tues–Sat 11am–7pm; Sun noon–5pm. Chinese-inspired gifts and modern soft furnishings, including porcelain and handmade leather bags.

Shanghai Trio

上海组合家居店

shàng hǎi zǔ hé jiā jū diàn

Unit 5, House 1, North Block, Xintiandi; Lane 181 Taikang Lu Art Street; workshop/showroom at No. 6, Lane 37 Fuxing Xi Lu; ⓦ www .shanghaitrio.com. See maps, p.73 & pp.70–71. Cotton and silk bags with traditional designs in vibrant colours. There's also a cute line of children's accessories and chic jewellery.

Simply Life

逸居生活

yì jū shēng huó

159 Madang Lu, Xintiandi; 9 Dongping Lu. See

maps, p.73 & pp.70–71. Chinese-themed knick-knacks and homeware; one of the more affordable shops in the area, this is a good place for some speedy souvenir shopping.

Spin

旋 陶艺

xuàn táo yì

758 Julu Lu, Building 3 (go through the car park), near Fumin Lu. Modern ceramics from Jingdezhen – the capital of china in China, as it were. None of that chintzy "lovers on a willow bridge" stuff that your gran had, this is modern and minimalist; it's used by Japanese restaurant *Shintori* nearby (see p.120).

Tree

树

shù

126 Wulumuqi Nan Lu, near Yongjia Lu. Custom-made leather shoulder bags (around ¥500), belts and cowboy boots (around ¥900) by designer Yan Feng.

Urban Tribe

城市山民

chéng shì shān mín

133 Fuxing Xi Lu. Daily 9.30am–10pm. Ethnic clothing, pottery and jewellery, with a lovely café tucked away in the back (see p.115).

Wholesale Pearl & Stone Market

上海时代城隍珠宝交易中心

shàng hǎi shí dài chéng huáng zhū bǎo jiāo yì zhōng xīn

First Asia Jewellery Plaza, 3rd floor, 333 Fuyou Lu. Daily 10am–6pm. See map, p.64. Wholesale market for pearls, stones and crystals. Plenty of ready-made jewellery is on offer but you can also design your own. To tell a fake pearl rub it across your teeth a real pearl – a cultivated or natural pearl will feel slightly gritty, while a plastic copy will feel smooth. Remember to bargain.

Souvenirs

For souvenirs, you can't go wrong with teapots, fans, signature chops and chopsticks, and you can get them all at **Yuyuan Bazaar**. But how about also: a tongue-in-cheek McStruggle T-shirt (Shirt Flag, see p.140); a calligraphy brush (art supply stores on Fuzhou Lu); a Peking opera costume (Nantai Costume Company, see below); silk slippers (Suzhou Cobblers, see p.141); Cultural Revolution picture postcards (Propaganda Poster Centre, see p.78); a replica of a *ding* pot (Shanghai Museum shop, see p.58); a flashing Buddha (Yufo Temple, see p.83), or a model Oriental TV Tower (vendors in Huangpu Park, see p.50).

Cang Bao Lou Market

藏宝楼市场

cáng bǎo lóu shì chǎng

457 Shanghai Lao Jie. See map, p.64. This five-storey mall is the wholesale market that supplies most of Yuyuan's shops, so everything should be a little cheaper than just outside. You'll still have to barter hard though. Great for a souvenir blitz.

Huangshan Tea Company

黄山茶业有限公司

huáng shān chá yè yǒu xiàn gōng sī

Basement, Hong Kong Plaza. Daily 10am–10pm. See map, pp.70–71. Teapots from the famous factories at Yixing, as well as loose Chinese teas sold by weight. Vendors will let you sample all the wares.

Nantai Costume Company

南泰戏剧服装用品有限公司

nán tài xì jù fú zhuāng yòng pǐn yǒu xiàn gōng sī

181 Henan Zhong Lu, near Fuzhou Lu. See map, p.48. Nantai kits out the local opera troupes

and sells fake beards, tasselled hats and the like. The shop mynah bird can say *ni hao*.

Shanghai Downtown Duty Free Shop

上海市内免税店

shàng hǎi shì nèi miǎn shuì diàn

Under no. 5 entrance to Shanghai Stadium metro. Daily 8.30am–6pm. Open only to foreign visitors, this shop offers luxury international goods at the same duty-free price you'll find at the airport. You'll have to present your international airline ticket and passport to order anything, which you pick up at the airport when you leave.

Yaoyang Teahouse

尧阳茶行

yáo yáng chá háng

North Block, Xintiandi, 181 Taicang Lu. Daily 10am–10pm. See map, p.73. Speciality Chinese teas; pricier than elsewhere, but the packaging is excellent, making them good gifts. Go for Longjing from Hangzhou or Geow Yong from Fujian.

143

Electronics, computer and photography equipment

There's not much point buying big-name-brand electronics here, or anything that's near the top of the range; prices are the same as in the West, and you'll get less after-sales support. But it is worth checking out the **local brands** that you've never heard of (Lenovo is the biggest) and mid-range brands from Japan and Korea such as Acer.

A basic Chinese **laptop** costs as little as ¥2500, though it may well have build quality issues. For twice that you can pick up one from a Korean company that will usually have an international warranty and will still cost two-thirds what it would cost in the West.

Simple **MP3 players** can be had for ¥200, **memory sticks** for computers, camera and phones start at around ¥100, and you can get similar value for **accessories** such as headphones, USB cameras, portable RAM, mobile phone adaptors and keyboards.

The best places to shop for such bargains are the giant **tech-souks** Cybermart (赛博数码广场; *sài bó shù mǎ guǎng chǎng*; 282 Huaihai Zhong Lu, at its intersection with Huangpi Nan Lu), Metro City (美罗城; *měi luó chéng*; 111 Zhaojiabang Lu, by Caoxi Bei Lu, in the basement of the mall shaped like a giant bubble; Xujiahui subway) and Pacific Digital Plaza (太平洋数码广场; *tài píng yáng shù mǎ guǎng chǎng*; 117 Zhaojiabang Lu; Xujiahui subway). Shop around, as many of the stalls sell the same things, and barter (though this isn't the fake market – you'll get at most fifteen percent off the asking price). Test everything thoroughly and remember that for the majority of this stuff the warranty is not valid internationally.

For **photography equipment**, head to the third floor of the Huanlong Department Store, at 360 Meiyuan Lu, by the train station (黄龙百货; *huáng lóng bǎi huò*). Prices are not as good as in Hong Kong but still cheaper than the West. Plenty of the stores sell second-hand and studio gear, but don't get anything printed here as you can't be sure of the quality.

Furniture

Middle-class locals might be flocking to the new IKEA, but foreign expats, it would seem, just can't get enough retro Chinese furniture, with four-poster beds, carved screens, and lacquered chairs the most popular of many lines. All shops will arrange shipping home. The majority is, of course, reproduction. See also Henry Antique Warehouse (p.139) and Paddy Field (p.142).

Art Deco
凹凸库家具
āo tū kù jiā jù
Building 7, 1st Floor, 50 Moganshan Lu. See map, pp.80–81. This was one of the first shops to arrive inside the Moganshan Art complex, and shows the way it will probably develop. A grand collection of old furniture from the 1920s to the 1940s collected by husband and wife team Ding Yi and Wang Yiwu.

No. D Gallery
D号创意艺术廊
dí hào chuàng yì yì shù láng
2F, No. 15, Peninsula Garden, Lane 1518, Xikang Lu, daily 11am–7pm; 223 Jianguo Xi Lu, daily 11am–9pm; ⓦwww.numberd.com. See maps, pp.80–81 & pp.70–71. Art Deco and retro Chinese furniture; more tasteful than its competitors.

Books, CDs and DVDs

It's not hard to find **books** in English in Shanghai. You can pick up those printed by local presses – usually dryly written guides, or classics – for around ¥20, though imported books are expensive at over ¥100. Fuzhou Lu may be known to locals as "Book Street", but there's not much English-language material in its huge bookshops.

You can buy **fake CDs and DVDs** from roadside stalls in just about any backstreet. They cost ¥5–8 (Westerners might have to barter the vendors down) and quality is unreliable; new releases almost never work, or are grainy prints filmed in a cinema. In addition, many Western films will be dubbed into Russian – because of anti-pirating measures in the west, the counterfeiters are now copying the Russian releases. You can guarantee to find a raft of stalls on Wujiang Lu Food Street (see p.111). The best shop selling fakes is Hollywood Hits on Taikang Lu, opposite and just east of the entrance to the Taikang Lu Arts Street. The Shanghai Theatre Shop and the Foreign Language Bookstore stock plenty of **authentic DVDs** (see p.146).

⑬

SHOPPING | Books, CDs and DVDs

Bored of shopping?

Anyone can tire of shopping, so here are a few alternative activities to keep you amused.

Go shooting. Strangely, there's a rifle range in the Old French Concession (7th floor, 701 Huahai Zhong Lu daily; 9am–midnight; the entrance is in the alleyway just off the main street, a short walk east from the Parkson Department Store). You can fire .22 rifles or pistols up to .357 calibre. Ammunition is ¥8 for small calibre bullets, ¥15 for large calibre bullets, with a minimum of ten bullets per person. You get to keep the paper target as a souvenir. It's a rapid way to spend money but when will you next have the opportunity to combine shooting with a shopping trip?

Do archery. Here's another oddity: a basement archery range-cum-bar at 293 Yunnan Nan Lu (daily; 9am–1am), just a few minutes walk east of Times Square mall. Staff will help you put on the equipment and teach you the rudiments of shooting compound bows – it's simple enough so it doesn't matter if you can't speak Chinese. At only ¥12 for a quiver of ten arrows, it's a lot cheaper (and more relaxing) than shooting guns.

Play dressing up. The Huayuan Photo Studio (Tower B, 25th floor, Heyi Building, 420 Jiangning Lu; ☏52280848) gives you the chance to get your picture taken dressed to the nines in a variety of historical Chinese costumes. The dresses for women are fantastic, but there's not much for men. It takes four hours (lots of make-up and hairpieces are involved) and costs ¥520, which gets you four costume changes. Pictures are delivered within five days.

Learn some magic tricks. Shanghai even has a magic school, on the fifth floor of the Grand Gateway Plaza (above Xujiazui subway stop). The dedicated young magicians who staff the shop here will teach you ten tricks for ¥300, which gets you as many lessons as you need to get good. If you're just around for the day you can learn one trick for ¥50. They can be simple and prop-based, card tricks, sleight of hand, or you can study some pretty advanced stuff. There's even a target to flick cards into.

145

Charterhouse

Basement, Times Square, 93 Huaihai Zhong Lu; 6th floor, 68 Superbrand Mall, 168 Lujiazui Lu. See maps p.64 & p.88. This is the best English-language bookstore in the city with an excellent selection of modern novels, non-fiction and magazines.

Foreign Language Bookstore

上海外文书店

shàng hǎi wài wén shū diàn

390 Fuzhou Lu. Daily 9.30am–6pm. See map, p.48. Though it's no longer the main source of English language material, there's still a good range of books in English about China, plus audiovisual material for those learning Chinese, maps, old film DVDs and classic fiction.

 Garden Books

韬奋西文书局

tāo fèn xī wén shū diàn

325 Changle Lu. See map, pp.70–71. One of the city's mellowest spaces, this is not just a good place to browse: the attached coffee shop is a great place both to cast a discreet eye over both your new acquisitions and the other customers. Fiction, art and coffee table books.

Shanghai Theatre Shop

Shanghai Theatre, People's Square. See map, p.58. Good selection of genuine DVDs, mostly documentaries and old films, from ¥12–30 – an excellent place to complete your Hitchcock or Kurosawa collections.

Timezone Books

50 Moganshan Lu. See map, pp.80–81. A surprisingly good art bookshop, with odd, pod-shaped display cases that invite browsing, and an attached coffee shop.

Excursions

Excursions

Around Shanghai

hanghai being the polluted, hectic, crowded urban jungle it is, it would be a rare visitor who never felt the urge at some point to escape to fresh air, trees and a bit of peace and quiet. Though you'll find no wilderness in the flat, wet and heavily populated outskirts, the nearby cities of **Suzhou** and **Hangzhou** are two of the most pleasant in China, and their landscaped gardens and parks will certainly restore stretched nerves; both are ideal for a two- or three-day break. A bus ride north of Hangzhou will bring you to the up-and-coming hill resort of **Moganshan**, which despite being only a couple of hours from Shanghai feels a world away in spirit. You'll get an even more comprehensive change of scene on the Buddhist island of **Putuo Shan**, a night's ferry ride from the city, with temples set in charmingly leafy surroundings. They're both great places to while away a few days.

There are a couple of worthwhile attractions closer to the city which make for ideal day-trips. At barely a hundred metres high, **She Shan**, about 30km south of Shanghai, might not be much as a hill but it does feature some

---

Getting around Shanghai's hinterland

Most **trains** leave Shanghai from the huge main Railway Station in the north of the city, though some bound for Hangzhou also leave from Shanghai South. Train **tickets** can be bought ten days in advance – worthwhile at peak times, such as over the Spring Festival, or the public holidays that begin on May 1 and October 1. At the main station there's a foreigners' booking office at the back of the "soft sleeper" waiting room, which is much more convenient than queuing up at the hectic ticket office. It's more convenient still to book your ticket from a hotel (for a small charge) or from one of the many booking offices around the city, where you'll rarely have to queue; there are handy ones at 230 Beijing Dong Lu, 121 Xizang Nan Lu (next door to the *YMCA Hotel*) and 73 Wanhangdu Lu (near Jing'an Temple), all of which are open daily 8am–5pm. Note that these offices will only sell the "soft class" tickets where you pay a little more for a well-padded seat.

For **buses** to all tourist destinations in the city outskirts, visit the Shanghai Stadium Sightseeing Bus Centre at 666 Tianyaoqiao Lu (information ☏64265555), on the south side of the Shanghai Stadium, a ten-minute walk from the metro stop of the same name. Tour buses leave between 7.30 and 10.30am, returning in the afternoon. Tickets are available up to a week in advance from the main booking office, where staff speak English. There are over a dozen routes, the most popular of which are to the canal towns. A guide is provided, though you are free to wander off on your own.

For information on **boat services** from Shanghai to Putuo Shan, see the box on p.169. For details of services between Suzhou and Hangzhou, see the box on p.159

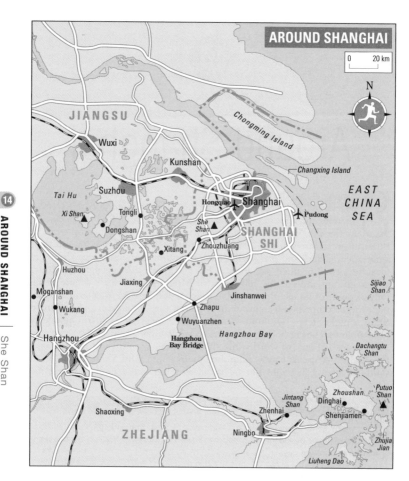

AROUND SHANGHAI

interesting historic buildings. And the **canal towns** of Zhouzhuang, Tongli and Xitang are attractive places to wander, though they are firmly on the tourist circuit. If it's at all possible, visit all of these places on a weekday; on weekends, they can get crowded.

She Shan

Such is the flatness of the surrounding land that **She Shan** (daily 7.30am– 4pm; ¥5), which only rises about 100m, is visible for miles around. The hill is crowned by an impressive **basilica**, a legacy of nineteenth-century European missionary work – She Shan has been under the ownership of a **Catholic** community since the 1850s – though the present church was not built until 1925.

She Shan	佘山	shé shān
Zhouzhuang	周庄	zhōu zhuāng
Shen House	沈厅	shěn tīng
Xitang	喜糖	xǐ táng
Xitang Youth Hostel	喜糖国际青年旅舍	xǐtáng guójì qīngnián lǚshè
Tongli	同里	tónglǐ
Tuisi Garden	退思园	tuìsī yuán
Sex Museum	中华性文化博物馆	zhōnghuá xìngwénhuà bówùguǎn

It's a pleasant walk up the hill at any time of year, or a cable-car ride if you prefer (¥20), past bamboo groves and the occasional ancient pagoda. Also on the hill are a **meteorological station** and an old **observatory**, the latter containing a small exhibition room displaying an ancient earthquake-detecting device – a dragon with steel balls in its mouth that is so firmly set in the ground that only movement of the earth itself, from the vibrations of distant earthquakes, can cause the balls to drop out. The more balls fall, the more serious the earthquake.

To reach She Shan, take a **bus** from the stop outside the Wenhua Guangchang on Shaanxi Nan Lu, just south of Fuxing Lu, or tour bus #1 from the Shanghai Stadium; services leave between 7 and 9am and return at around 3pm (¥12).

The canal towns

An extensive canal system once transported goods all around imperial China, and the attractive water towns that grew up around them – notably **Zhouzhuang**, **Xitang** and **Tongli** – present some of eastern China's most distinctive urban environments. Whitewashed Ming and Qing timber buildings back onto the narrow waterways, which are crossed by charming humpback stone bridges; travel is by foot or punt as the alleys are too narrow for cars.

Today, these sleepy towns are a popular escape from the city, and each has become a nostalgia theme park for the urban sophisticate. They're fine as daytrips but don't expect much authenticity – there are far more comb shops than dwellings – and don't come on weekends, when they're overrun. All charge an **entrance fee**, which also gets you into the historical buildings, mostly the grand old houses of wealthy merchants.

Zhouzhuang

Twenty kilometres west of the city, just across the border into Jiangsu province, **ZHOUZHUANG** (¥120) is the most accessible of the canal towns. Buses make the run regularly from the Sightseeing Bus Centre stop by Shanghai Stadium (1hr 30min; buses depart at 7am, 8.30am, 9am, 9.30am and 10am, and return between 4.30 and 5.30pm).

Lying astride the large Jinghang Canal connecting Suzhou and Shanghai, Zhouzhuang grew prosperous from the area's brisk grain, silk and pottery trade during the Ming dynasty. Many rich government officials, scholars and artisans moved here and constructed beautiful villas, while investing money into developing the stately stone bridges and tree-lined canals that now provide the city's main attractions.

The biggest mansion is the **Shen House** in the east of town, built in 1742. Over a hundred rooms (not all of them open) are connected by covered colonnades, with grand public halls at the front and the more intimate family chambers at the back. Period furnishings help evoke a lost age of opulence, though it is all rather dark; the neat gardens offer a pleasant contrast. An exhibition of folk instruments in the Xiaotong Tower at the rear is worth seeking out, as is the nearby statue of the mansion's founder, Shen, looking rather pleased with himself.

Zhouzhuang's most highly rated views are of the pretty sixteenth-century twin **stone bridges** in the northeast of town. Also firmly on the itinerary are a **boat ride** round the canals (¥80) and lunch – there are no shortage of restaurants, all offering the local specialities of pig's thigh, meatballs and clams as a set meal (around ¥60 per head).

Xitang

XITANG (¥60), sixty kilometres southwest of Shanghai, was popularized by its appearance in *Mission Impossible III*, and you won't forget the fact; bizarrely, there are posters of Tom Cruise all over the place. Though short on specific sights, the lanes, canals and bridges are undeniably picturesque. And if it rains, at least you'll be dry: the locals, tired of the wet climate, built roofs over the main alleyways, the biggest of which is over a kilometre long. It runs alongside the central canal, and is lined with restaurants and stalls housed in half-timbered buildings.

To get to Xitang, take a sightseeing bus from Shanghai Stadium, which leaves at 8.45am and returns at 4pm; the journey takes two hours. If you want to stay the night, head for the *Xitang Youth Hostel* at 6 Tangjia Lane, off Xi Xia Jie on the west side of town, which offers simple rooms and dorms (℡0512/65218885; ❶).

▲ Punting on the canal, Zhouzhuang

Tongli

Of all the canal towns, **TONGLI** (¥60), around eighty kilometres from Shanghai, has the best sights, and with more than forty humpback bridges (some more than a thouand years old) and fifteen canals it offers plenty of photo ops. The town's highlight is the UNESCO-listed **Tuisi Garden** (daily 8am–6pm; ¥20), built by disillusioned retired official Ren Lansheng in 1886 as a place to retreat and meditate – though you'll have to come in the early morning, before the tour groups arrive, to appreciate the peacefulness of the place. With its harmonious arrangements of rockeries, pavilions and bridges, zigzagging over carp-filled ponds, it is comparable to anything in Suzhou. The nearby **Sex Museum** (daily 8am–5.30pm; ¥20), housed in a former girls' school, is a branch of the museum in Pudong (see p.89), with similar exhibits – figurines of Tang dynasty prostitutes, special coins for use in brothels, and a wide range of occasionally eye-watering dildos.

There is no sightseeing bus from Shanghai to Tongli; the easiest way to get here is by bus or cab from Suzhou (see below), only twenty kilometres away.

Suzhou

SUZHOU, about ninety kilometres west of Shanghai, is famous for its gardens, beautiful women and silk. The city is said to have been founded in 600 BC by He Lu, semi-mythical ruler of the Kingdom of Wu, as his capital, but it was the arrival of the **Grand Canal** more than a thousand years later that marked the beginning of its prosperity as a centre for the production of wood block and the weaving of silk. In the late thirteenth century, Marco Polo reported "six thousand bridges, clever merchants, cunning men of all crafts, very wise men called Sages and great natural physicians". These were the people responsible for carving out the intricate **gardens** that are now Suzhou's primary attractions.

Arrival, information and orientation

From Shanghai Railway Station, fast double-decker **trains** make the fifty-minute run to Suzhou every morning from 6 till 11am; after this time, they are slower, taking one hour thirty minutes. **Buses** to Suzhou leave every half-hour from Shanghai Hengfeng Station, Xujiazui station and from outside the train station, taking almost two hours.

From the **train station**, you can get into town on buses #1 and #20. Directly across the street from the train station exit is a small **tourist office** and jetty where you can sign up for **boat tours** around Suzhou (¥60 for a ride around the city moat) and to Tongli (see above; trip leaves 8am; ¥150). **Minibus tours** of the city, on which you get ferried to all the sights (without commentary) depart from the train station square at 7.30am, returning at 4.30pm; they cost ¥15 exclusive of admission charges and can be booked on the day or in advance at the tourist office. City tours can also be arranged by CITS, next to the *Lexiang Hotel* on Dajing Lu (☏0512/65155207).

Suzhou has two main **bus stations**. The North Bus Station, which has half-hourly connections with Shanghai, is directly to the east of the train station. The South Bus Station, which sees arrivals from points south including Hangzhou and Zhouzhuang, is on Nanyuan Nan Lu just south of Nanhuan Dong Lu. Just

Suzhou	苏州	*sūzhōu*
North Bus Station	北公共汽车站	*běi gōnggòng qìchēzhàn*
South Bus Station	南公共汽车站	*nán gōnggòng qìchēzhàn*
Nanmen Dock	南门客运码头	*nánmén kèyùn mǎtóu*
Bamboo Grove	竹辉饭店	*zhúhuī fàndiàn*
Dongwu	东吴饭店	*dōngwú fàndiàn*
Lexiang	乐乡饭店	*lèxiāng fàndiàn*
Nanlin	南林饭店	*nánlín fàndiàn*
New Century	新世纪大酒店	*xīnshìjì dàjiǔdiàn*
Sheraton	喜来登大酒店	*xǐláidēng dàjiǔdiàn*
Suzhou International Youth Hostel	苏州国际青年旅社	*sūzhōu guójì qīngnián lüshè*
Beisi Ta	北寺塔	*běisì tǎ*
Silk Museum	丝绸博物馆	*sīchóu bówùguǎn*
Suzhou Museum	苏州博物馆	*sūzhōu bówùguǎn*
Zhuozheng Yuan	拙政园	*zhuózhèng yuán*
Shizi Lin	狮子林	*shīzi lín*
Xuanmiao Guan	玄妙观	*xuánmiào guàn*
Yi Yuan	怡园	*yíyuán*
Museum of Opera and Theatre	戏曲博物馆	*xìqǔ bówùguǎn*
Ou Yuan	耦园	*ǒuyuán*
Shuang Ta	双塔	*shuāng tǎ*
Canglang Ting	沧浪亭	*cānglàng tíng*
Wangshi Yuan	网师园	*wǎngshī yuán*
Pan Men	盘门	*pánmén*
Wumen Qiao	吴门桥	*wúmén qiáo*
Ruiguang Ta	瑞光塔	*ruìguāng tǎ*
Dianyun Fanzhuang	滇云饭庄	*diànyún fànzhuāng*
Korea Restaurant	汉城韩国料理	*hànchénghánguó liàolǐ*
Songhelou Caiguan	松鹤楼	*sōnghèlóu*

east of Renmin Lu on the southern stretch of the city moat is **Nanmen Dock**, for canal boats to and from Hangzhou.

The city itself is an easy place in which to get your bearings. **Renmin Lu**, the main street, zooms south through the centre from the train station. The traditional commercial centre of the city lies around **Guanqian Jie**, halfway down Renmin Lu, an area of cramped, animated streets thronged with small shops, teahouses and restaurants. The best way to get around is by **bike**; there are many bike rental places along Shiquan Jie and a couple on Renmin Lu, charging ¥15–25 for a day with a deposit of a few hundred yuan.

Accommodation

The main **hotel** area, and the heaviest concentration of gardens and historic buildings, is in the south of the city, around Shiquan Jie. Out of season (Oct–May), you should be able to get rooms in all the hotels listed below at a discount of at least twenty percent if you ask.

Bamboo Grove 168 Zhuhui Lu ☏0512/65205601, ⓦ www.bg-hotel.com. A tour-group favourite, this efficient

Japanese-run four-star hotel imitates local style with black and white walls and abundant bamboo in the garden. There are a couple of good restaurants on site. ⑧

Dongwu 24 Wu Ya Chang, Shiquan Jie ☎0512/65193681. The best budget hotel option, this large place run by Suzhou University is central but quiet, and offers rooms either in the main building or - the cheaper option - in the foreign students' pleasant guesthouse at the back. There's a very cheap canteen on site too. ③

Lexiang 18 Dajin Xiang, the third lane south of Guanqian Jie, east off Renmin Lu ☎0512/65228888. A very good, friendly, central hotel – one of the best options in its

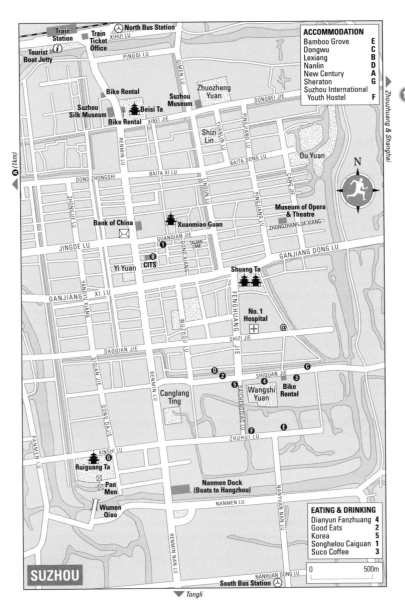

ACCOMMODATION
Bamboo Grove	E
Dongwu	C
Lexiang	B
Nanlin	D
New Century	A
Sheraton	G
Suzhou International Youth Hostel	F

EATING & DRINKING
Dianyun Fanzhuang	4
Good Eats	2
Korea	5
Songhelou Caiguan	1
Suco Coffee	3

SUZHOU

0   500m

price bracket – with CITS next door, and convenient for some good restaurants. The three- or four-bed rooms can work out fairly cheap if you bring enough friends to fill them. ❻

Nanlin 20 Gun Xiu Fang, Shiquan Jie ☎0512/68017888, ⊛www.nanlin.cn. A sprawling mansion with an immaculate lobby, surrounded by spacious and leafy gardens. The new wing has luxury rooms, while the old wing still offers reasonably priced doubles and triples. ❽

New Century 23 Guangji Lu ☎0512/65338888. Out in the west of the city, beyond the moat (take bus #7 from the train station), with nicely decorated, airy rooms. ❻

Sheraton 259 Xinshi Lu, near Pan Men in the southwest of town ☎0512/65103388, ⊛www.sheraton.com/suzhou. A pastiche Chinese mansion sprawling over two city blocks, Suzhou's best (and most expensive) international-standard hotel has double rooms from ¥1560. A stream runs through the middle of the grounds, and there are serene gardens and indoor and outdoor swimming pools. ❾

Suzhou International Youth Hostel 186 Zhuhui Lu ☎0512/65180266. A bit out of the way, but worth it for their decent dorm beds (though stick with the *Dongwu* if you want a room). They also rent out bikes for ¥20 a day. From the station, take bus #2 and get off outside the *Bamboo Grove Hotel*. Dorm beds ¥50. ❹

The City

The three most famous gardens – **Wangshi Yuan**, **Shizi Lin** and **Zhuozheng Yuan** – attract a stream of visitors all year round, but many of the equally beautiful yet lesser-known gardens, notably **Canglang Ting** and **Ou Yuan**, are comparatively serene and crowd-free. Seasons make surprisingly little difference as the gardens can be appreciated at any time of year, although springtime brings more blossom and brighter colours. Suzhou also has some rather charming **temples** and **pagodas**, and a couple of decent **museums**.

Beisi Ta and the Suzhou Silk Museum

A few minutes' walk south down Renmin Lu from the train station, the sixteenth-century **Beisi Ta** (North Temple Pagoda; daily 7.45am–5pm; ¥25) looms up unmistakeably. At 76m the pagoda is the tallest Chinese pagoda south of the Yangzi, though it retains only nine of its original eleven storeys. Climbing it gives an excellent view over some of Suzhou's more conspicuous features – the Shuang Ta, the Xuanmiao Guan, and, in the far southwest corner, the Ruiguang Ta. There's also a pleasant teahouse on site.

Virtually opposite, also on Renmin Lu, the **Suzhou Silk Museum** (daily 9am–5.30pm; ¥7) is one of China's better-presented museums, labelled in English throughout. Starting from the legendary inventor of silk, Lei Zu, the

---

Chinese gardens

Gardens, above all, are what Suzhou is all about. They have been laid out here since the Song dynasty, a thousand years ago, and in their Ming and Qing heyday it is said that the city had two hundred of them.

Chinese gardens do not set out to improve upon a slice of nature or to look natural. As with painting, sculpture and poetry, the aim is to produce for contemplation the **balance**, **harmony**, **proportion** and **variety** which the Chinese seek in life. Little pavilions and terraces are used to suggest a larger scale, undulating covered walkways and galleries to give a downward view, and intricate interlocking groups of rock and bamboo to hint at, and half conceal, what lies beyond. Almost everything you see has some symbolic significance – the pine tree and the crane for long life, mandarin ducks for married bliss, for example.

concubine of the equally legendary emperor Huang Di, it traces the history of silk production and its use from 4000 BC to the present day. There are displays of looms and weaving machines, and reproductions of early silk patterns, but the most riveting display – and something of a shock – is the room full of silkworms munching mulberry leaves and spinning cocoons, and copulating moths.

Suzhou Museum, the Zhuozheng Yuan and Shizi Lin

Suzhou seems proud of the new **Suzhou Museum** (daily 8.15am–4.15pm; ¥20), at the intersection of Dongbei Lu and Qimen Lu; you'll see plenty of pictures of it around town. It was designed by "starchitect" I.M. Pei, and is the most successful attempt at updating the Suzhou's characteristic white-wall and black-beam building style. The collection is small but choice, and includes some exquisite decorative objects, mostly china and jade; look out for the ugly toad carved out of jasper and the elaborate carvings of Buddhist scenes onto bamboo roots.

Next door on Dongbei Lu you'll find the largest of Suzhou's gardens. Covering forty thousand square metres, the **Zhuozheng Yuan** (Humble Administrator's Garden; ¥70) is based on water and set out in three linked sections: the eastern part (just inside the entrance) consists of a small lotus pond and pavilions; the centre is largely water, with two small islands connected by zigzag bridges; while the western part has unusually open green spaces. Built at the time of the Ming by an imperial censor, Wang Xianchen, who had just resigned his post, the garden was named by its creator as an ironic lament on the fact that this was now all he could administer.

A couple of minutes south of the Zhuozheng Yuan is another must-see garden, the **Shizi Lin** (Lion Grove; daily 7.30am–4.30pm; ¥30). Laid out by monk Tian Ru in 1342, it largely consists of rocks that are supposed to resemble lions. Part of the rockery takes the form of a convoluted labyrinth, from the top of which you emerge occasionally to gaze down at the water reflecting the trees and stones.

Xuanmiao Guan and Yi Yuan

Moving south from here, you arrive at the **Xuanmiao Guan** (Taoist Temple of Mystery; daily 7.30am–4.30pm; ¥10), just north of Guanqian Jie and rather incongruously at the heart of the modern city's consumer zone. Founded during the Jin Dynasty in the third century AD, the temple has been destroyed, rebuilt, burnt down and put back together many times during its history. Nowadays the attractive complex basically consists of a vast entrance court full of resting locals with, at its far end, a hall of Taoist deities and symbols; it's all encircled by a newly constructed park.

A few minutes south of Guanqian Jie, on the northwest corner of the Renmin Lu and Ganjiang Lu junction, is one of the lesser gardens, **Yi Yuan** (Joyous Garden; daily 7.30am–11pm; ¥15), laid out in the late Qing Dynasty by official Gu Wenbin. Considerably newer than the others, it is supposed to encompass all the key features of a Chinese garden; unusually, it also has formal flowerbeds and arrangements of coloured pebbles.

The Museum of Opera and Theatre and Ou Yuan

A ten-minute walk along narrow lanes due east from the end of Guanqian Jie, the unusual **Museum of Opera and Theatre** stands on Zhongzhangjia Xiang (daily 8.30am–4.30pm; ¥8). The rooms are filled with costumes, masks, musical instruments, and even a full-sized model orchestra, complete with cups of tea, though the building itself is the star, a Ming dynasty theatre made of latticed wood. The Suzhou area is the home of the 5000-year-old **Kun Opera** style, China's oldest operatic form. Kun is distinguished by storytelling and ballad singing but can be hard to follow (even if you speak Chinese) as it is performed in the obscure Suzhou dialect.

A five-minute walk northeast of the museum, abutting the outer moat and along a canal, the **Ou Yuan** (daily 8am–5pm; ¥15) is a quiet garden, free from the loudhailer-toting tour groups. Here a series of hallways and corridors opens onto an intimate courtyard, with a pond in the middle surrounded by abstract rock formations and relaxing teahouses.

Shuang Ta and Canglang Ting

Several blocks east of Renmin Lu and immediately south of Ganjiang Xi Lu, the **Shuang Ta** (Twin Pagodas; daily 7am–4.30pm; ¥4) are matching slender towers built during the Song dynasty by a group of successful candidates in the imperial examinations who wanted to honour their teacher. The teahouse here is crowded in summer with old folk fanning themselves against the heat.

A kilometre or so farther southwest of here, just beyond Shiquan Jie, the intriguing **Canglang Ting** (Dark Blue Wave Pavilion; daily 8am–5pm; ¥15) is the oldest of the major surviving gardens. Originally built by scholar Su Zimei around 1044 AD, it's approached through a grand stone bridge and ceremonial marble archway. The curious Five Hundred Sage Temple in the south of the garden is lined with stone tablets recording the names and achievements of Suzhou's statesmen, heroes and poets.

Wangshi Yuan

The intimate **Wangshi Yuan** (Master of the Nets Garden; daily 7.30am–5pm; ¥20) is down a narrow alleyway on the south side of Shiquan Jie. The garden, so named because the owner, a retired official, decided he wanted to become a fisherman, was started in 1140, but was later abandoned and not restored to its present layout until 1770. Considered by garden connoisseurs to be the finest of them all, it boasts an attractive central lake, minuscule connecting halls, pavilions with pocket-handkerchief courtyards and carved wooden doors – and rather more visitors than it can cope with. The garden is said to be best seen on moonlit nights, when the moon can be seen three times over from the Moon-watching Pavilion – in the sky, in the water and in a mirror. Other features include its delicate latticework and fretted windows. Outside the winter months the garden plays host to nightly arts performances (see opposite).

Pan Men and around

In the far southwestern corner of the moated area is one of the city's most pleasant areas, centred around **Pan Men** (Coiled Gate) and a stretch of the original city wall, built in 514 BC; the gate is the only surviving one of eight that once surrounded Suzhou. The best approach is from the south, via **Wumen Qiao**, a delightful high-arched bridge (the tallest in Suzhou) with steps built into it; it's a great vantage point for watching the canal traffic (bus #7 from the train station passes the southern edge of the moat). Just inside Pan Men sits the dramatic **Ruiguang Ta** (¥6), a thousand-year-old pagoda now rebuilt from ruins.

Eating, drinking and entertainment

Suzhou has a good range of **places to eat** and the local cuisine, with its emphasis on fish from the nearby lakes and rivers, is justly renowned; specialities include *yinyu* ("silver fish") and *kaobing* (grilled pancakes with sweet filling). For **nightlife**, there is a slew of touristy bars scattered along Shiquan Jie near Wangshi Yuan.

The best **entertainment** in town is the nightly opera extravaganza at Wangshi Yuan (March–Oct 7.30–10pm; ¥80 including admission to garden), featuring eight displays of the most prominent forms of Chinese performance arts, from Beijing opera to folk dancing and storytelling. For the latest information, check ⓦwww.whatsoninsuzhou.com.

Restaurants and cafés

Dianyun Fanzhuang 519 Shiquan Jie. A friendly, inexpensive place for rice noodles and other specialities from Yunnan province – sit by the window for a view of the tourists plying Shiquan Jie. Open 24hr.

Good Eats 694 Shiquan Jie. An American-style café selling hot dogs, burgers and fish and chips. Open till 4am so it's a good place to end a night out.

Korea 579 Daichengqiao Lu, at the Shiquan Jie intersection. One of the best of a host of unimaginatively named Korean restaurants, with good barbecued beef, cooked at the table.

 Songhelou Caiguan On Taijian Lane, 200m east of Renmin Lu. The most famous restaurant in town – it claims to be old enough to have served Emperor Qianlong. The menu is elaborate and long on fish and seafood (crab, eel, squirrel fish and the like), though not cheap at around ¥150 a head. Flanking *Songhelou* are four other restaurants of repute, all claiming more than 100 years of history: the *Dasanyuan*, *Deyuelou*, *Wangsi* and *Laozhengxing*. They're all big, busy and good for a splurge on local dishes, with foreigner-friendly staff and menus.

Suco Coffee 357 Shiquan Jie. The best café in town, with excellent smoothies (¥28), wireless and comfortable seating.

Hangzhou

HANGZHOU, one of China's most established tourist attractions, lies in the north of Zhejiang province at the head of Hangzhou Bay, two hours by train from Shanghai South station. The modern city is not of much interest in itself, but **Xi Hu** – the lake around which Hangzhou curls – and its shores still offer wonderful Chinese vistas of trees, hills, flowers, old causeways over the lake, fishing boats, pavilions and pagodas.

With the building of the Grand Canal at the end of the sixth century, Hangzhou became the centre for trade between north and south China, the Yellow and Yangzi river basins. Under the **Tang dynasty** it was a rich and thriving city, but its position made it vulnerable to the fierce equinox tides in Hangzhou Bay. When Tang-dynasty governors were building locks and dykes to control the waters round Hangzhou, a contemporaneous writer, describing the beginning of a sea wall in 910 AD, explained that "archers were stationed on the shore to shoot down the waves while a poem was recited to propitiate the King of Dragons and Government of the Waters." The problem of floods – and the search for remedies – was to recur down the centuries.

During the **Song dynasty**, Hangzhou became the **imperial capital**, setting off a boom in all the trades that waited upon the court, particularly silk. Marco Polo, writing of Hangzhou towards the end of the thirteenth century, spoke of "the City of Heaven, the most beautiful and magnificent in the world." Though its role as imperial capital ceased when the Southern Song dynasty was overthrown by the Mongols in 1279, it remained an important centre of

Hangzhou and Moganshan

Hangzhou	杭州	*hángzhōu*
Wulin Pier	武林 陆巷码头	*wǔlín lùxiàng mǎtóu*
Dahua	大华饭店	*dàhuá fàndiàn*
Dongpo	东坡宾馆	*dōngpō bīnguǎn*
Huaqiao	华侨饭店	*huáqiáo fàndiàn*
Mingtown Hangzhou Youth Hostel	华美达广场杭州海华大酒店	*huáměidá guǎngchǎng*
Ramada Plaza Hangzhou Haihua	香格里拉饭店	*xiānggélǐlā fàndiàn*
Shangri-La	新桥饭店	*xīnqiáo fàndiàn*
Xinxin	浙江大学招待所	*zhèjiāng dàxué zhāodàisuǒ*
Zhonghua	中国美术学院国际教育学院	*zhōngguó měishù xuéyuàn*
Xi Hu	西湖	*xīhú*
Bai Di	白堤	*báidī*
Gu Shan	孤山	*gūshān*
Zhejiang Provincial Museum	浙江博物馆	*zhèjiāng bówùguǎn*
Xiling Seal Engravers' Society	西泠印社	*xīlíng yìnshè*
Su Di	苏堤	*sūdī*
Santaninyue	三潭印月	*sāntán yìnyuè*
Baoshu Ta	保淑塔	*bǎoshū tǎ*
Qixia Shan	栖霞山	*qīxiá shān*
Baopu Daoist Compound	包朴道院	*bāopǔ dàoyuàn*
Yuefei Mu	岳飞墓	*yuèfēi mù*
Huanglong Dong Park	黄龙洞公园	*huánglóngdòng gōngyuán*
Feilai Feng	飞来峰	*fēilái fēng*
Lingyin Temple	灵隐寺	*língyǐn sì*
Tea Museum	茶博物馆	*cha bówùguǎn*
Longjing	龙井	*lóngjǐng*
Hupaomeng Quan	虎跑梦泉	*hǔpǎomèng quán*
Kaiyuan Guan	奎元馆	*kuíyuán guǎn*
Louwailou	楼外楼	*lóuwài lóu*
Tianwaitian	天外天	*tiānwài tiān*
Zhiweiguan	知味观	*zhīwèi guàn*
Moganshan	莫干山	*mògānshān*
Songliang Shanzhuang	松梁山庄	*sōngliáng shānzhuāng*
Du Yuesheng Villa	杜月笙别墅	*dùyuèshēng biéshù*

commerce. **Ming** rulers repaired the city walls and deepened the Grand Canal so that large ships could go all the way from Hangzhou to Beijing, and two great **Qing** emperors, Kangxi and Qianlong, built villas, temples and gardens by the lake. Although largely destroyed in the Taiping Rebellion (see p.177), it recovered quickly, and the **foreign concessions** that were established towards the end of the century – followed by the building of rail lines from Shanghai and Ningbo – stimulated the growth of new industries alongside traditional silk and brocade manufacturing.

Arrival, information and city transport

Hangzhou has two halves; to the east and north of the lake is **downtown**, with its shops and tourist facilities, while to the west and south you'll find greenery and scenic spots. The commercial centre of town is the area around the Jiefang Lu/Yan'an Lu intersection, where you'll find accommodation, restaurants and shops; buses around the lake also leave from here. Hangzhou's gateway to the sea, the **Qiantang River**, flows well to the south and west, on the outskirts of the city.

Hangzhou's main **train station** is 2km east of Xi Hu. Reaching the lake from here on foot takes about forty minutes; otherwise, take bus #7 direct to the lake or #151 as far as Yan'an Lu. Buses from Shanghai pull in at the **North Bus Station**, 9km north of the city (bus #155 plies the route), though private buses on this route use the train station square, as do services from Suzhou. Boats from Suzhou arrive in the early morning at **Wulin Pier** on the Grand Canal, north of the city centre and also accessible on bus #155.

The **Hangzhou Tourist Centre** (☏0571/96123) has a booth in front of the train station, between the public bus stops; they run one-day **tours** of Hangzhou and surrounding canal towns and cities, as well as shuttles to Shanghai's Pudong airport. Their main office is at 3 Huanglong Lu, northwest of the lake. **CITS** is on the north shore of the lake, on a hillock above the junction of Beishan Lu and Baoshu Lu. Walk through the main gate and you'll find the office a couple of minutes' walk ahead to the left (☏0571/85059033; daily 8.30am–5pm). Nearly all Hangzhou's hotels have their own travel agencies, usually more helpful than CITS.

As for transport, a ¥10 **taxi** ride should cover any destination in central Hangzhou. Alternatively, **cycling** is a great way to get around the city. Hangzhou's Freedom Network Bike Rental is one of the best operations of its kind in China, with locations around the lake and the option to return your bike to any of their outlets. One convenient outlet is the small corner office at 175 Nanshan Lu (☏0571/87131718), in a freestanding grey building 200m south of Jiefang Lu. Rentals cost ¥10/hr or ¥50/day, with a ¥400 deposit.

Accommodation

There are some excellent **hotels** in Hangzhou, particularly on the lakefront, and a handful of **hostels** have opened in recent years. Rooms fill fast in season, so you may want to book in advance.

Dahua 171 Nanshan Lu ☏0571/87181888. On the lakeside, several blocks south of Jiefang Lu. Spacious grounds with comfortable rooms and attentive service justify the prices – this is actually better value than many of its competitors. Mao Zedong and Zhou Enlai stayed here whenever they visited Hangzhou. ❼

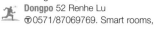 **Dongpo** 52 Renhe Lu ☏0571/87069769. Smart rooms,

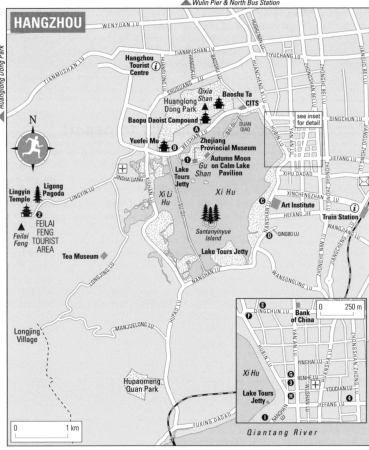

ACCOMMODATION						EATING	
Dahua	I	Mingtown Hangzhou		Shangri-La	B	Kuiyuan Guan	4
Dongpo	G	Youth Hostel	C	Xinxin	A	Louwailou	1
Holiday Wuyang	D	Ramada Plaza		Zhonghua	H	Tianwaitian	2
Huaqiao	F	Hangzhou Haihua	E			Zhiweiguan	3

a beautiful six-storey central atrium and friendly staff make this just about the best deal in town. ❹

Holiday Wuyang 109 Qingbo Lu, off Nanhan Lu, by Xi Hu ☎0571/87655678. Recently renovated and in a promising location, near the lake but tucked away on a side street. Rooms are decent but modular. ❼

Huaqiao 39 Hubin Lu ☎0571/87074401. This four-star offering has spacious if slightly overpriced rooms, in a great location on the lakefront just south of Qingchun Lu. ❻

Mingtown Hangzhou Youth Hostel 101 Nanshan Lu ☎0571/87918948. Down an alley directly across from the Chinese Art Institute, with a range of rooms, including a few with lake views and private bathroom. ❷

Ramada Plaza Hangzhou Haihua 298 Qingchun Lu ☎0571/87215888, ⓦwww .ramadainternational.com. One of the more upmarket offerings from this international hotel chain, with luxurious and tastefully designed rooms. The grand lobby features an imposing staircase. Rooms overlooking the lake command a premium. ⑨

Shangri-La Beishan Lu, next to the Yuefei Mu ☎0571/87977951, ⑩www.shangri-la .com. Total air-conditioned luxury in beautiful, secluded grounds, overhung by trees, on the northern shore of the lake. There's an expensive but tasty breakfast buffet. ⑧

Xinxin 58 Beishan Lu ☎0571/87999090. Standard, mildly worn rooms, but it does have one of the nicest locations, overlooking the Xi Hu's northern shore. ⑦

Zhonghua 55 Youdian Lu ☎0571/87027094. Very central, between the lakefront and Yan'an Lu, this place offers clean and well-designed single and double rooms. ⑥

The City

Hangzhou encompasses large areas of greenery that might normally be classified as countryside. This is mainly thanks to **Xi Hu** itself – so central and dominant a role has the lake played in the city's history that even today a trip right round its shores does not feel like an excursion out of the city.

Within the lake are various **islands** and causeways, while the shores are home to endless **parks** holding Hangzhou's most famous individual sights. These range from the extravagant and historic **Yuefei Mu** (Tomb of Yuefei) to the ancient hillside Buddhist carvings of **Feilai Feng** and its associated temple, the **Lingyin Temple**, one of China's largest and most renowned. Farther afield, beautiful tea plantations nestle around the village of **Longjing**, while south down to the **Qiantang River** are excellent walking opportunities.

With most of Hangzhou's sights located on or near the lakeshore, you'll find that the ideal way to get between them is by **bike**.

Xi Hu

Xi Hu forms a series of landscapes with rock, trees, grass and lakeside buildings all reflected in the water and backed by luxuriant wooded hills. The lake itself stretches just over 3km from north to south and just under 3km from east to west, though the surrounding parks and associated sights spread far beyond this. On a sunny day the colours are brilliant, but even with grey skies and choppy waters, the lake views are soothing and tranquil; for the Chinese they are also laden with literary and historic associations. Although the crowds and hawkers are sometimes distracting, the area is so large that you can find places to escape the hubbub.

As early as the Tang dynasty, work was taking place to control the waters of the lake with dykes and locks, and the two **causeways** that now cross sections of the lake, Bai Di across the north and Su Di across the west, originated in these ancient embankments. Mainly used by pedestrians and cyclists, the causeways offer instant escape from the noise and smog of the built-up area to the east. The western end of Bai Di supposedly offers the best vantage point over the lake.

Boat trips on Xi Hu

One of the most pleasant things to do on a visit to Hangzhou is to take a boat trip on the lake. Tourist boats (¥45, including entrance fees for Santanyinyue) launch from the two lake tour jetties and head directly for the **islands**. Then there are the freelance boatmen who charge ¥80/hr for up to six people. You can also take a boat out on your own – either electric putt-putters for four people (¥30 for 30min; ¥200 deposit), or paddle boats (¥15–20 for 30min).

Bai Di and Gu Shan

Bai Di is the shorter and more popular of the two causeways, about 1500m in length. Starting in the northwest of the lake near the *Shangri-La Hotel*, it runs along the outer edge of Gu Shan before crossing back to the northeastern shore, enclosing a small strip known as Beili Hu (North Inner Lake). The little island of **Gu Shan** in the middle of the causeway is one of Hangzhou's highlights, a great place to relax under a shady tree. Dotted with pavilions and pagodas, this tiny area was originally landscaped under the Tang, but the present style dates from the Qing, when Emperor Qianlong built himself a palace here. Part of the palace itself, facing south to the centre of the lake, is now the **Zhejiang Provincial Museum** (Mon noon–4pm, Tues–Sun 9am–4pm; free), a huge place with English captions throughout. The main building in front of the entrance houses historical relics, including some superb bronzes from the eleventh to the eighth century BC. Another hall centres on coin collections and has specimens of the world's first banknotes, dating to the Northern Song; you'll get an appreciation of the deep conservatism of Chinese society from its coinage, which remained fundamentally unchanged for two thousand years from the Han to the Qing dynasties. New galleries outside hold displays of painting and Tibetan Buddha statues.

The curious **Xiling Seal Engravers' Society** (daily 9am–5pm; ¥5), founded in 1904, occupies the western side of the hill, next to the *Louwailou Restaurant*. Its tiny park encloses a pavilion with a pleasant blend of steps, carved stone tablets, shrubbery, and nearby a small early Buddhist stupa. On the southeastern side of the hill by the water is another of Qianlong's buildings, the **Autumn Moon on a Calm Lake Pavilion**, which is the perfect place to watch the full moon. It's a teahouse now, very popular after sunset and full of honeymooners. The low stone **Duan Qiao** (Broken Bridge), at the far eastern end of the causeway, gets its name because winter snow melts first on the hump of the bridge, creating the illusion of a gap.

Su Di and Santanyinyue Island

The longer causeway, **Su Di**, named after the Song-dynasty poet-official Su Dong Po, who was governor of Hangzhou, starts from the southwest corner of the lake and runs its full length to the northern shore close to Yuefei Mu. Consisting of embankments planted with banana trees, weeping willows and plum trees, linked by six stone arch bridges, the causeway encloses a narrow stretch of water, **Xili Hu** (West Inner Lake). East of the causeway and in the southern part of the lake is the largest of the islands here, **Xiaoying**, built up in 1607. It's better known as **Santanyinyue** (Three Flags Reflecting the Moon) after the three "flags" in the water – actually stone pagodas, said to control the evil spirits lurking in the deepest spots of the lake. Bridges link across from north to south and east to west so that the whole thing seems like a wheel with four spokes, plus a central hub just large enough for a pavilion, which doubles as a shop and a restaurant. The ¥20 admission fee to get onto the island is usually included if you take one of the tourist boat rides here.

The lake shore and Huanglong Dong Park

Starting from the northeast of the lake on Beishan Lu and heading anticlockwise, the seven-storey **Baoshu Ta** on Baoshi Shan is the first sight you'll encounter. Looming up on the hillside to your right, the pagoda is a 1933 reconstruction of a Song dynasty tower, and a nice place to walk to along

▲ Pavilion, Xi Hu

hillside paths. From Beishan Lu a small lane leads up behind some buildings to the pagoda. Tracks continue beyond, and you can climb right up to **Qixia Shan** (Mountain Where Rosy Clouds Linger) above the lake. About halfway along this path you'll see a yellow-walled monastery with black roofs lurking below to your left, the **Baopu Daoist Compound**. It's well worth a stop, especially in the late afternoon, if only because you might be able to watch discreetly one of the ancestral worship ceremonies that are held here, with priests clad in colourful garb and widows clutching long black necklaces. If you climb the stairs, you will find several smaller halls where old men practise their calligraphy and young women play the *pipa*.

Continuing west, the **Yuefei Mu** (Tomb of Yuefei; daily 7.30am–5.30pm; ¥25) is one of Hangzhou's big draws, the twelfth-century Song general Yuefei being considered a hero in modern China thanks to his unquestioning patriotism. Having emerged victorious from a war against barbarian invaders from the north, Yuefei was falsely charged with treachery by a jealous prime minister, and executed at the age of 39. Twenty years later, the subsequent emperor annulled all charges against him and had him reburied here with full honours. Walk through the temple to reach the tomb itself – a tiny bridge over water, a small double row of stone men and animals, steles, a mound with old pine trees and four cast-iron statues of the villains, kneeling in shame with their hands behind their backs. The calligraphy on the front wall of the tomb reads, "Be loyal to your country".

Immediately west of Yuefei's tomb is a lane leading away from the lake and north into the hills behind. Thirty minutes' walk along here eventually leads to the **Huanglong Dong Park** (Yellow Dragon Cave Park; daily 6.30am–4pm; ¥15), to the north of Qixia Shan. The park can also be approached from the roads to the north of here, south of Hangzhou University. The main area of the park is charmingly secluded, sunk between sharply rising hills with a pond, teahouses, a shrine to Yue Lao (the Chinese god of arranging marriages), and a pavilion where musicians perform traditional music.

Feilai Feng and Lingyin Temple

Three kilometres west of the lake (bus #7 from Yuefei Mu to its terminus), Hangzhou's most famous sights are scattered around **Feilai Feng** (daily 5.30am–5.30pm; ¥25). The hill's name –"The Hill that Flew Here" – derives from the tale of an Indian Buddhist named Hui Li who, upon arrival in Hangzhou, thought he recognized the hill from one back home, and asked when it had flown here. Near the entrance is the **Ligong Pagoda**, constructed for him. If you turn left shortly after entering the site, you'll come to a surprisingly impressive group of fake rock carvings, replicas of giant Buddhas from all over China. To the right of the entrance you'll find a snack bar and beautiful views over the neighbouring tea plantations up the hill.

The main feature of Feilai Feng is the hundreds of **Buddhist sculptures** carved into its limestone rocks. These date from between the tenth and fourteenth centuries and are the most important examples of their type to be found south of the Yangzi. Today the little Buddhas and other figurines are dotted about everywhere, moss-covered and laughing among the foliage. It's possible to follow trails right up to the top of the hill to escape the tourist hubbub.

Deep inside the Feilai Feng tourist area you'll eventually arrive at **Lingyin Temple** (Temple of the Soul's Retreat; daily 7.30am–4.30pm; ¥20), one of the biggest temple complexes in China. Founded in 326 AD by Hui Li, who is buried nearby, it was the largest and most important monastery in Hangzhou and once had three thousand monks, nine towers, eighteen pavilions and 75 halls and rooms. Today it is an attractive working temple with daily services, usually in the early morning or after 3pm.

The temple was so badly riddled with woodworm that in the 1940s the main crossbeams collapsed onto the statues; the eighteen-metre-high Tang statue of Sakyamuni is a replica, carved in 1956 from 24 pieces of camphorwood. Elsewhere in the temple, the old frequently brushes against the new – the **Hall of the Heavenly King** contains four large and highly painted Guardians of the Four Directions made in the 1930s, while the Guardian of the Buddhist Law and Order, who shields the Maitreya, was carved from a single piece of wood eight hundred years ago.

South of the lake

Down in the southwestern quarter of the city, in the direction of the village of Longjing, the dominant theme is **tea production**: gleaming green tea bushes sweep up and down the land, and old ladies pester tourists into buying fresh tea leaves. Fittingly, this is where you'll find the **Tea Museum** (daily 8am–5pm; free), a smart place with lots of captions in English, covering themes such as the history of tea and the etiquette of tea drinking. There are displays on different varieties of tea, cultivation techniques, the development of special teaware, and finally, reconstructed tearooms in various ethnic styles, such as Tibetan and Yunnanese. Bus #27 from Pinghai Lu in the town centre comes here; get off more or less opposite the former *Zhejiang Hotel*, then head southwest to the museum along a small lane just to the north of, and parallel to, the main road.

A couple of kilometres further southwest, the village of **Longjing** ("Dragon Well"), with tea terraces rising on all sides behind the houses, is famous as the origin of **Longjing Tea**, perhaps the finest variety of green tea produced in China. Depending on the season, a stroll around here affords glimpses of leaves in different stages of processing – being cut, sorted or dried. You'll be hassled to sit at an overpriced teahouse or to buy leaves when you get off the bus – have a good look around first, as there is a very complex grading system and a huge range in quality and price. The **Dragon Well** itself is at the end of the village, a group of buildings around a spring, done up in a rather touristy fashion. Bus #27 runs to Longjing from the northwestern lakeshore, near Yuefei Mu.

East of Longjing and south of Xi Hu, the area extending down to the Qiantang River is full of trees and gentle slopes. Of all the parks in this part of the city, perhaps the most attractive is the **Hupaomeng Quan** (Tiger Running Dream Spring; daily 8am–5pm; ¥15). The spring here – according to legend, originally found by a ninth-century Zen Buddhist monk with the help of two tigers – is said to produce the purest water around, which serious connoisseurs use for brewing the best Longjing teas. For centuries, this has been a popular site for hermits to settle; now largely forested, it is dotted with teahouses, shrines, waterfalls and pagodas. Bus #504 and tourist bus #5 both run to Hupaomeng Quan from the city centre, down the eastern shore of the lake, while tourist bus #3 passes close by on the way down from Longjing.

Eating and drinking

As a busy resort for local tourists, Hangzhou has plenty of good **places to eat**. The wedge-shaped neighbourhood between Hubin Lu and Yan'an Lu is home to a number of Chinese restaurants and fast-food joints. Touristy Jiefang Lu is a good spot to make for, with a variety of Chinese restaurants and snacks.

Many Chinese tourists make it a point to visit one of the famous **historical restaurants** in town: both *Louwailou* (Tower Beyond Tower) and *Tianwaitian* (Sky Beyond Sky) serve local specialities at reasonable prices, while a third, *Shanwaishan* (Mountain Beyond Mountain), has garnered a bad reputation over the years. All three restaurants were named after a line in Southern Song poet Lin Hejin's most famous poem: "Mountain beyond mountain and tower beyond tower/Could song and dance by West Lake be ended anyhow?"

For **nightlife**, try the smattering of clubs across from the Chinese Art Institute, none of which stands out from the pack.

Restaurants and cafés

Kuiyuan Guan Jiefang Lu, just west of Zhongshan Zhong Lu (go through the entrance with Chinese lanterns hanging outside, and it's on the left, upstairs). Specializes in more than 40 noodle dishes for all tastes, from the mundane (beef noodle soup) to the acquired (pig intestines and kidneys), and also offers a range of local seafood delicacies. If you stay away from the exotica and you'll find it reasonably priced around ¥20 a bowl.

Louwailou Gu Shan Island. The best-known restaurant in Hangzhou, whose specialities include *dongpo* pork, fish-shred soup and beggar's chicken (a whole chicken cooked inside a ball of mud, which is broken and removed at

your table). Lu Xun and Zhou Enlai, among others, have dined here. Standard dishes cost ¥30–45.

Tianwaitian At the gate to Feilai Feng. Chinese tourists flock here to sample the fresh seafood, supposedly caught from Xi Hu, though it's not as good as *Louwailou*. Dishes are ¥40–55 each.

Zhiweiguan Renhe Lu, half a block east of the lake. In a very urbane atmosphere, with piped Western classical music, you can enjoy assorted *dianxin* by the plate for around ¥20, including *xiao long bao* (small, fine stuffed dumplings) and *mao erduo* (fried, crunchy stuffed dumplings). The *huntun tang* (wonton soup) and *jiu miao* (fried chives) are also good.

Moganshan

The hill station of **MOGANSHAN**, 60km north of Huangzhou, was popular with the fast foreign set before the war and has recently resumed its former role as a resort to escape Shanghai's stifling summer heat. The old stone villas and po-faced communist-style sanatoriums are being restored and turned into guesthouses, bars and cafés; it's lovely, actually, but get here sooner rather than later, before it all gets overdeveloped. There's nothing much to do except for wander around the village – which with its cobbles and neat gardens manages to look almost English – enjoy the views and head out into the local bamboo woods.

Buses from Hangzhou's North bus station take an hour and a half to San Qiao, just before the little town of Wukang; a taxi the rest of the way will cost around ¥30. If you're coming from Shanghai, change in Hangzhou. There's a charge of ¥80 for entering the resort. Note that there are no **ATMs** in town, so arrive with enough money to last your stay.

Accommodation options include a surfeit of faded and functional Chinese-style, two-star hotels; try the *Songliang Shanzhuang*, at the south end of Yinshan Jie, the main road (☎0572/803381; ②), or the higher *Baiyun Hotel* (☎0572/8033382, ⓦwww.mogan-mountain.com; ②). The *Du Yuesheng Villa*, once owned by the gangster himself (see p.179), is now operated by the Radisson; exteriors are period and rather lovely, but the rooms themselves are ordinary, so it feels a little overpriced (☎0572/3033601; ②).

Yinshan Jie is lined with **restaurants** offering local specialities such as wild game, but the best place to eat is *Moganshan Lodge* (☎0572/8033011), a bar and restaurant in a wing of the *Songliang Shanzhuang*. The food, all Western staples, is excellent – though you have to order in advance so that they can buy supplies – and the helpful foreign owners will point you in the right direction for walks. It's also the most conducive place for a drink in the evening.

Putuo Shan

An overnight boat ride south of Shanghai takes you to the island of **Putuo Shan**, just twelve square kilometres in area and divided by a narrow channel from the much larger Zhoushan Island. The island has no honking cars or department stores, only vistas of blue sea, sandy beaches and lush green hills dotted with ancient monasteries, making it an ideal place to escape the noise, traffic and dirt of Shanghai, with endless opportunities for walking. Although bursts of local tourists at weekends and in summer threaten the serenity, you should still be able to avoid the hordes if you schedule your visit on a weekday or in the off season; the best times to come are April, May, September and October.

Arrival, information and orientation

The island is long and thin, with the **ferry jetty**, where all visitors arrive, in the far south; a ¥120 entry fee is payable when you set foot on dry land. About 1km north from here is the main "town", a tiny collection of hotels, shops and restaurants, with a central square faced to the north by Puji Temple. There are only a few roads, travelled by a handful of **minibuses** (¥4–6) which connect the port with Puji Temple and other sights farther north.

Boats to Putuo Shan from Shanghai run from Wusong Dock at 251 Songbao Lu (☏021/56575500), in the far south of town. **Overnight services** leave at 8pm daily and arrive at Putou Shan at 7am. The cheapest tickets (¥100) are for the large common room, but you're better off in second class: ¥158 gets you a berth in a four-bunk cabin with a washbasin; travelling first class gets you a two-bed cabin (¥350) but doesn't offer much more comfort. Bring some food as the meals on board aren't up to much.

There is also a **fast service** (4hr; ¥221), which leaves from a dock more than an hour south of the city; your ticket includes the bus journey there from a pick-up point at 1588 Waima Lu, just south of the Bund. Boats leave at 9.30am, 10am and 3.30pm. Tickets for all boats can be bought in advance from Shanghai CITS or from the dingy booking office at 59 Jinling Dong Lu.

Leaving Putuo Shan, there are several fast ferries back to Shanghai in the morning, plus one or two slow overnight departures which leave at 4.30pm (¥80–350, depending on class). You can buy tickets for outbound boats from any of the island's hotels or at the jetty office (daily 6am–6pm). The slow service is worth considering: chugging back into the city just after sunrise, it provides a memorable view of the awakening metropolis.

Upon arrival, you can reach the town by following either the road heading west or the one east from the jetty, or by picking up a bus from the car park just east of the arrival gate. The westerly route is slightly shorter and takes you past most of the modern buildings and facilities on the island, including the **Bank of China** (daily 8–11am & 1–4.30pm) and the **CITS** office. A little farther north is the **post office**.

Accommodation and eating

There are several decent **hotels** on Putuo Shan, including a number of converted monasteries, but be warned that in the peak summer months, and especially during the weekend stampede out of Shanghai, you may face a trek around town to find an empty room, not to mention very expensive rates. The price codes in the reviews represent peak season, outside of which rates fall sharply. Another option is to stay in a **private house**, standard practice for Chinese tourists on Putuo Shan though technically illegal for foreigners, so use your discretion. It's not hard to find people with houses to let – they congregate at the jetty pier, and you should be able to bargain them down to around ¥100–150 per person, depending on the season.

Eating is not likely to be the highlight of your trip to Putuo Shan – most food must be brought in from the mainland, and is therefore expensive. Dingy-looking eating houses can be found along the lane running northeast away from Puji Temple and on the road between the jetty departure and arrival points. These places specialize in **seafood** ranging from fish to molluscs and eel, though they also do standard dishes and noodles. Otherwise, there are vegetarian restaurants at all the main temples and an upscale vegetarian eaterie in the *Putuoshan Hotel*.

Hotels

Fu Quan Not far north of the jetty, on the eastern route into town. ☏0580/6092069. The sign is only in Chinese and easy to miss. Basic but agreeable rooms. ❹

Putuoshan Hotel On the main west road from the jetty to the town ☏0580/6092828, ℱ6091818. Very easy to spot, thanks to its spacious grounds and opulent design, this

Putuo Shan	普陀山	pǔtuóshān
Fu Quan	福泉山庄	fúquán shānzhuāng
Putuoshan Hotel	普陀山大酒店	pǔtuóshān dàjiǔdiàn
Putuo Shanzhuang	普陀山庄宾馆	pǔtuóshānzhuāng
Ronglai Yuan Guesthouse	融来院	rónglái yuàn
Sanshengtang	三圣堂饭店	sānshèngtáng fàndiàn
Puji Temple	普济寺	pǔjì sì
Duabao Pagoda	多宝塔	duōbǎo tǎ
Qianbu Sha	千步沙	qiānbù shā
Baibu Sha	百步沙	bǎibù shā
Chaoyang Dong	潮阳洞	cháoyáng dòng
Chaoyin Dong	潮音洞	cháoyīn dòng
Zizhu Temple	紫竹寺	zǐzhú sì
Guanyintiao	观音跳	guānyīn tiào
Huiji Temple	慧济寺	huìjì sì
Foding Shan	佛顶山	fódǐng shān
Fayu Temple	法雨寺	fǎyǔ sì

is the best hotel on the island, with prices to match. Furniture in the classier rooms and the dining areas is in traditional Chinese style. ⑤

Putuo Shanzhuang Just south of the *Sanshengtang* ☎0580/6091530, ⑰6091228. A beautiful, relatively isolated and extremely comfortable option set on the wooded hillside opposite Puji Temple. ⑥

Ronglai Yuan Guesthouse In the middle of town ☎0580/6091262, ⑰6091235. Walk past Puji Temple to its eastern end, through an arch, then turn left (north) up the first alley. The alley first bends slightly to the right, then seriously to the left (the hotel is actually directly behind Puji Si). Foreigners aren't allowed to stay in the main building, a converted ancient monastery overhung by giant trees, but can use the small annexe across the street, where the rooms are comfortable enough, if slightly cramped. The genteel owner speaks no English but is always helpful. ⑥

Sanshengtang ☎0580/6091277, ⑰6091140. On the eastern route from the jetty to town, this is just a couple of minutes due south of the centre along a small path. Though the rooms themselves are unremarkable, this is quite an attractive place, styled like a temple. Note though that they have an irritating habit of attempting to surcharge foreigners by fifty percent. ④

The island

The main **temples** on the island are in extremely good condition, recently renovated, with yellow–ochre walls offsetting the deep green of the mature trees in their forecourts. They're squarely geared up for tourism, each charging around ¥8 to get in, though they are also frequented by plenty of pilgrims too. As well as temples, two **caves** are firmly on the pilgrim circuit and there are even a couple of **beaches**.

The two temples in the northern half of the island are conveniently connected to the southern half by minibuses, which depart from the bus stop just southeast of the central square in the town; there are minibuses between the temples as well. The best way to get around, however, is to walk; you can do the two halves of the island in two days.

The south of the island

The town itself is unremarkable, but it does hold one of the island's star attractions, the **Puji Temple** (daily 6am–9pm; ¥5), which was built in 1080 and enlarged by successive dynasties. Standing among magnificent camphor trees, it boasts a bridge lined with statues and an elegantly tall pagoda with an enormous iron bell.

South of here and just to the east of the square pond you'll find the town's other major religious structure, the five-storey **Duobao Pagoda**. It was built in 1334 using stones brought over from Tai Hu in Jiangsu province, it has Buddhist inscriptions on all four sides.

A couple of minutes walk east from here, two decent beaches line the eastern shore, **Qianbu Sha** (Thousand Step Beach; ¥12 until 5pm, free afterwards) and **Baibu Sha** (Hundred Step Beach; ¥10 until 5pm, free afterwards). In summer, it's possible to bring a sleeping bag and camp out on either beach – be sure to bring all your supplies as there are no stores nearby. The beaches are separated by a small headland hiding the **Chaoyang Dong**, a little cave inside which there's a teahouse and a seating area overlooking the sea. At the southern end of Baibu Sha is a second cave, **Chaoyin Dong**, which is frequented by pilgrims who stand with their ears cupped; the din of crashing waves is thought to resemble the call of Buddha. The neighbouring **Zizhu Temple** (Purple Bamboo Temple; daily 6am–6pm; ¥5, which includes admission to Chaoyin Dong) is one of the less-touristed temples on the island and, for that reason alone, a good spot to observe the monks' daily rituals.

A kilometre south of here, lying on a headland on the island's southernmost tip, the **Guanyintiao** (Guanyin Leap; daily 7am–5pm; ¥6), a spectacular 33-metre-high bronze-plated statue of the Goddess of Mercy visible from much of the island, is Putuo's most prominent sight. In her left hand, Guanyin holds a steering wheel, symbolically protecting fishermen (not to mention travelling monks) from violent seastorms. The pavilion at the base of the statue houses a small exhibit of wooden murals recounting how Guanyin has aided Putuo villagers and fishermen over the years, while in a small room directly underneath the statue sit four hundred statues representing the various spiritual incarnations of the goddess. The view from the statue's base over the surrounding islands and fishing boats is sublime, especially on a clear day.

The north of the island

It's a bracing, three-kilometre uphill walk north from town to **Huiji Temple** (daily 6.30am–5pm; ¥5), on the summit of **Foding Shan**, though once there you'll be rewarded with great views of the sea and surrounding temples. You'll likely be walking alone, as pilgrims take the bus or the **cable car** from the minibus stand (daily 7am–5pm; ¥25 up, ¥15 down). The temple itself, built mainly between 1793 and 1851, occupies a beautiful site, surrounded by green tea plantations. Its halls stand in a flattened area between hoary trees and bamboo groves, the greens, reds, blues and gold of their enamelled tiles gleaming magnificently in the sunshine. There's also a vegetarian restaurant here.

Head down a marked path towards the island's third major temple, Fayu Temple (see p.172). Shortly after setting off, you'll see a secondary track branching away to the east. It takes you to the **Ancient Buddha Cave**, a delightfully secluded spot by a sandy beach on the northeastern coast of the island; give yourself a couple of hours to get there and back. Back on the main path, the steep steps bring you to the **Xiangyun Pavilion**, where you can rest and drink tea with the friendly monks.

A twenty-minute walk south from here will bring you to the **Fayu Temple** (daily 6.30am–5.30pm; ¥5), another superb collection of over two hundred halls amid huge trees, built up in levels against the slope during the Ming. With the mountain behind and the sea just in front, it's a delightful place to sit in peaceful contemplation. The Daxiong Hall has been brilliantly restored, while the Dayuan Hall has a unique beamless arched roof and a dome, around the inside of which squirm nine carved wooden dragons. This hall is said to have been moved here from Nanjing by Emperor Kangxi in 1689. Its great **statue of Guanyin**, flanked by monks and nuns, is the focal point of the goddess's birthday celebrations in early April, when thousands of pilgrims and sightseers crowd onto the island for chanting and ceremonies which last all evening.

Contexts

Contexts

A short history of Shanghai

Shanghai's history as a metropolis is distinct from that of the nation as a whole, as the machinations of thousands of years of imperial dynasties have not much influenced its destiny. In fact, it's a young city (for China) whose story is dominated by trade rather than politics, by international forces as much as domestic ones.

The port on the Yangzi

Contrary to Western interpretations, Shanghai's history did not begin with the founding of the foreign concessions. Located at the head of the **Yangzi River**, Shanghai grew from a fishing village (Shanghai simply means "on the sea") into a major commercial port during the Song dynasty. By the time of the Qing dynasty, huge **mercantile guilds**, dealing in lucrative local products – silk, cotton, and tea – often organized by trade and bearing superficial resemblance to their Dutch counterparts, had established economic and, to some extent, political control of the city. The Yangzi basin reaches half of China, and this formidable route to the interior was bolstered by almost a million kilometres of **canals** – vital trade routes in a country with very few roads. It was this unprecedented accessibility, noted by its first foreign visitor, Hugh Lindsay of the British East India Company, that was to prove so alluring to the foreign powers, and set the city off down its unique, tempestuous path. The story of **foreign intervention** in China began in morally murky waters (and, some would say, remained there): it started with a dispute over drugs and money.

Ocean barbarians

The **Qing dynasty**, established in 1644, followed the pattern of China's long and repetitive history; a rebellion, in this case by the Manchus from the north, overthrew the emperor and established a new dynasty which ran, as usual, on a feudal, Confucian social model – everyone from peasant to emperor knew their place in a rigid hierarchy. By the eighteenth century the Qing had lost their early vigour and grown conservative and decadent, the out-of-touch royal court embroiled in intrigue. As with all previous dynasties, they were little troubled by outsiders. For thousands of years, China had remained alone and aloof, isolated from the rest of the world; the only foreigners in the Chinese experience were nomadic tribesmen at the fringes of the empire – savages to be treated with disdain.

So when the **British East India Company** arrived in the early seventeenth century the Manchu officials were not much interested. The "ocean barbarians" began trading in Canton in the far south, China's only open port – they sold English textiles to India, took Indian cotton to China, and bought Chinese tea, porcelain and silk. The Chinese wanted no British manufacturing in return, only silver.

Even this much trade was begrudged by the Qing, whose policies ensured that the East India Company always bought more than it sold, with the result that the British exchequer reluctantly made up the balance with hard currency. The Company's infamous solution to this trade imbalance was to get the country hooked. **Opium** grown in India was exported to China, and proved a great success; in 1760 more than a thousand chests, each weighing more than a hundred pounds, were imported; fifty years later, this had grown to more than forty thousand. Stupefied addicts numbered more than two million and now the trade imbalance was firmly in the other direction.

In 1839, fearing a crippled economy, Emperor Daoguang abruptly declared the trade illegal and British merchants were forced to watch their opium cargo hurled overboard their ships. It was a typically ill-judged response. The British countered by **seizing Hong Kong** (then a minor outpost) and sending an expeditionary force to attack Canton, triggering the **First Opium War**. Chinese tactics such as sending monkeys with fireworks to set enemy ships alight were inventive but hardly effective; the superior technology of the British meant that the result was never in doubt.

In 1842 the defeated Manchu were forced to sign the unequal **Treaty of Nanjing**, which ceded Hong Kong to the British and opened Shanghai, then a small fortified town, as well as four other ports (Fuzhou, Xiamen, Guangzhou and Ningbo), to foreign trade. This, the first of many unequal treaties, marks the beginning of modern Chinese history, on a sour note of national humiliation.

The concession era

Of the new open ports, Shanghai was the most ideally situated – at the midpoint of China's coast, close to established trading routes between the West and Japan, and offering a route straight into the heart of China. The town was soon booming, and other nations scrambled to get a foothold in the alluring new market that the British had prised open. France, Belgium, Norway and Russia all began to make their own demands on the Qing administration, but it was the **Americans** who proved most influential. An envoy sent by President Tyler "to save the Chinese from being an exclusive monopoly of England" managed, in the 1844 Treaty of Wangxia, to hack out the principle that was to prove vital to Shanghai's development, the idea of "**extra-territoriality**"; foreigners resident in the treaty ports would be subject to the laws of their own nation rather than those of China. This guaranteed the safety and property of traders – and of course, set them completely apart from the local population.

Shanghai was divided up between trading powers, with each claiming a riverside frontage: the British along the Bund and the area to the north of the Chinese city, the **French** in an area to the southwest, centred on the site of a cathedral a French missionary had founded two centuries earlier. Later the Americans, in 1863, came to tack their own areas onto the British Concession, which expanded into the so-called **International Settlement**. Each section was a mini state, with its own police force, and a municipal council voted in by prominent traders. The borders of these states had not been fixed, so the foreigners used every excuse to extend them. It was colonialism in all but name; but whereas in other colonial territories, such as British India, a degree of mixing occurred between peoples, in Shanghai the Chinese and the foreigners lived in isolation from each other, in a state of mutual contempt.

The Huangpu riverfront swelled as the **great trading houses** such as Jardine Matheson and Swire from Hong Kong rushed to open godowns (warehouses) and offices. Silk, tea and opium (still technically illegal) remained important but insurance and banking proved lucrative new moneymakers. Behind the river, homesick merchants built mansions in imitation of the ones they had left behind in Europe, with large gardens. By 1853 there were several hundred foreign ships making regular trips into the Chinese interior, and almost a thousand resident foreigners, most of them British. Still, even the largest firms had only a dozen or so foreign staff. Shanghai might have continued to grow incrementally for decades; it would take a catastrophic civil war to kick the city's development into a much higher gear.

The Taiping Rebellion and beyond

China's humiliation by foreigners, and the corruption and decadence of her ineffectual overlords, caused instability in Shanghai's giant, mysterious hinterland. Between 1740 and 1840 the Chinese population tripled, and vast numbers of peasantry became poverty-stricken and rootless. Arbitrary taxes and lawlessness compounded their plight. Resentment crystallized around the unlikely figure of charismatic cult leader **Hong Xiuquan**, a failed scholar who declared himself the younger brother of Jesus Christ. His egalitarian philosophy proved wildly popular, and he attracted millions of followers. Declaring their intention to build a Taiping Tianguo, or "Heavenly Kingdom of Great Peace", with Hong as its absolute ruler, these **Taipings** stormed across southern China, capturing Nanjing in 1854 and making it their capital. They abolished slavery, redistributed the land and replaced Confucianism with a heretical form of Christianity.

A sister organization, the **Small Sword Society**, took over the Chinese quarter at the centre of Shanghai. Alarmed by these fanatical revolutionaries, the city's foreign residents joined forces with the armies of the Qing against them. The fighting devastated the countryside around Shanghai, and more than twenty million are thought to have died (more than a hundred million if natural disasters and famine are added) – making this obscure rebellion, little known in the West, the world's bloodiest ever civil war. Hong retreated into the sensual distractions of his harem, and the drive of the Taiping faltered; the final blows were administered with the help of foreign mercenaries in 1865.

For Shanghai, the crisis proved an opportunity. Chinese **refugees** from the conflict swarmed, for safety, into the city's foreign concessions. Previously, foreigners had banned Chinese from living in their exclusive enclaves, but plenty of the new arrivals had gold enough to make them overcome any scruples. Now Shanghai's greatest asset became land, as the average price of an acre in the foreign concessions shot up from £70 to more than £10,000 in less than a decade. The merchants demolished their spacious villas, sold their grounds, and annexed local farms in a feverish **real-estate boom**. The Chinese population exploded from fewer than a thousand souls in 1850 to more than 70,000 by 1870.

A pattern was set: as Manchu misrule continued and warlords blighted millions of lives, Shanghai profited by offering haven under the racist but at least orderly rule of the foreigners. This is when the city began to take its modern shape, with Nanjing Lu emerging as the busiest shopping street, and the French

Concession providing the most desirable residences. The Chinese were not allowed any say in running the city, though their taxes paid for improvements such as gas lighting, electricity, tarmacked roads and, in 1905, a tramline.

The seeds of revolution

It was the arrival of a new foreign power, who played by different rules to the old colonial nations, that caused Shanghai's next spurt of growth. For the **Japanese**, dealings with the West had proved much more positive than for the Chinese and by the mid-nineteenth century Japan had successfully transformed itself into a modern industrial nation. Following their defeat of the Qing in a conflict over the vassal state of Korea in 1895, the Japanese copied the Western tactic of extracting unequal treaties, and won for themselves the right to start **manufacturing** in Shanghai. It was a clever move; coal and electricity were cheap, and, with the city stuffed with desperate refugees, labour even cheaper. The Western powers followed, factories replaced the godowns along the Huangpu and the city grew from a trading port to an industrial powerhouse.

Squalid living conditions, outbreaks of unemployment and glaring abuses of Chinese labour by foreign investors made the city a natural breeding ground for **revolutionary ferment**. But just as influential was first-hand experience of foreign technology, ideologies and administration. To Shanghai's urban intellectuals, especially those who had been educated abroad, it became clear that the old imperial order had to be overthrown. Just as clearly, the foreigner had to be expelled – from now on, far being aloof from China's political life, the city was about to be thrown into the centre of it.

By the early twentieth century, mass **civil disorder** had broken out across the country. Attempts to reform the administration had been quashed by the conservative Dowager Empress Cixi, and her death in 1908 further destabilized the country. In 1911, the dynasty finally collapsed, in large part due to the influence of the Shanghai intellectual, **Sun Yatsen**, leader of the Nationalists and a champion of Chinese self-determination. Steeped in international culture, this ex-medical student was a fine product of the city's intellectual foment. Yet against men such as this, who understood the need to modernize, warlords maintained China's old ideological model, and fought to establish a new dynasty. No one succeeded, and with the absence of central government, chaos reigned.

In 1921, the **Chinese Communist Party** was founded in Shanghai. Four years later, in protest at the indiscriminate killing of protesting students by settlement police, the CCP organized China's first strike. Two hundred thousand workers downed tools; some even marched under the slogan "No taxation without representation!" Much to the chagrin of Shanghai's foreign overlords, the Chinese were beginning to develop political consciousness.

Nationalists versus Communists

The most powerful of the new groups, however, was the **Nationalist Party**, now led by the wily **Chiang Kaishek**. In 1927 he attempted to unite the country in an alliance with the Communists. Curfews and labour unrest froze the city as the Nationalists and Communists fought Shanghai's own warlords. Having won that battle, Chiang promptly turned on his allies and launched a surprise attack against the Communists, with the help of the city's ruthless criminal mastermind, **Du Yuesheng**. In what came to be known as the White Terror, Du's hoods, dressed in Nationalist uniforms, rampaged across the city, killing anyone with any association with communism; at least twelve thousand died, most of them executed in cold blood.

But even during the chaos, the party continued, and the foreign concessions remained an enclave of privilege. Foreign Shanghai was at its decadent height in the 1920s and 1930s, and it was during this age of inequality and decadence that Shanghai got its reputation as the "**Paris of the East**" or, less politely, "whore of the Orient". A visiting missionary sniffed, "if God allows Shanghai to endure, he owes Sodom and Gomorrah an apology." For foreigners, no visa or passport was needed and every new arrival, it was said, had something to hide. White Russian émigres (see p.76) filled the chorus lines at the Paramount and the Majestic, and their unluckier sisters joined the Chinese girls at the only institutions more popular than the cabaret, the brothels. In certain areas of the city the visitor was grabbed by girls in *qipaos* with, an American visitor observed, "the Chinese equivalent of the rugby tackle". The traps that a destitute woman could fall in to were many, yet only in Shanghai could a Chinese girl receive an education, reject an arranged marriage, or carve out a career. Film stars such as Ruan Lingyu, China's Garbo, personified the new independent spirit, in both her roles and her life – though the latter ended in tragedy, with her suicide.

Inevitably, the show could not last. By 1928 Chiang Kaishek had defeated enough warlords to form a tentative **National Government**, with its capital in Nanjing. Now he courted the Western powers and, partly to prove that he was a modernizer, converted to Christianity and married Song Meiling, whose father had been a close ally of Sun Yatsen. Though he was explicit about his desire to rid China of the foreigners, the powers in Shanghai backed him as the man to control the country. They were forced to renege some of the more outrageous racist policies, such as the ruling that kept the Chinese out of Shanghai's parks; more importantly, Chinese were allowed to vote in municipal elections.

But Chiang had not rooted out all of Shanghai's Communists; by 1931 they had regrouped, and a messy civil war began. To compound the nation's woes, the same year the **Japanese snatched Manchuria** (China's northeastern province, present-day Dongbei) and Chiang found himself fighting two conflicts. Believing the Communists to be the more serious threat, he fled west with his government to avoid a showdown that he feared losing. The Japanese now struck against the interior, and in 1937 succeeded in occupying the valley of the Yangzi River, thus cutting off river trade, and depriving Shanghai of its source of wealth. Hobbled by the depression at home, weary of fighting losing battles against China's resurgent nationalism, the Western powers lost their appetite for interference in the country's chaotic affairs, and Shanghai was left to decline. By the time the Japanese marched in 1941, the life had already drained from the metropolis.

Shanghai under the Communists

It took nearly a decade for China to become once more united, this time under the Communist Party, led by **Mao Zedong**. Communism might have come from abroad, but the manner of its triumph and rule – shrewd charismatic leader leads a peasants' revolt, then becomes an all-powerful despot – were a rerun of dynastic models. They might have been born there, but the Communists distrusted Shanghai; associating it with imperialism, squalor and bourgeois individualism, they deliberately ran the city down. The worst slums were replaced by apartments, the gangsters and prostitutes were taken away for "re-education", and foreign capital was ruthlessly taxed if not confiscated outright (although Chiang Kaishek did manage to spirit away the gold reserves of the Bank of China to Taiwan, leaving the city broke). For 35 years Western influences were forcibly suppressed.

Perhaps eager to please its new bosses, the city became a centre of radicalism, and Mao, stifled by Beijing bureaucracy, launched his **Cultural Revolution** here in 1966 – officially a campaign to rid China of its counter-revolutionaries, but really a way to regain control of the party after a string of economic failures. Fervent Red Guards even proclaimed a Shanghai Workers' Commune, modelled on the Paris Commune, but the whole affair quickly descended into wanton destruction and petty vindictiveness. After Mao's death in 1976, Shanghai was the last stronghold of hardcore Maoists, the Gang of Four, in their struggle for the succession, though their planned coup never materialized.

The Shanghainese never lost their ability to make waves for themselves; their chance came when following the death of Mao – and the failure of his experiment – China's communists became **one-party capitalists**. Its economic renaissance dates from 1990 when Shanghai became an autonomous municipality and the paddy fields of Pudong were designated a "Special Economic Zone". The pragmatic leader **Deng Xiaoping** declared an end to the destructiveness of ideological politicking by declaring "it doesn't matter if the cat is black or white, as long as it catches mice" – though the dictum of his that Shanghai has really taken to heart is "to get rich is glorious".

Shanghai today

Having opened for business, **Shanghai's growth** has never dipped below ten percent a year. The city has been torn up and built anew (locals quip that its new mascot is the crane), and now has more skyscrapers than New York. In fifteen years the population has almost doubled to 21 million people. Per capita incomes have risen from US$1000 per year in 1977 to US$6000 in 2007. Accounting for a third of China's foreign imports and attracting a quarter of all foreign investment into the country, the city is the white-hot core of the nation's astonishing boom.

As well as batteries of skyscrapers, there has been massive investment in **infrastructure projects**, most notably the Maglev train and the new, US$2 billion Pudong International Airport. Prestige ventures such as the Oriental Arts Centre have joined high-profile projects such as the World Financial Centre in expressing the city's breezy new swagger. With a booming new **stock exchange**, its next target is to become Asia's biggest financial centre. And just as Beijing is using the 2008 Olympics to focus on its development, Shanghai plans to garner global attention as host of the **World Expo** in 2010, which is expected to bring 70 million visitors to the city.

Of course there are problems. Shanghai's destiny is still controlled by outside forces, today in the form of the technocrats of Beijing. Despite huge gains economically, China is **politically stagnant**. Corruption is rife – more than US$15 billion is embezzled annually from state coffers. Dissident voices are easy to control while the economy remains healthy but any slowdown will surely bring an upswell of dissent. Until recently, many key modernizing officials in the central government were from the Shanghai area; Jiang Zemin and Zhu Rongji were both former mayors. But the arrest in 2007 of Shanghai's mayor Han Zheng and Party Secretary Chen Liangyu on corruption charges is an attempt by Beijing to rein in the influential "Shanghai clique", and bring a halt to its favouritism. China's grotesque **income disparities** have begun to worry the Party, which is attempting to funnel wealth away from the coast into the poor interior. Simply dealing with the products of success has become a considerable headache. The city is almost four times as dense as New York, and the flow of new arrivals is constant, many of then poor migrant workers from the countryside in search of work. Not unionized, they are often exploited, and – though the majority are family men who send their wages home – widely resented.

Shanghai's attitude to the **environment**, along with the rest of China, is that the clean up will start just as soon as the city gets rich; the result is that the air quality is poor, and the rivers filthy – five million tons of untreated sewage and industrial waste are deposited in the mouth of the Yangzi every day. Finally, the city is becoming a victim of its own success – all those skyscrapers are causing it to **sink** at the rate of about a centimetre a year, so the city government has had to cap new build.

Never mind; Shanghai is a natural survivor, and will surely cope with whatever new vicissitudes history throws – it's not as if it hasn't had practise. As the business heart of the world's newest superpower, it's booming in all directions, and the sheer buzz of a city on the make is intoxicating. It might not have had much of a past, but it's guaranteed a future.

Books

D
on't expect too much variety in English-language reading material
in Shanghai, and what is available will mostly be expensive imports.
You will, though, find, cheap editions of Chinese and Western classics
published in English by Chinese publishers. In the reviews below, titles
marked with a 🏃 are particularly recommended.

History

Robert Bickers *Empire Made Me: An Englishman Adrift in Shanghai* (Allen Lane, UK). This readable but carefully researched tale humanizes the concession era by focusing on one English policeman who is both toughened and corrupted by his experiences.

Nien Cheng *Life and Death in Shanghai* (Flamingo, UK; Penguin, US). One of many "my years of hell in the Cultural Revolution" books, but this one is better than most, with absorbing descriptions of life in Shanghai in the bad old days of dour ideological purity.

🏃 **Stella Dong** *Shanghai: The Rise and Fall of a Decadent City 1842–1949* (HarperCollins, UK; Harper Perennial, US). Excellent popular history, vivid and readable, though with rather an anti-foreigner bias. Plenty of salacious stories of opium, flower girls, squalor and debauchery.

Harriet Sargeant *Shanghai* (John Murray, UK). Academic and broad-ranging exploration of the city during the concession era, giving equal weight to both Chinese and foreign inhabitants, and particularly good on their interrelations.

Society and business

Radha Chadha and Paul Husband *The Cult of the Luxury Brand: Inside Asia's Love Affair with Luxury* (Nicholas Brealey). Why do so many Chinese girls spend two months' salary on a purse? This examination of the cult of branding will help you get to grips with the mores of modern Shanghai.

🏃 **Tim Clissold** *Mister China* (Constable & Robinson, UK). Engaging and eye-opening real-life horror story of how a Western venture capitalist lost US$400 million in China, thanks largely to fraud and malfeasance by his local partners. It's not Shanghai-specific but is a must for anyone thinking of tackling China's "eccentric" business environment.

James Farrer *Opening Up: Youth Sex Culture & Market Reform in Shanghai* (University of Chicago Press, US). An original and engrossing piece of social anthropology, based on interviews, that uses an examination of Shanghai's sexual revolution to make some telling points.

🏃 **Sun Tzu** *The Art of War.* "Lure them with the prospect of gain, then take them by confusion"; this classic treatise on military strategy is as relevant now as it was when it was written, nearly three thousand years ago. Short and to the point, it's full of pithy maxims that can be applied to many aspects of life, particularly business.

Pamela Yatsko *New Shanghai* (John Wiley). This journalistic introduction to the vagaries of the twenty-first-century's new metropolis is an expat essential, as it's breezy and well informed on both business and culture.

Fiction

J.G. Ballard *Empire of the Sun* (Flamingo, UK; Simon & Schuster, US). This, the best literary evocation of old Shanghai, is a compelling tale of how the gilded life of expat Shanghai collapsed into chaos with the onset of war, based on the author's own experience growing up in a Japanese internment camp. It was subsequently made into a pretty decent film by Steven Spielberg. Ballard's science fiction novels – some of the greatest of the twentieth century – are spookily relevant to the contemporary city; both *High Rise* and *Concrete Island* could be set in Pudong.

Tom Bradby *The Master of Rain* (Corgi, UK; Anchor, USA). A breathless if overlong novel of murder and betrayal in 1920s Shanghai.

Hergé *The Blue Lotus* (Mammoth, UK; Casterman Editions, US). One of the best Tintin yarns, a tale of drugs and derring-do set in Shanghai during the Sino–Japanese conflicts of the 1930s.

Kazuo Ishiguro *When We Were Orphans* (Faber & Faber, UK). Ishiguro is a great writer but this postmodern detective story set in Shanghai between the wars is a little too clever and doesn't quite deliver.

Mian Mian *Candy* (Back Bay, US). Salacious if meandering *roman-à-clef*, with plenty of sex, drugs and rock and roll, by one of China's modern *enfants terribles*. Though set in the 1980s and 90s, it already seems very dated.

Qiu Xiaolong *When Red is Black*; *Death of a Red Heroine*; *A Case of Two Cities*; *A Loyal Character Dancer* (Sceptre, UK; Soho Crime, US). Procedural detective fiction, featuring the poetry-loving Inspector Chen of the Shanghai PSB. Though sometimes Qiu seems more interested in examining Shanghai society and morals than in weaving a mystery, his stories of corrupt officials, sharp operators and compromised cops are the best evocations of the city and its people written in English.

Wei Hui *Shanghai Baby* (Constable & Robinson). Infamous chick-lit, banned in China for its louche moral tone, concerning a girl torn between her impotent Chinese boyfriend and married Western lover – though her true love is for designer labels. Self-absorbed, over-hyped, with rather more style than substance – very Shanghai.

Zhang Henshui *Shanghai Express* (University of Hawaii Press, US). A pulp novel from the 1930s, very popular in its day. Lots of incidental detail enlivens a melodramatic tale of seduction and betrayal set on a train ride from Beijing to Shanghai.

Food

Chen Ciliang *Shanghai Cool Restaurants* (teNeues, Germany). Lavishly illustrated, multilingual guide to froufrou food. Just don't be surprised if you blow your budget.

Lee Hwa Lin *Chinese Cuisine: Shanghai Style* (Wei-Chuan, US). Well-illustrated cookbook, one of a series, essential for anyone wishing to try their hand at Shanghai cuisine.

Two Hundred Best Restaurants (Shanghai Tatler). Is the lobster bisque a trifle outré? Where can I get my car valeted while I eat? These and other vital questions are considered in this definitive guide to upscale dining in the city.

Language

Language

Chinese

Though you'll certainly hear the local Shanghai dialect being spoken, **Mandarin Chinese**, derived from the language of officialdom in the Beijing area, is the city's primary tongue. It's been systematically promoted over the past hundred years as the official, unifying language of the Chinese people, much as modern French, for example, is based on the original Parisian dialect. It is known in mainland China as **putonghua**, "common language".

Chinese **grammar** is delightfully simple. There is no need to conjugate verbs, decline nouns or make adjectives agree – Chinese characters are immutable, so Chinese words simply cannot have different "endings". Instead, context and fairly rigid rules about word order are relied on to make those distinctions of time, number and gender that Indo-European languages are so concerned with. Instead of cumbersome tenses, the Chinese make use of words such as "yesterday" or "tomorrow" to indicate when things happen; instead of plural endings they simply state how many things there are. For English speakers, Chinese word order is very familiar, and you'll find that by simply stringing words together you'll be producing perfectly grammatical Chinese. Basic sentences follow the subject-verb-object format; adjectives, as well as all qualifying and describing phrases, precede nouns.

From the point of view of foreigners, the main thing that distinguishes Mandarin from familiar languages is that it's a **tonal language**. In order to pronounce a word correctly, it is necessary to know not only the sounds of its consonants and vowels but also its correct tone – though with the help of context, intelligent listeners should be able to work out what you are trying to say even if you don't get the tones quite right.

Pinyin

Back in the 1950s it was hoped eventually to replace Chinese characters with an alphabet of Roman letters, and to this end the **pinyin system**, a precise and exact means of representing all the sounds of Mandarin Chinese, was devised. It comprises all the Roman letters of the English alphabet (except "v"), with the four tones represented by diacritical marks, or accents, which appear above each syllable. The old aim of replacing Chinese characters with *pinyin* was abandoned long ago, but in the meantime *pinyin* has one very important function, that of helping foreigners pronounce Chinese words. However, there is the added complication that in *pinyin* the letters don't all have the sounds you would expect, and you'll need to spend an hour or two learning the correct sounds (see p.188).

You'll often see *pinyin* in Shanghai, on street signs and shop displays, but only well-educated locals know the system very well. The Chinese names in this book have been given both in characters and in *pinyin*; the pronunciation guide below is your first step to making yourself comprehensible. For more information, see the *Rough Guide Mandarin Chinese Phrasebook* or *Pocket Interpreter* (FLP, Beijing; it's available at Shanghai's Foreign Language Bookstore).

Pronunciation

There are four possible **tones** in Mandarin Chinese, and every syllable of every word is characterized by one of them, except for a few syllables, which are considered toneless. In English, to change the tone is to change the mood or the emphasis; in Chinese, to change the tone is to change the word itself. The tones are:

First or "high" *a e i o u*. In English this level tone is used when mimicking robotic or very boring, flat voices.

Second or "rising" *á é í ó ú*. Used in English when asking a question showing surprise, for example "*eh?*"

Third or "falling-rising" *ǎ ě ǐ ǒ ǔ*. Used in English when echoing someone's words with a measure of incredulity. For example, "John's dead." "*De-ad?!*"

Fourth or "falling" *à è ì ò ù*. Often used in English when counting in a brusque manner – "*One! Two! Three! Four!*".

Toneless A few syllables do not have a tone accent. These are pronounced without emphasis, such as in the English **u**pon.

Note that when two words with the third tone occur consecutively, the first word is pronounced as though it carries the second tone. Thus *nǐ* (meaning "you") and *hǎo* ("well, good"), when combined, are pronounced *ní hǎo*, meaning "how are you?"

Consonants

Most consonants, as written in *pinyin*, are pronounced in a similar way to their English equivalents, with the following exceptions:

c as in ha**ts**
g is hard as in **g**od (except when preceded by "n", when it sounds like sa**ng**)
q as in **ch**eese
x has no direct equivalent in English, but you can make the sound by sliding from an "s" to an "sh" sound and stopping midway between the two
z as in su**ds**
zh as in fu**dge**

Vowels and diphthongs

As in most languages, the vowel sounds are rather harder to quantify than the consonants. The examples below give a rough description of the sound of each vowel as written in *pinyin*.

a usually somewhere between f**a**r and m**a**n
ai as in **eye**
ao as in c**ow**
e usually as in f**ur**
ei as in g**ay**
en as in hyph**en**
eng as in s**ung**
er as in b**ar** with a pronounced "r"
i usually as in b**ee**, except in *zi, ci, si, ri, zhi, chi* and *shi*, when *i* is a short, clipped sound, like the American military "**sir**".
ia as in **ya**k
ian as in **yen**
ie as in **yeah**
o as in s**aw**
ou as in sh**ow**

ü as in the German **ü** (make an "ee" sound and glide slowly into an "oo"; at the mid-point between the two sounds you should hit the ü-sound.

u usually as in f**oo**l, though whenever *u* follows *j, q, x* or *y*, it is always pronounced **ü**

ua as in s**ua**ve

uai as in **why**

ue as though contracting "you" and "air" together, **you'air**

ui as in **way**

uo as in **wo**re

Useful words and phrases

When writing or saying the name of a Chinese person, the surname is given first; thus Mao Zedong's family name is Mao.

Basics

I	我	wǒ
You (singular)	你	nǐ
He	他	tā
She	她	tā
We	我们	wǒmen
You (plural)	你们	nǐmen
They	他们	tāmen
I want...	我要	wǒ yào...
No, I don't want...	我不要	wǒ bú yào…
Is it possible...?	可不可以...	kěbù kěyǐ...?
It is (not) possible	(不)可以...	(bù)kěyǐ
Is there any/Have you got any...?	你有没有...	yǒu méi yǒu...?
There is/I have	有...	yǒu…
There isn't/I haven't	没有...	méi yǒu
Please help me	请帮我忙..	qǐng bāng wǒ máng
Mr...	.....先生	xiānshēng
Mrs...	.....太太	tàitai
Miss...	.....小姐	xiǎojiě

Communicating

I don't speak Chinese	我不会说中文	wǒ búhuì shuō zhōngwén
Can you speak English?	你会说英语吗?	nǐ huì shuō yīngyǔ ma?
Can you get someone who speaks English?	请给我找一个会说英文的人?	qǐng gěi wǒ zhǎo yī gè huì shuō yīngyǔ de rén?
Please speak slowly	请说得慢一点	qǐng shuōde màn yīdiǎn
Please say that again	请再说一遍	qǐng zài shuō yī biàn
I understand	我听得懂	wǒ tīngdedǒng
I don't understand	我听不懂	wǒ tīngbùdǒng
I can't read Chinese characters	我看不懂汉字	wǒ kànbùdǒng hànzì
What does this mean?	这是什么意思?	zhè shì shénme yìsi?
How do you pronounce this character?	这个字怎么念?	zhègè zì zěnme niàn?

Greetings and basic courtesies

Hello/How do you do/ How are you?	你好	nǐ hǎo
I'm fine	我很好	wǒ hěn hǎo
Thank you	谢谢	xièxie
Don't mention it/ You're welcome	不客气	búkèqi
Sorry to bother you...	麻烦你	máfán nǐ
Sorry/I apologize	对不起	duìbùqǐ
It's not important/No problem	没关系	méi guānxi
Goodbye	再见	zài jiàn
Excuse me	对不起	dúi bù qǐ

Chitchat

What country are you from?	你是哪个国家的?	nǐ shì nǎge guójiā de?
Britain	英国	yīngguó
England	英国/英格兰	yīngguó/yīnggélán
Scotland	苏格兰	sūgélán
Wales	威尔士	wēi'ěrshì
Ireland	爱尔兰	ài'érlán
America	美国	měiguó
Canada	加拿大	jiānádà
Australia	澳大利亚	àodàlìyà
New Zealand	新西兰	xīnxīlán
South Africa	南非	nán fēi
China	中国	zhōngguó
Outside China	外国	wàiguó
What's your name?	你叫什么名字?	nǐ jiào shénme míngzi?
My name is...	我叫....	wǒ jiào...
Are you married?	你结婚了吗?	nǐ jiéhūn le ma?
I am (not) married	我(没有)结婚(了)	wǒ (méiyǒu) jiéhūn (le)
Have you got (children)?	你有没有孩子?	nǐ yǒu méiyǒu háizi?
Do you like...?	你喜不喜欢.....?	nǐ xǐ bù xǐhuān....?
I (don't) like...	我不喜欢....	wǒ (bù) xǐhuān...
What's your job?	你干什么工作?	nǐ gàn shénme gōngzuò?
I'm a foreign student	我是留学生	wǒ shì liúxuéshēng
I'm a teacher	我是老师	wǒ shì lǎoshī
I work in a company	我在一个公司工作	wǒ zài yígè gōngsī gōngzuò
I don't work	我不工作	wǒ bù gōngzuò
I'm retired	我退休了	wǒ tuìxiū le
Clean/dirty	干净/脏	gānjìng/zāng
Hot/cold	热/冷	rè/lěng
Fast/slow	快/慢	kuài/màn
Good/Bad	好/坏	hǎo/huài
Big/Small	大/小	dà/xiǎo
Pretty	漂亮	piàoliang
Interesting	有意思	yǒuyìsi

Numbers

Zero	零	líng
One	一	yī
Two	二/两	èr/liǎng*
Three	三	sān
Four	四	sì
Five	五	wǔ
Six	六	liù
Seven	七	qī
Eight	八	bā
Nine	九	jiǔ
Ten	十	shí
Eleven	十一	shíyi
Twelve	十二	shíèr
Twenty	二十	èrshí
Twenty-one	二十一	èrshíyi
One hundred	一百	yìbǎi
Two hundred	二百	èrbǎi
One thousand	一千	yìqiān
Ten thousand	一万	yìwàn
One hundred thousand	十万	shíwàn
One million	一百万	yìbǎiwàn
One hundred million	一亿	yìyì
One billion	十亿	shíyì

* 两/liǎng is used when enumerating, for example "two people" ír liǎng gè rén. 二 /èr is used when counting.

Time

Now	现在	xiànzài
Today	今天	jīntian
(In the) morning	早上	zǎoshàng
(In the) afternoon	下午	xiàwǔ
(In the) evening	晚上	wǎnshàng
Tomorrow	明天	míngtiān
The day after tomorrow	后天	hòutiān
Yesterday	昨天	zuótiān
Week/month/year	星期/月/年	xīngqī/yuè/nián
Next/last week/month/year	下/上 星期/月/年	xià/shàng xīngqī/yuè/nián
Monday	星期一	xīngqī yī
Tuesday	星期二	xīngqī èr
Wednesday	星期三	xīngqī sān
Thursday	星期四	xīngqī sì
Friday	星期五	xīngqī wǔ
Saturday	星期六	xīngqī liù
Sunday	星期天	xīngqī tiān
What's the time?	几点了?	jǐdiǎn le?

morning	早上	zǎoshàng
afternoon	中午	zhōngwǔ
10 o'clock	十点钟	shídiǎn zhōng
10.20	十点二十	shídiǎn èrshí
10.30	十点半	shídiǎn bàn

Travelling and getting around town

North	北	běi
South	南	nán
East	东	dōng
West	西	xī
Airport	机场	jīchǎng
Ferry dock	船码头	chuánmǎtóu
Left-luggage office	寄存处	jìcún chù
Ticket office	售票处	shòupiào chù
Ticket	票	piào
Can you sell me a ticket to...?	可不可以给我买到 .....的票?	kěbùkěyǐ gěi wǒ mǎi dào....de piào?
I want to go to...	我想到.....去	wǒ xiǎng dào … qù
I want to leave at (8 o'clock)	我想(八点钟)离开	wǒ xiǎng (bā diǎn zhōng) líkāi
When does it leave?	什么时候出发?	shénme shíhòu chūfā?
When does it arrive?	什么时候到?	shénme shíhòu dào?
How long does it take?	路上得多长时间?	lùshàng děi duōcháng shíjiān?
CITS	中国国际旅行社	zhōngguó guójì lǚxíngshè
Train	火车	huǒchē
(Main) Train station	主要火车站	(zhǔyào) huǒchēzhàn
Bus	公共汽车	gōnggòng qìchēzhàn
Bus station	汽车站	qìchēzhàn
Long-distance bus station	长途汽车站	chángtú qìchēzhàn
Express train/bus	特快车	tèkuài chē
Fast train/bus	快车	kuài chē
Ordinary train/bus	普通车	pǔtōng chē
Timetable	时间表	shíjiān biǎo
Map	地图	dìtú
Where is...?	.....在 哪里?	…zài nǎlǐ?
Go straight on	往前走	wǎng qián zǒu
Turn right	往右走	wǎng yòu zǒu
Turn left	往左拐	wǎng zuǒ guǎi
Taxi	出租车	chūzū chē
Please use the meter	请打开记价器	qǐng dǎkāi jìjiàqì
Underground/Subway station	地铁站	dìtiě zhàn
Bicycle	自行车	zìxíngchē
Can I borrow your bicycle?	能不能借你的自行车?	néng bùnéng jiè nǐ dēzìxíngchē?
Bus	公共汽车	gōnggòngqìchē
Which bus goes to...?	几路车到......去?	jǐ lù chē dào … qù?

Number (10) bus	（十）路车	(shí) lù chē
Does this bus go to...?	这车到……去吗?	zhè chē dào … qù ma?
When is the next bus?	下一班车几点开?	xià yì bān chē jǐ diǎn kāi?
The first bus	头班车	tóubān chē
The last bus	末班车	mòbān chē
Please tell me where to get off	请告诉我在哪里下车	qǐng gàosù wǒ zài nǎlǐ xià chē?
Museum	博物馆	bówùguǎn
Temple	寺庙	sìyuàn
Church	教堂	jiàotáng

Accommodation

Accommodation	住宿	zhùsù
Hotel (upmarket)	宾馆	bīnguǎn
Hotel (cheap)	招待所, 旅馆	zhāodàisuǒ, lüguǎn
Hostel	旅社	lüshè
Do you have a room available?	你们有房间吗?	nǐmen yǒu fángjiān ma?
Can I have a look at the room?	能不能看一下方向?	néng bù néng kàn yíxià fángjiān?
I want the cheapest bed you've got	我要你这里最便宜的床位	wǒ yào nǐ zhèlǐ zuì piányi de chuángwèi
Single room	单人房	dānrénfáng
Twin room	双人房	shuāngrénfáng
Double room with a big bed	双人房间带大床	shuāngrén fángjiān dài dàchuáng
Three-bed room	三人房	sānrénfáng
Dormitory	多人房	duōrénfáng
Suite	套房	tàofáng
(Large) bed	（大）床	(dà) chuáng
Passport	护照	hùzhào
Deposit	押金	yājīn
Key	钥匙	yàoshi
I want to change my room	我想换一个房间	wǒ xiǎng huàn yí gèfángjiān

Shopping, money and the police

How much is it?	这是多少钱?	zhè shì duōshǎo qián?
That's too expensive	太贵了	tài guì le
I haven't got any cash	我没有现金	wǒ méiyǒu xiànjīn
Have you got anything cheaper?	你没有便宜一点的?	yǒu méiyǒu piányi yìdiǎn de?
Do you accept credit cards?	可不可以用信用卡	kě bù kěyǐ yòng xìnyòngkǎ?
Department store	百货商店	bǎihuò shāngdiàn
Market	市场	shìchǎng
¥1 (RMB)	一块（人民币）	yí kuài (rénmínbì)
US$1	一块美金	yí kuài měijīn
£1	一个英镑	yí gè yīngbàng
Change money	换钱	huàn qián
Bank	银行	yínháng

Traveller's cheques	旅行支票	lǚxíngzhīpiào
ATM	提款机	tí kuǎn jī
PSB	公安局	gōng'ān jú

Communications

Post office	邮电局	yóudiànjú
Envelope	信封	xìnfēng
Stamp	邮票	yóupiào
Airmail	航空信	hángkōngxìn
Surface mail	平信	píngxìn
Telephone	电话	diànhuà
Mobile phone	手机	tourshǒu jī
SMS message	短信	duǎn xìn
International telephone call	国际电话	guójì diànhuà
Reverse charges/collect call	对方付钱电话	duìfāngfùqián diànhuà
Fax	传真	chuánzhēn
Telephone card	电话卡	diànhuàkǎ
I want to make a telephone call to (Britain)	我想给（英国）打电话	wǒ xiǎng gěi (yīngguó) dǎ diànhuà
I want to send an email to the US	我想发一个邮件到美国	wǒ xiǎng fāyīgè yóujiàn dào měiguó
Internet	网吧	wǎngbā
Email	电邮	diàn yóu

Health

Hospital	医院	yīyuàn
Pharmacy	药店	yàodiàn
Medicine	药	yào
Chinese medicine	中药	zhōngyào
Diarrhoea	腹泻	fùxiè
Vomit	呕吐	ǒutù
Fever	发烧	fāshāo
I'm ill	我生病了	wǒ shēngbìng le
I've got flu	我感冒了	wǒ gǎnmào le
I'm (not) allergic to...	我对……(不)过敏	wǒ duì … (bù) guòmin
Antibiotics	抗生素	kàngshēngsù
Condom	避孕套	bìyùntào
Tampons	卫生棉条	wèishēng miántiáo

Menu reader

General

Restaurant	餐厅	cān tīng
House speciality	拿手好菜	náshǒuhǎocài
How much is that?	多少钱?	duōshǎo qián?

I don't eat (meat)	我不吃(肉)	wǒ bù chī (ròu)
I would like...	我想要....	wǒ xiǎng yào...
Local dishes	地方菜	dìfang cài
Snacks	小吃	xiǎochī
Menu/set menu/English menu	菜单/套菜/英文菜单	càidan/tàocài/yīngwén càidan
Small portion	少量	shǎoliàng
Chopsticks	筷子	kuàizi
Knife and fork	刀叉	dā ochā
Spoon	勺子	sháozi
Waiter/waitress	服务员	fúwùyuán
Bill/cheque	买单	mǎidān
Cook these ingredients together	一快儿做	yíkuàir zuò
Not spicy/no chilli please	请不要辣椒	qing búyào làjiao
Only a little spice/chilli	一点辣椒	yìdian làjiao
50 grams	两	liǎng
250 grams	半斤	bànjīn
500 grams	斤	jīn
1 kilo	公斤	gōngjīn

Drinks

Beer	啤酒	píjiǔ
Coffee	咖啡	kā fēi
Milk	牛奶	niúnǎi
(Mineral) water	(矿泉)水	(kuàngquán) shuǐ
Wine	葡萄酒	pútáojiǔ
Yoghurt	酸奶	suānnǎi
Tea	茶	chá
Black tea	红茶	hóng chá
Green tea	绿茶	lü`chá
Jasmine tea	茉莉花茶	mòlìhuā chá

Staple foods

Aubergine	茄子	qiézi
Bamboo shoots	笋尖	sǔnjiān
Bean sprouts	豆芽	dòuyá
Beans	豆	dòu
Beef	牛肉	niúròu
Bitter gourd	葫芦	húlu
Black bean sauce	黑豆豉	heidòuchǐ
Bread	面包	miànbāo
Buns (filled)	包子	bāozi
Buns (plain)	馒头	mántou
Carrot	胡萝卜	húluóbo
Cashew nuts	腰果	yaoguǒ
Cauliflower	菜花	càihuā
Chicken	鸡	jī

Chilli	辣椒	làjiao
Chocolate	巧克力	qiǎokèlì
Coriander (leaves)	香菜	xiāngcài
Crab	蟹	xiè
Cucumber	黄瓜	huángguā
Duck	鸭	yā
Eel	鳝鱼	shànyú
Eggs (fried)	煎鸡蛋	jiānjīdàn
Fish	鱼	yú
Fried dough stick	油条	yóutiáo
Garlic	大蒜	dàsuàn
Ginger	姜	jiāng
Green pepper (capsicum)	青椒	qīngjiāo
Green vegetables	绿叶素菜	lǜ yè sùcài
Jiaozi (dumplings, steamed or boiled)	饺子	jiǎozi
Lamb	羊肉	yángròu
Lotus root	莲心	liánxīn
MSG	味精	wèijīng
Mushrooms	磨菇	mógū
Noodles	面条	miàntiáo
Omelette	摊鸡蛋	tānjīdàn
Onions	洋葱	yángcōng
Oyster sauce	蚝油	háoyóu
Pancake	摊饼	tā nbǐng
Peanut	花生	huā shēng
Pork	猪肉	zhūròu
Potato (stir-fried)	(炒)土豆	(chǎo) tǔdòu
Prawns	虾	xiā
Preserved egg	皮蛋	pídàn
Rice noodles	河粉	héfěn
Rice porridge (aka congee)	粥	zhōu
Rice, boiled	白饭	báifàn
Rice, fried	炒饭	chaofàn
Salt	盐	yán
Sesame oil	芝麻油	zhīma yóu
Shuijiao (dumplings in soup)	水铰	shuǐjiāo
Sichuan pepper	四川辣椒	sìchuān làjiao
Snake	蛇肉	shéròu
Soup	汤	tāng
Soy sauce	酱油	jiàngyóu
Squid	鱿鱼	yóuyú
Straw mushrooms	草菇	cǎogū
Sugar	糖	táng
Tofu	豆腐	dòufu
Tomato	蕃茄	fānqié

Vinegar	醋	cù
Water chestnuts	马蹄	mǎtí
White radish	白萝卜	báiluóbo
Wood ear fungus	木耳	mùěr
Yam	芋头	yùtóu

Cooking methods

Boiled	煮	zhǔ
Casseroled (see also "Claypot")	焙	bèi
Deep-fried	油煎	yóujiān
Fried	炒	chǎo
Poached	白煮	báizhǔ
Red-cooked (stewed in soy sauce)	红烧	hóngshāo
Roast	烤	kǎo
Steamed	蒸	zhēng
Stir-fried	清炒	qīngchǎo

Shanghai specialities

Beggars' chicken (baked)	叫花鸡	jiàohuā jī
Braised pig trotters	蹄膀	tí pang
Brine duck	盐水鸭	yánshuǐ yā
Crab soup	蟹肉汤	xièròu tāng
Crispy eel	香酥脆	xiang sū cuì
Crystal prawns	水晶虾仁	shuǐ jīng xiā rén
Dongpo pork casserole (steamed in wine)	东坡焙肉	dōngpō bèiròu
Drunken chicken (chicken cooked in wine)	醉鸡	zuì jī
Drunken prawns	醉虾	zuìxiā
Fish-shred soup	鱼丝汤	yúsī táng
Five-flower pork (steamed in lotus leaves)	五花肉	wǔhuā ròu
Fried crab with eggs	蟹肉鸡蛋	xièròu jidàn
Hairy crab	大闸蟹	dàzhá xiè
Pearl balls (rice grain-coated, steamed rissoles)	珍珠球	zhēnzhūqiú
Shaoxing chicken	绍兴鸡	shàoxīng jī
Shengjian dumplings	生煎包	shēnjiān bāo
Smoked fish	熏鱼	xún yú
Soup dumplings (steamed, containing jellied stock)	汤包	tāngbāo
Sour and hot soup with eel and chicken	龙凤酸辣汤	lóngfèng suānlà tāng
Steamed "lionshead" (mincemeat)	清蒸狮子头	qīngzhēng shīzitóu
Steamed sea bass	清蒸鲈鱼	qīngzhēnglúyú

Stuffed green peppers	馅青椒	xiànqīngjiāo
Sweet and sour spare ribs	糖醋小排	tángcù xiǎopái
West Lake fish (braised in a sour sauce)	西湖醋鱼	xīhúcùyú
White-cut beef (spiced and steamed)	白切牛肉	báiqie niúròu
Xiaolong dumplings	小笼包	xiǎolóng bāo
Yangzhou fried rice	杨州炒饭	yángzhōu chǎofàn

Everyday dishes

Braised duck with vegetables	炖鸭素菜	dùnya sùcài
Cabbage rolls (stuffed with meat or vegetables)	卷心菜	juǎnxīncài
Chicken and sweetcorn soup	玉米鸡丝汤	yùmǐ jīsī tāng
Chicken with bamboo shoots and babycorn	笋尖嫩玉米炒鸡片	sǔnjiān nènyùmi chaojipiàn
Chicken with cashew nuts	腰果鸡片	yāoguǒ jīpiàn
Claypot/sandpot (casserole)	沙锅	shāguō
Crispy aromatic duck	香酥鸭	xiāngsūyā
Egg flower soup with tomato	蕃茄蛋汤	fānqié dàn tāng
Egg fried rice	蛋炒饭	dànchaofàn
Fish ball soup with white radish	萝卜鱼蛋汤	luóbo yúdàn tāng
Fish casserole	焙鱼	bèiyú
Fried shredded pork with garlic and chilli	大蒜辣椒炒肉片	dàsuàn làjiao chaoròupiàn
Kebab	串肉	chuànròu
Noodle soup	汤面	tāngmiàn
Pork and mustard greens	芥末肉片	jièmò ròupiàn
Pork and water chestnut	马蹄猪肉	matí zhūròu
Prawn with garlic sauce	大蒜炒虾	dàsuàn chǎoxiā
Pulled noodles	拉面	lā miàn
Roast duck	烤鸭	kǎoyā
Scrambled egg with pork on rice	滑蛋猪肉饭	huádàn zhuròufàn
Sliced pork with yellow bean sauce	黄豆肉片	huángdòu ròupiàn
Squid with green pepper and black beans	豆豉青椒炒鱿鱼	dòuchǐ qīngjiāo chaoyóuyú
Steamed eel with black beans	豆豉蒸鳝	dòuchi zhēngshàn
Steamed rice packets wrapped in lotus leaves	荷叶蒸饭	héyè zhēngfàn
Stewed pork belly with vegetables	回锅肉	huíguoròu
Stir-fried chicken and bamboo shoots	笋尖炒鸡片	sǔnjiān chǎojipiàn
Stuffed bean-curd soup	豆腐汤	dòufutāng
Sweet bean paste pancakes	赤豆摊饼	chìdòu tānbǐng
White radish soup	白萝卜汤	báiluóbo tāng
Wonton soup	馄饨汤	húntun tāng

Vegetables and eggs

Aubergine with chilli and garlic sauce	大蒜辣椒炒茄子	dàsuàn làjiao chǎoqiézi
Aubergine with sesame sauce	拌茄子片	bànqiézipiàn
Bean curd and spinach soup	菠菜豆腐汤	bocài dòufu tāng
Bean-curd slivers	豆腐花	dòufuhuā
Bean curd with chestnuts	马蹄豆腐	matí dòufu
Pressed bean curd with cabbage	卷心菜豆腐	juǎnxīncài dòufu
Egg fried with tomatoes	蕃茄炒蛋	fānqié chǎodàn
Fried bean curd with vegetables	豆腐素菜	dòufu sùcài
Fried bean sprouts	炒豆芽	chǎodòuyá
Spicy braised aubergine	香茄子条	xiā ngqiézitiáo
Stir-fried bamboo shoots	炒冬笋	chǎodōngsǔn
Stir-fried mushrooms	炒鲜菇	chǎoxiāngū
Vegetable soup	素菜汤	sùcài tāng

Regional dishes

Northern

Aromatic fried lamb	炒羊肉	chǎoyángròu
Beijing (Peking) duck	北京烤鸭	běijīng kǎoyā
Fish with ham and vegetables	火腿素菜鱼片	huǒtuǐ sùcài yúpiàn
Fried prawn balls	炒虾球	chǎoxiaqiú
Hotpot	火锅	huǒguō
Lion's head (pork rissoles casseroled with greens)	狮子头	shīzitóu
Red-cooked lamb	红烧羊肉	hóngshāo yángròu

Sichuan Western Chinese

Boiled beef slices (spicy)	水煮牛肉	shuǐzhu niúròu
Crackling-rice with pork	爆米肉片	bàomi ròupiàn
Crossing-the-bridge noodles	过桥面	guòqiáomiàn
Carry-pole noodles (with a chilli-vinegar-sesame sauce)	担担面	dàndànmiàn
Deep-fried green beans with garlic	大蒜刀豆	dàsuàn daodòu
Dong'an chicken (poached in spicy sauce)	东安鸡子	dōng'ān jīzi
Doubled-cooked pork	回锅肉	huíguoròu
Dry-fried pork shreds	油炸肉丝	yóuzhá ròusi
Fish-flavoured aubergine	鱼香茄子	yúxiāng qiézi
Fish with pickled vegetables	酸菜鱼	suān cài yú
Gongbao chicken (with chillies and peanuts)	公保鸡丁	gōngbǎo jīdīng
Green pepper with spring onion and black bean sauce	豆豉青椒	dòuchī qīngjiāo

Hot and sour soup (flavoured with vinegar and white pepper)	酸辣汤	suānlà tāng
Hot-spiced bean curd	麻婆豆腐	mápódòufu
Rice-flour balls, stuffed with sweet paste	汤圆	tāngyuán
Smoked duck	熏鸭	xūnyā
Strange flavoured chicken (with sesame-garlic-chilli)	怪味鸡	guàiwèiji
Stuffed aubergine slices	馅茄子	xiànqiézi
Tangerine chicken	桔子鸡	júzijī
Tiger-skin peppers (pan-fried with salt)	虎皮炒椒	hupí chǎojiāo
Wind-cured ham	火腿	huǒtuǐ

Southern Chinese/Cantonese

Baked crab with chilli and black beans	辣椒豆豉焙蟹	làjiao dòuchǐ bèixiè
Barbecued pork (char siew)	叉烧	chā shāo
Casseroled bean curd stuffed with pork mince	豆腐煲	dòufubāo
Claypot rice with sweet sausage	香肠饭	xiangchángfàn
Crisp-skinned pork on rice	脆皮肉饭	cuìpíròufàn
Fish-head casserole	焙鱼头	bèiyútóu
Fish steamed with ginger and spring onion	清蒸鱼	qīngzhēngyú
Fried chicken with yam	芋头炒鸡片	yùtóu chǎojīpiàn
Honey-roast pork	叉烧	chā shāo
Lemon chicken	柠檬鸡	níngméngjī
Litchi (lychee) pork	荔枝肉片	lìzhiròupiàn
Salt-baked chicken	盐鸡	yánjī

Dim sum

Dim sum	点心	diǎnxīn
Barbecued pork bun	叉烧包	chā shāo bāo
Crab and prawn dumpling	蟹肉虾饺	xièròu xiā jiāo
Custard tart	蛋挞	dàntà
Doughnut	炸面饼圈	zhá miànbǐngquān
Pork and prawn dumpling	烧麦	shāomài
Fried taro and mince dumpling	蕃薯糊饺	fānshǔ hújiāo
Lotus paste bun	莲蓉糕	liánrónggāo
Moon cake (sweet bean paste in flaky pastry)	月饼	yuèbǐng
Paper-wrapped prawns	纸包虾	zhǐbāoxiā
Prawn crackers	虾片	xiā piàn
Prawn dumpling	虾饺	xiā jiāo
Spring roll	春卷	chūnjuǎn
Steamed spare ribs and chilli	排骨	páigǔ

Stuffed rice-flour roll	肠粉	chángfěn
Stuffed green peppers with black bean sauce	豆豉馅青椒	dòuchi xiànqīngjiāo
Sweet sesame balls	芝麻球	zhima qiú

Fruit

Fruit	水果	shǔiguǒ
Apple	苹果	píngguǒ
Banana	香蕉	xiāngjiāo
Grape	葡萄	pútáo
Honeydew melon	哈密瓜	hāmì guā
Longan	龙眼	lóngyǎn
Lychee	荔枝	lìzhī
Mandarin orange	橘子	júzi
Mango	果	mángguǒ
Orange	橙子	chéngzi
Peach	桃子	táozi
Pear	梨	lí
Persimmon	柿子	shìzi
Plum	李子	lǐzi
Pomegranate	石榴	shíliú
Pomelo	柚子	yòuzi
Watermelon	西瓜	xīguā

Glossary

Arhat Buddhist saint

Bei North

Concession A section of Shanghai under the control of a foreign power during the nineteenth and twentieth centuries; a colonial territory in all but name.

Cultural Revolution Ten-year period beginning in 1966 and characterized by destruction, persecution and fanatical devotion to Mao.

CCP Chinese Communist Party

Ding An ancient three-legged vessel, used for cooking and ceremonial purposes.

Dingpeng Literally a nail shed, the cheapest kind of brothel in concession-era Shanghai.

Dougong Ornate, load-bearing bracket used in temple roofs

Dagoba Another name for a stupa

Dong East

Fen Smallest denomination of Chinese currency – there are one hundred fen to the yuan.

Feng Peak

Feng shui A system of geomancy used to determine the positioning of buildings.

Gong Palace

Guan Temple

Guanyin The ubiquitous Buddhist Goddess of Mercy, who postponed her entry into paradise in order to help ease human misery. Derived from the Indian deity Avalokiteshvara, she is often depicted with up to a thousand arms.

Guomindang (GMD) The Nationalist Peoples' Party. Under Chiang Kaishek, the GMD fought Communist forces for 25 years before being defeated and moving to Taiwan in 1949, where it remains a major political party.

Han Chinese The main body of the Chinese people, as distinct from other ethnic groups such as Uigur, Miao, Hui or Tibetan.

Hu Lake

Jiao (or mao) Ten fen

Jie Street

Little Red Book A selection of "Quotations from Chairman Mao Zedong", produced in 1966 as a philosophical treatise for Red Guards during the Cultural Revolution.

Longtang A narrow lane lined with shikumen houses

Lu Street

Maitreya Buddha The Buddha of the future, at present awaiting rebirth.

Men Gate/door

Miao Temple

Ming Chinese dynasty that ruled from 1368 to 1644, before being overthrown by the Manchus from the north.

Nan South

PLA The People's Liberation Army, the official name of the Communist military forces since 1949.

PSB Public Security Bureau, the branch of China's police force which deals directly with foreigners.

Pagoda Tower with distinctively tapering structure.

Pipa A traditional string instrument

Pinyin The official system of transliterating Chinese script into Roman characters.

Putonghua Mandarin Chinese; literally "Common Language".

Qiao Bridge

Qipao The characteristic Chinese long fitted dress.

Qing The last of the great Chinese dynasties (1644–1911), administered from Beijing.

Red Guards The unruly factional forces unleashed by Mao during the Cultural Revolution to find and destroy brutally any "reactionaries" among the populace.

Renmin The people

Shan Mountain

Shikumen Terraced housing created in the nineteenth century by the British

Shuyu A high-class courtesan, like a geisha, skilled in singing and dancing as well as love.

Si Temple, usually Buddhist

Song A Chinese Dynasty (960–1279 AD) administered first from Kaifeng and later from Hangzhou, regarded as mercantilist and progressive.

Stele Freestanding stone tablet carved with text.

Stupa Multi-tiered tower associated with Buddhist temples that usually contains sacred objects.

Ta Tower or pagoda

Tang Arguably the greatest Chinese dynasty (618–907 AD). The Tang was outward looking and stable. The era also represented a high watermark for the Chinese arts.

Taxi girls Girls who danced for money in concession-era Shanghai.

Tai ji A discipline of physical exercise, characterized by slow, deliberate, balletic movements.

Tea dances Organized dances in concession Shanghai, rather less innocent than the name implies.

Tian Heaven or the sky

Xi West

Yuan China's unit of currency. Also a courtyard or garden.

Zhan Station

Zhou Villa or manor

Travel store

D: Rough Guide
DIRECTIONS for
short breaks

Available from all good bookstores

For more information go to www.roughguides.com

Visit us online
www.roughguides.com
Information on over 25,000 destinations around the world

- **Read** Rough Guides' trusted travel info
- **Access** exclusive articles from Rough Guides authors
- **Update** yourself on new books, maps, CDs and other products
- **Enter** our competitions and win travel prizes
- **Share** ideas, journals, photos & travel advice with other users
- **Earn** points every time you contribute to the Rough Guide
  community and get rewards

BROADEN YOUR HORIZONS

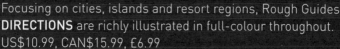

Avoid Guilt Trips

Buy fair trade coffee + bananas ✓

Save energy – use low energy bulbs ✓

– don't leave tv on standby ✓

Offset carbon emissions from flight to Madrid ✓

Send goat to Africa ✓

Join Tourism Concern today ✓

Slowly, the world is changing.
Together we can, and will, make a difference.

Tourism Concern is the only UK registered charity fighting exploitation in one of the largest industries on earth: people forced from their homes in order that holiday resorts can be built, sweatshop labour conditions in hotels and destruction of the environment are just some of the issues that we tackle.

Sending people on a guilt trip is not something we do. We know as well as anyone that holidays are precious. But you can help us to ensure that tourism always benefits the local communities involved.

Call 020 7133 3330
or visit **tourismconcern.org.uk** to find out how.

A year's membership of Tourism Concern costs just £20 (£12 unwaged)
– that's 38 pence a week, less than the cost of a pint of milk, organic of course.

Small print and

Index

A Rough Guide to Rough Guides

Published in 1982, the first Rough Guide – to Greece – was a student scheme that became a publishing phenomenon. Mark Ellingham, a recent graduate in English from Bristol University, had been travelling in Greece the previous summer and couldn't find the right guidebook. With a small group of friends he wrote his own guide, combining a highly contemporary, journalistic style with a thoroughly practical approach to travellers' needs.

The immediate success of the book spawned a series that rapidly covered dozens of destinations. And, in addition to impecunious backpackers, Rough Guides soon acquired a much broader and older readership that relished the guides' wit and inquisitiveness as much as their enthusiastic, critical approach and value-for-money ethos.

These days, Rough Guides include recommendations from shoestring to luxury and cover more than 200 destinations around the globe, including almost every country in the Americas and Europe, more than half of Africa and most of Asia and Australasia. Our ever-growing team of authors and photographers is spread all over the world, particularly in Europe, the USA and Australia.

In the early 1990s, Rough Guides branched out of travel, with the publication of Rough Guides to World Music, Classical Music and the Internet. All three have become benchmark titles in their fields, spearheading the publication of a wide range of books under the Rough Guide name.

Including the travel series, Rough Guides now number more than 350 titles, covering: phrasebooks, waterproof maps, music guides from Opera to Heavy Metal, reference works as diverse as Conspiracy Theories and Shakespeare, and popular culture books from iPods to Poker. Rough Guides also produce a series of more than 120 World Music CDs in partnership with World Music Network.

Visit www.roughguides.com to see our latest publications.

Rough Guide travel images are available for commercial licensing at www.roughguidespictures.com

Rough Guide credits

Text editor: Edward Aves
Layout: Umesh Aggarwal
Cartography: Ed Wright
Picture editor: Sarah Cummins
Production: Vicky Baldwin
Proofreader: Karen Parker
Cover design: Chloë Roberts
Photographer: Tim Draper
Editorial: **London** Kate Berens, Claire Saunders, Ruth Blackmore, Alison Murchie, Karoline Densley, Andy Turner, Keith Drew, Alice Park, Lucy White, Jo Kirby, James Smart, Natasha Foges, Róisín Cameron, Emma Traynor, Emma Gibbs, Kathryn Lane, Joe Staines, Duncan Clark, Peter Buckley, Matthew Milton, Tracy Hopkins, Ruth Tidball; **New York** Andrew Rosenberg, Steven Horak, AnneLise Sorensen, Amy Hegarty, April Isaacs, Ella Steim, Anna Owens, Joseph Petta, Sean Mahoney; **Delhi** Madhavi Singh, Karen D'Souza
Design & Pictures: **London** Scott Stickland, Dan May, Diana Jarvis, Mark Thomas, Nicole Newman; **Delhi** Ajay Verma, Jessica Subramanian, Ankur Guha, Pradeep Thapliyal,

Sachin Tanwar, Anita Singh, Nikhil Agarwal
Production: Rebecca Short
Cartography: **London** Maxine Repath, Katie Lloyd-Jones; **Delhi** Jai Prakash Mishra, Rajesh Chhibber, Ashutosh Bharti, Rajesh Mishra, Animesh Pathak, Jasbir Sandhu, Karobi Gogoi, Amod Singh, Alakananda Bhattacharya, Swati Handoo
Online: Narender Kumar, Rakesh Kumar, Amit Verma, Rahul Kumar, Ganesh Sharma, Debojit Borah
Marketing & Publicity: **London** Liz Statham, Niki Hanmer, Louise Maher, Jess Carter, Vanessa Godden, Vivienne Watton, Anna Paynton, Rachel Sprackett; **New York** Geoff Colquitt, Megan Kennedy, Katy Ball; **Delhi** Ragini Govind
Manager India: Punita Singh
Series Editor: Mark Ellingham
Reference Director: Andrew Lockett
Publishing Coordinator: Helen Phillips
Publishing Director: Martin Dunford
Commercial Manager: Gino Magnotta
Managing Director: John Duhigg

Publishing information

This first edition published March 2008 by
Rough Guides Ltd,
80 Strand, London WC2R 0RL
345 Hudson St, 4th Floor,
New York, NY 10014, USA
14 Local Shopping Centre, Panchsheel Park,
New Delhi 110017, India
Distributed by the Penguin Group
Penguin Books Ltd,
80 Strand, London WC2R 0RL
Penguin Group (USA)
375 Hudson Street, NY 10014, USA
Penguin Group (Australia)
250 Camberwell Road, Camberwell,
Victoria 3124, Australia
Penguin Books Canada Ltd,
10 Alcorn Avenue, Toronto, Ontario,
Canada M4V 1E4
Penguin Group (NZ)
67 Apollo Drive, Mairangi Bay, Auckland 1310,
New Zealand

Cover concept by Peter Dyer.
Typeset in Bembo and Helvetica to an original design by Henry Iles.
Printed and bound in China
© Simon Lewis 2008
No part of this book may be reproduced in any form without permission from the publisher except for the quotation of brief passages in reviews.
224pp includes index
A catalogue record for this book is available from the British Library
ISBN: 978-1-84353-869-1

The publishers and authors have done their best to ensure the accuracy and currency of all the information in **The Rough Guide to Shanghai**, however, they can accept no responsibility for any loss, injury, or inconvenience sustained by any traveller as a result of information or advice contained in the guide.

1   3   5   7   9   8   6   4   2

Help us update

We've gone to a lot of effort to ensure that the first edition of **The Rough Guide to Shanghai** is accurate and up to date. However, things change – places get "discovered", opening hours are notoriously fickle, restaurants and rooms raise prices or lower standards. If you feel we've got it wrong or left something out, we'd like to know, and if you can remember the address, the price, the hours, the phone number, so much the better.

Please send your comments with the subject line "**Rough Guide Shanghai Update**" to ©mail @roughguides.com, or by post to the address above. We'll credit all contributions and send a copy of the next edition (or any other Rough Guide if you prefer) for the very best emails.
  Have your questions answered and tell others about your trip at
Ⓦcommunity.roughguides.com

SMALL PRINT

ROUGH
GUIDES

Acknowledgements

The author thanks: Noe, Kathrene, Du Ying Nan, Shen Ye, Xiao Song, Ling Ling, Phil, Juliette, Penny, Yen, Rain, Tim, Maggie and Mark.

Photo credits

All photos © Rough Guides except the following:

Title page
Pudong skyline from the Bund © Photolibrary

Introduction
p.5 Maglev train © Keren Su/China Span/Alamy
p.6 M on the Bund © Alamy
p.9 The Bund at night © PanoramaStock/Robert Harding

Things not to miss
01 View from the Jinmao Tower observation deck © Alamy
05 The Bund © Photolibrary
06 Renmin Park © Alamy
08 Xintiandi at night © Getty Images
12 Xi Hu, Hangzhou © Photolibrary

High hopes: Shanghai's architectural boom colour section
Pudong at night © Luis Veiga/Getty Images
Bank of China building at night © John W. Banagan/Getty Images
Shanghai Grand Theatre © Getty Images
Jiushi Corporation Headquarters © arcspace.com
Oriental Arts Centre © LIU JIN/AFP/Getty Images

China's regional cuisines colour section
Dim sum © Getty Images
Hairy crabs © Corbis

Black and whites
p.165 Xi Hu, Hangzhou © Photolibrary

SMALL PRINT

Index

Map entries are in colour.

Map symbols

maps are listed in the full index using coloured text

Provincial boundary	Temple/monastery
Major road	Pagoda
Minor road	Public gardens
Pedestrianized road	Bridge
Steps	Bus station/depot
Tunnel	Minibus stand/bus stop
Path	Hospital
Railway	Information office
Metro station & line	Post office
Ferry route	Gate/park entrance
Waterway	Building
Wall	Church/cathedral
Airport	Stadium
Mountain peak	Park/cemetery

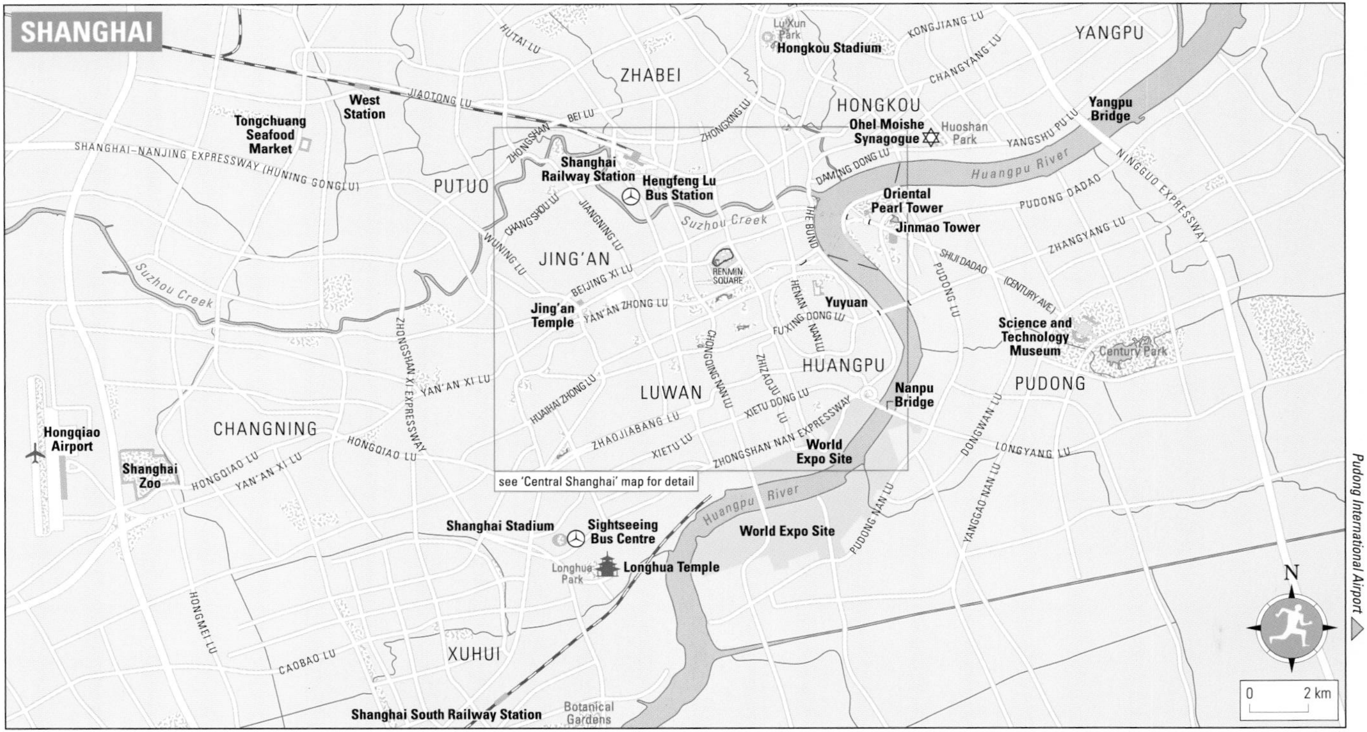

SHANGHAI
Pudong International Airport
N
0
2 km
YANGPU
ZHABEI
HONGKOU
PUTUO
JING'AN
HUANGPU
LUWAN
PUDONG
CHANGNING
XUHUI
Lu Xun Park
Hongkou Stadium
KONGJIANG LU
CHANGYANG LU
HUTAI LU
West Station
JIAOTONG LU
Yangpu Bridge
BEI LU
ZHONGXING LU
Ohel Moishe Synagogue
Huoshan Park
YANGSHU PU LU
Tongchuang Seafood Market
SHANGHAI–NANJING EXPRESSWAY (HUNING GONGLU)
ZHONGSHAN
Shanghai Railway Station
Hengfeng Lu Bus Station
DAMING DONG LU
Huangpu River
NINGGUO EXPRESSWAY
Oriental Pearl Tower
PUDONG DADAO
Suzhou Creek
THE BUND
Jinmao Tower
ZHANGYANG LU
CHANGSHOU LU
JIANGNING LU
WUNING LU
SHIJI DADAO
(CENTURY AVE)
PUDONG LU
RENMIN SQUARE
BEIJING XI LU
HENAN NAN LU
Yuyuan
Jing'an Temple
YAN'AN ZHONG LU
FUXING DONG LU
Science and Technology Museum
Century Park
ZHONGSHAN XI EXPRESSWAY
CHONGQING NAN LU
ZHIZAOJU LU
YAN'AN XI LU
HUAIHAI ZHONG LU
XIETU DONG LU
Nanpu Bridge
ZHONGSHAN NAN EXPRESSWAY
DONGWAN LU
ZHAOJIABANG LU
XIETU LU
World Expo Site
LONGYANG LU
Hongqiao Airport
HONGQIAO LU
Shanghai Zoo
HONGQIAO LU
YAN'AN XI LU
see 'Central Shanghai' map for detail
YANGGAO NAN LU
PUDONG NAN LU
World Expo Site
Shanghai Stadium
Sightseeing Bus Centre
Longhua Park
Longhua Temple
HONGMEI LU
CAOBAO LU
Shanghai South Railway Station
Botanical Gardens

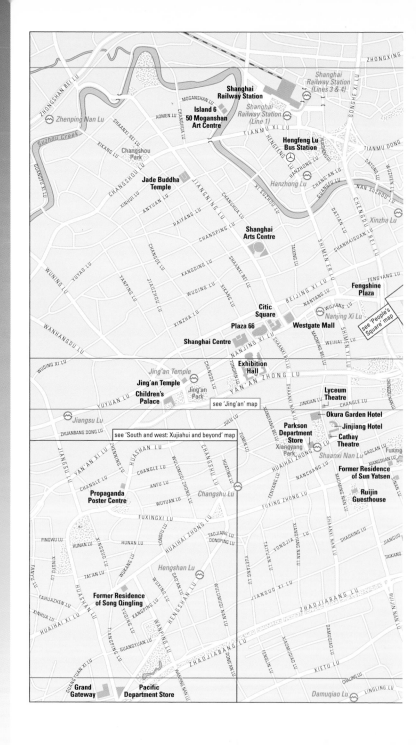

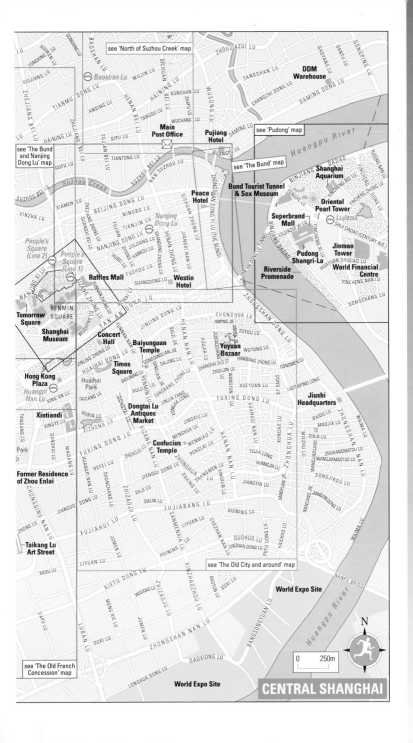

CENTRAL SHANGHAI

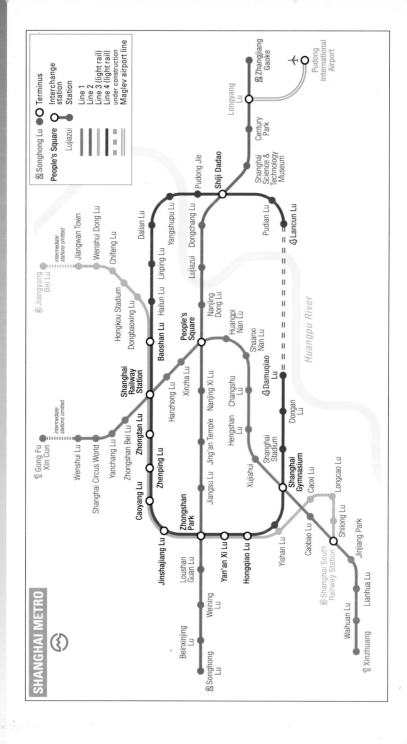